THE
GODFATHER OF
BRITISH CRIME

THE
GODFATHER OF BRITISH CRIME

FREDDIE FOREMAN

JB

First published in the UK by John Blake Publishing
an imprint of Bonnier Books UK
4th Floor, Victoria House
Bloomsbury Square,
London, WC1B 4DA
England

Owned by Bonnier Books
Sveavägen 56, Stockholm, Sweden

www.facebook.com/johnblakebooks ⊙
twitter.com/jblakebooks ▣

First published in paperback in 2009
This edition published in 2018

Paperback: 978-1-78606-894-1
Ebook: 978-1-78219-501-6

British Library Cataloguing-in-Publication Data:

A catalogue record for this book is available from the British Library.

Text design by www.envydesign.co.uk

Printed and bound in Great Britain by Clays Ltd, Elcograf S.p.A.

5 7 9 10 8 6 4

John Blake Publishing is an imprint of Bonnier Books UK
www.bonnierbooks.co.uk

'**Brown Bread:** Dead. One London criminal is known admiringly among his peers as Brown Bread Fread after the number of bodies, rightly or wongly, attributed to him.'

Gang Slang, A Dictionary of Criminal Slang.

'People do get over familiar. I was at a boxing show and a guy said: "Hi Fred. Have you killed anyone recently?" I just stopped and looked at him. I said, "The night is not over yet." '

Freddie Foreman, *The Book of Criminal Quotations*

CONTENTS

	PROLOGUE	ix
1	THE EARLY YEARS	1
2	HARD TIME	11
3	YOUR COUNTRY NEEDS YOU	23
4	THE JUMP-UP	43
5	FIRM FRIENDS	57
6	EAST ENDERS	73
7	THE PERFECT TEAM	83
8	BATTLE OF BOW	103
9	'GOT ANY GOLD BARS DOWN THERE, FRED?'	111
10	PANAMA GOLD	123
11	'GIVE ME A NAME'	135
12	BUILDING THE EMPIRE	151
13	THE MAD AXEMAN	169
14	MUDDY WATERS	183
15	BANGED UP	197

16 SNOOKERED 215
17 OPERATION WRECKER 221
18 BREAKING AMERICA 229
19 SECURITY EXPRESS 241
20 KIDNAPPED 255
21 TRIALS AND TRIBULATIONS 261
22 FREDDIE TODAY 277
23 TIME TELLS ALL 287
 EPILOGUE 301

PROLOGUE

The snowfall began late on Good Friday. Blanketing the hills of north-east England and the Midlands, by Saturday it had painted white the entire eastern side of Britain, from Scotland to Norfolk. As Sunday slowly became Easter Monday, light snowflakes began to drift across east London – dissolving into the tarmac of Curtain Road, and scattering across the yard of the famous Security Express depot.

The air was as crisp as a £5 note, and, while snow at this time of year was most unusual, for the five men crouched behind the walls and buildings of that yard, it was the only part of the morning that was unplanned. They'd carefully pinpointed the section of wall unscrutinised by the electronic gaze of closed-circuit television, and dropped over. They'd calculated that they could hide inside this fortress – known to locals as 'Fort Knox' – completely undetected. And, most importantly, they had learned that one man's routine of an early-morning cuppa would leave the entire alarm system temporarily disabled, and the treasures locked deep inside the building open for the taking.

As these five men sat waiting through the night, they contemplated what would be the most audacious crime ever undertaken in London's Square Mile: to rob the headquarters of Security Express of £7 million in cash. The redbrick complex had 12-foot-high walls and steel-shuttered doors. Alarms and cameras were strategically placed around the entire building and it was considered impenetrable. The next most difficult job would have been to relieve the Tower of London of the Crown Jewels.

'What's the time?' whispered one man, for a third time.

'Nearly four o'clock,' was the hushed reply.

The floor was ice-cold beneath them, and the wait almost unbearable. As is normal on a holiday weekend, the City of London was a ghost town, yet the Firm were alert to every sound. Goods trains rumbled along the steel tracks, their brakes screeching along the approach to nearby Liverpool Street Station. The mild hum of a motorbike would occasionally zoom down the adjoining Great Eastern Street, while distant sirens caused the more nervous members of the gang to prick up their ears, their minds racing with images of squad cars, armed response units and dogs.

'What time is it now?' the voice came again.

'It's still nearly four o'clock.'

'For fuck's sake, shut up!' came another voice in the darkness. As the figure leaned forward into the sodium light, all that was visible was a plastic fancy-dress party mask in his right hand.

No one said a word for the next few hours. They knew that escape routes had been planned, vehicles assembled, safe houses prepared and route familiarisation practised. The Firm were at work on a regular basis, so tools were constantly in use and were already at hand, but strict instructions had been given that nobody should get hurt. Threatened, yes. But no physical violence. Everyone involved would wear face masks and gloves and everything brought inside the premises would be taken away. This included cigarette butts, apple cores and even tissue paper. No clues would be left behind for forensic examination.

Above the gang's hiding place, high above the floodlights that cast deep shadows across the yard, stood a derelict office block, once owned by Security Express. Ironically, it was from there that the Firm had kept watch on the premises of the country's leading security firm for several months. They had been shown around by estate agents and had taken imprints of the keys. There, with sleeping bags and thermoses, they had taken it in turns to watch the comings and goings of the bright-yellow-and-green armoured vehicles by day and night.

'We should have just done the vans...' hissed another voice in the dark, but he was shushed before he'd finished.

Months previously, in the early stages of planning this job, there was talk that they should simply jump over and steal bags of silver coins from the vans left overnight. But careful observation and planning revealed there was a much greater prize on offer.

This weekend, the vaults would be overflowing with five tons of cash in silver and paper money. The country was enjoying an economic boom under Margaret Thatcher's Conservative government, and the City of London was swimming with cash. But, with no banks open, much of it – including profits from the *Daily Mail* Ideal Homes Exhibition – sat idle in the vaults.

Patiently, the gang waited three more freezing hours for the door to open. They *knew* it would open. And it did, at just after 7am. The golden opportunity came as guard Greg Counsell took over from the nightshift man. He had poured steaming water over the teabag in his brown mug, and now walked through the compound to fetch a pint of milk left at the front gate. Thinking he was perfectly safe, he left the door to the back of the building open, meaning that he had to switch the entire alarm system off.

The Firm heard the heavy bolt slide along, and knew it was time for action. They listened intently as his keys jangled, playing like a tambourine against his thigh with every step, getting louder and louder. For a minute, Counsell hesitated. Perhaps he had noticed something unusual. But it was too late: now a figure swiftly jumped out of the shadows and took him hostage. 'Keep your head to the fucking floor!' he shouted. 'Look down!'

It was on. Adrenaline pumping inside them, the other raiders raced inside the building. Two members of the Firm were disguised with monkey masks; the rest wore balaclavas. All wore boiler suits and gloves and were tooled up. Counsell did the sensible thing for someone at the wrong end of a shotgun – he 'cooperated'. He opened the glass doors of the main reception area, allowing the Firm inside.

'How many of you are there in here?' snarled one of the gang, through the hole in his balaclava.

'Just me,' came Counsell's shaking reply.

'Don't fucking lie to us!' shouted another voice from behind them. It was hard to believe, but Counsell was telling the truth: there was, in fact, just one guard on duty.

With the preliminaries successfully completed, the gang now had to wait several hours for the timer to release some of the locking mechanisms on three of the main underground vaults. After that, it would require the 'cooperation' of several guards holding passwords and keys before the vaults could be opened. A further seven employees were due to arrive during the course of the afternoon and they would have to be taken care of one by one and 'cooperate' fully with the Firm.

The second employee to arrive that day came in soon after 1pm. Counsell was told to sit at his desk and not even look at the man. A flicker of the eye, one little mistake, and he could give away the whole game. One of the Firm lay concealed under his desk, poking a shotgun into Counsell's bollocks to persuade him he should follow their advice.

One by one, the guards were wrapped up with women's stockings and a plaster put over their mouths and, by 2pm, all staff had been accounted for. The task of waiting for them had been long and arduous and required strong nerves. The Firm could not afford to make a single mistake.

Now came the delicate task of opening the vaults without setting off alarms. When turning a lock, it had to be opened in a prescribed sequence. One wrong turn and the bells would ring. Keys also had to be put into locks in the right sequence. It would require the 'cooperation' of two members of staff, each of whom held a required key. With time on their hands, the Firm were able to rehearse the lock-opening procedure with the guards to make sure they were not given wrong information. The guards were told to repeat the methods and codes over and over again. Experience had taught the Firm that, by separating employees first, they would reveal everything – but they wouldn't while others were listening. When they'd got all the information they needed, they made the guards lie down together. If any further problems arose, the man responsible would be taken out on his own and asked to repeat codes and numbers and procedures until they got it right.

They had to employ psychology. If one of the guards had made a simple error, or lied about procedure, the whole operation would have been doomed. At one point, keys to the main vault were found to be missing. Lighter fluid was poured on to a guard's legs and a matchbox rattled by his ear. The Firm threatened to torch him if the keys weren't found. One of the guards quickly showed them where they were hidden. Threats were made, but nobody was battered. They were all well treated and offered cigarettes and a drop of tea, although the Firm did eat one of the guards' sandwiches and an apple. Phone calls by customers to Security Express were answered and no suspicions were aroused, even when Counsell's wife rang. 'Don't forget to bring a loaf of bread home with you,' she told him, unaware that as she spoke her husband was being held at gunpoint.

Once the vault doors were open, the Firm transferred the cash to trolleys and sent them up on a lift to loading bays, where a 7-ton truck was waiting. The operation to move 5 tons of cash took only about an hour. Forming a human chain, they passed bag after bag, heavy with currency, into the back of the van. Their muscles began to ache, and the bags began to feel increasingly heavy, but knowing each sack contained another £100,000 drove the men to fill the van to the ceiling.

'Get in! Get in!' yelled one of the gang, as they emptied the vault of almost its very last pound. But the truck was so full of cash there was no room for one of the men, as planned.

'Do the doors!' they shouted to the last man, who had just slammed shut the back of the truck. To escape, a button had to be pressed inside a control box in the corner of the yard. After throwing the switch, the last man would have to race across the yard like a sprinter to escape before those gates automatically slid shut again. He did exactly that, as the van's engine, loud and throaty, fired up first time. The man turned on his heels, knowing the gates were about to close.

Across the yard, the van gradually built up speed. The driver pulled the gear stick from first to second, then almost immediately punched it forward to third as its back double axle cleared the gate with ease, and growled gently on to the east London streets. The rest of gang followed, walking quietly to waiting getaway cars. As rehearsed, the escape was calm, cool and collected – a screech of brakes or broken speed limit could attract unwanted attention.

But still that last man was fighting his way across the yard, heaving lungfuls of cold air into his body as his legs pumped towards freedom. Hours of throwing around 5 tons of cash, coupled with nerve-racking tension, had left his legs heavy as lead. Still he pushed on as the metal gates drew agonisingly to a close before him.

The driver of one of the Firm's cars, searched his wing mirror for any sign of his colleague, but saw none. As the gate was closing, it left the man just enough space to drag his sweaty body to freedom.

Jumping out of the Peugeot to help, the driver watched as the last man struggled and squeezed his way free. Relieved, the two men both clambered in the car and pulled away. It was 3.30pm as they drove away calmly, yet eager to put as many miles between them and the scene of this amazing crime. Northwards they fled, to freedom.

It was a long journey to the flophouse, but the bank holiday traffic was light. Inside the van there was no celebration. Not yet. Instead, they sat, still alert, listening to the windscreen wipers rhythmically sweep patterns in the snow that continued to fall on the windscreen. Gradually, the snowflakes subsided, and as the van sped on a thaw crept in, melting the snow into nothing.

And that was exactly what would have to happen to the millions of pounds of used notes packed tightly into the back of the van. They'd blend into the underground, melt away and disappear. But laundering 5 tons of stolen banknotes was no easy task. It had taken criminal genius to commit the robbery, but the hardest part would be getting away with it.

In the years following, these banknotes would come to be responsible for treachery, greed and double crossings. The story would grip the nation and take over newspaper front pages for decades, while the worldwide police investigation would end in the dramatic kidnapping – on foreign soil – of one man the police believed was behind the crime. A man with a kaleidoscopically colourful criminal history, yet who came from very humble beginnings…

CHAPTER 1
THE EARLY YEARS

I was born on Sheepcote Lane on Saturday, 5 March 1932. Every part of London had one street where villains came from, and in our area it was Sheepcote Lane. I was an unexpected arrival, the youngest of five brothers – the last thing my mother wanted was another boy! I was unwanted, but loved. My father was from Irish stock and my mother from a middle-class London family. Father's family was huge. There were 13 children: six sisters and seven brothers. My father was christened Herbert Albert Foreman, but his brothers called him Sonny. Confusingly, my mother called him Alf; he called her Lou, short for Louise.

Number 22 Sheepcote Lane was a terraced house, two-up and two-down. You stepped from the street straight into the front room. The kitchen was at the back with an outside lavatory and two bedrooms upstairs. We five brothers shared one bedroom.

The week's highlights came on a Saturday night. Poor as they were, the family would hold legendary parties after the pubs had closed. As kids, we weren't allowed inside the pubs, but we'd linger about and wait for the action that usually began after the last drinks had been served.

We were rarely let down. Differences of opinion and heated exchanges would always arise, leading to the eagerly awaited spectacle of a bare-knuckle fight. This would take place on the street outside The Flag pub and every now and then my father would be one of the combatants.

My brothers would let me watch others fight and hoist me on to a window ledge outside the pub, from where I would get a glimpse of the fighters' heads and shoulders as they threw punch after punch. If they fell to the ground and rolled about, someone would take the part of referee and break them up so they could shape up and start again. The drunken crowd would form a circle, shouting and encouraging their respective mates into action, oblivious to the blood and sweat that sprayed in their direction.

There was a lot of drunkenness around in those days – and snuff-taking was also popular with older people at the time. My grandmother, and others of her generation, would take it on a regular basis, like people do coke today, and you could identify the snuff-takers by the brown stains under their noses and on their smudged handkerchiefs. From a little boy's point of view it was disgusting – especially when the old girl tried to kiss you!

Some parties at our house would turn out much the same way as the pub evenings – beginning with a song and dance and ending in a fight. Two of my father's sisters were on the boards at the Upper Brixton Empire and part of their repertoire included clog dancing and singing popular tunes around the piano. Lizzie Mayne, my aunt, was a lively entertainer. Her special number was 'There's a Blue Ridge Round My Heart, Virginia', which my father, a little worse for drink, would follow with a rendition of 'Are We to Part Like This, Dear?', which he sang to my mother.

We kids used to sit on the stairs and enjoy the mixed procession of people including boxers, market traders, vendors and musicians wandering in and out of our tiny house. Musicians were always welcome and from time to time, just for the crack, the Salvation Army band would be invited to play. Huge wooden firkins of beer would arrive on willing shoulders as well as quart bottles of brown ale, four to a crate. Later, to help soak up the alcohol, big doorstep sandwiches filled with cheese and mustard pickle and large jars of pickled onions would appear and be wolfed down. As the evening wore on and my old man became more spirited, he would disappear to the pigeon loft in the back garden with a crate of ale and two or three of his favoured cronies. They would sit there telling each other stories until one of the wives dragged them out to join the party.

The loft had been built by my brother Wally, the second eldest, and it still holds poignant memories for me today. A big tomcat once got in there and slaughtered all Wally's prized pigeons. Some time later, my mother heard a horrendous commotion in the garden and ran outside in a panic. Wally had caught the offending cat, swung it around in circles by its tail and projected it across three neighbouring gardens, never to be seen again.

With the reduced pigeon population, the loft became a useful watering hole for my father and his friends. But having drunk all their liquor, they'd return to the house and the fighting would begin. The old man's regular opponent was his brother-in-law, Johnny Wicker, who was as tough and as game as he was.

The pair would be at it hammer and tongs, battering the daylights out of one another with bare fists. They were constantly brawling and had fought each other so often that their contests had become a game of one-upmanship: win one, lose one, call it a draw, it went on and on, party after party. They never got fed up with bashing each other. I did not enjoy these spectacles, seeing my father bloodied and hurt. Those times were violent and very physical – proving one's manhood in those days was an essential part of survival.

I never discovered whether my father spent time in a civilian jail. If he did, we were never told, although there were certainly periods when he was not around. In those days, judges or stipendiary magistrates didn't give long sentences. You'd get two to three months for assault and battery, or for beating up the police – which was done on a regular basis. The coppers were quite into it themselves and would return for a 'straightener' scrap.

Hitting a police officer was considered acceptable. Talking to one was not, even if you had the misfortune of being a relative. My mother's brother, Ted White, who ended up being Chief Constable of Durham, would drop in to see my mother if he was on a job in London. But, on the rare occasion that he visited us, my father refused to acknowledge his presence, let alone speak to him. He'd put on his hat and coat and walk out of the house. No self-respecting citizen of Sheepcote Lane would ever be seen in the company of a policeman.

My father's hatred of authority was universal and led to a spell inside a military prison before I was born. Like my four brothers, he too had fought for King and Country, joining the army at 17. Previously, he'd been apprenticed as a blacksmith, but, when his arm was shattered by German shrapnel in the Battle of the Somme, it put an end to his blacksmith career. He returned to Aldershot, where he fell foul of a sergeant major. The sergeant poked him with his stick and my father, a young man with lots of spirit, lost his rag and whacked him with the butt of his rifle. Rather than face a court martial, he made his getaway by stealing a bicycle and cycling all the way home to London.

They eventually caught him in the bar at the Super Palace Casino, Clapham, and there was a hell of a fight. He was battered and unceremoniously dragged down to one of the military police wagons and then off to the nick.

After a further period in barracks, he was sent back into action, though not to the front line. His injuries at the Somme prevented him from using a rifle and he was packed off with a pistol to Ireland as part of the peacekeeping force. My father was of good Irish stock, so this didn't sit well with him at all, as you can imagine – but he had little choice.

I take after him. I can't stand being told what to do by people who abuse authority and that has got me into trouble over the years. While in custody all I have ever demanded is that which anyone else is entitled to: to be treated fairly and with civility and to be spoken to like a human being.

My old man used to say, 'A little civility costs nothing', and those words have stuck with me throughout my life. As a young child, I can remember he once took me for a special treat to a café, where he bought me a meat pudding and two veg. He couldn't afford one for himself and, by the time my food was served, it was quite late and they began clearing up. As I got stuck into my meal, this guy came around and started sweeping up. Dust went everywhere. Then he began putting chairs on tables, ignoring the fact that I was a customer. My father asked him to stop, but the geezer either ignored him or made a rude comment. That was too much. My father looked menacingly at him and said, 'Put that fucking broom down and wait for my kid to finish his meal.' At this point I was getting embarrassed and trying to eat my food as quickly as possible because, knowing the old man, it looked like being a right fight any second now. But the man took my father's threat seriously and stopped clearing up.

My father wasn't a man who would take liberties, nor did he expect them to be taken. He never laid a finger on any of us five boys, although the threat was always there. Mum would give you a clump, but not viciously. And never around the head. When she got the hump with you, you'd run for the coat rack and cover yourself with the heavy khaki greatcoat from WWI. She'd then get down and smack your legs, the only exposed area she could find.

In those days, we were so poor that in winter us boys would huddle together in bed sharing the greatcoat and a couple of blankets for warmth. Gas stoves were still a luxury and there was no electricity in the house.

I was the youngest brother, and there was a considerable gap between our ages. Herbie was older by 12 years, Wally by 10, George by eight and Bert by five. Herbie was the only one to have the luxury of a single bed to himself, but he shared the same small bare room with the rest of us.

We made do with gas-fired mantel lamps above the fireplace. They would spit and splutter, occasionally making gentle popping sounds and throwing moving shadows on to the wall. Huddled together around the cooking range, toasting bread while listening to favourite programmes on our pride and joy, one crystal set radio – happy memories!

If you were the youngest, bath time could be a dirty affair. The ritual cleansing took place on Friday nights, when the tin bath was carried in from the yard and set up in the kitchen. The older boys jumped in first, so I always ended up in a tepid bath with scum floating on top – not such happy memories!

Our toilet was in the yard next to the big wooden coal bunker. Years later, after they had demolished the house, we discovered railway sleepers in the foundations. The house had probably been built on a disused railway track. In front of our place was a brick railway embankment leading to the Southern Railways trucks and wagons, which were shunted and left above some stables. Locals in Sheepcote Lane would break into these on a regular basis and nick saleable goods. Throwing caution to the wind, they would then pitch a stall and sell the goods on their front doorstep.

Nice cars were a target for us local urchins. We'd jump on to the running boards for a game and honk their horns in innocent fun. This was our street and we didn't like outsiders. They'd interfere with our football and cricket and another game called bridge where as many boys as possible would leapfrog on your back and cling on until you collapsed under their combined weight. If nothing else, the game built up your strength.

My immediate family were amazed that I developed strong bones and a strong physical presence, because as a very young boy I was sent to a nursery suffering from malnutrition. I had rickets, so they put me in callipers to keep my legs straight and fed me all this cod-liver oil, malt and egg custard. A nurse would go around to everyone with a big spoonful of enriched vitamin mixture, which you had to take and lick clean.

As poor as my parents were, they would not have anyone say I was undernourished; they did everything to make sure I got enough to eat and exercised my little muscles. Mum used to have a mangle which, with great effort, I turned in order to squeeze dry her washing, and she'd say, 'My, you're a strong little boy, Freddie,' as I swung on the handle and struggled to pull it round. She used to go to Shaftesbury Welcome, a church hall run by a charity, where they'd sing a few hymns and say some prayers. On their way out, the mothers would get a quarter of tea, a pound of sugar and a packet of biscuits. It was a hard life.

Living at Sheepcote Lane was like being part of a permanent fairground. Horse-drawn carts would constantly rumble past our house, scattering chickens as they went. Street traders came with candy floss and choc-ices. The knife sharpener would loudly announce himself and out you would run with all your mother's knives.

Another horse-and-cart man with a small hand-driven carousel would play music as you sat in tiny wooden seats and rode slowly around a central glass dome with two figures, like a wedding couple inside. The kids loved it.

Billy goats chased us children down the lane, and every now and again you'd see policemen grappling with men resisting arrest. The muffin man would come by regularly, with trays of muffins on his head. But the most exotic attraction was 'the coloured man' – Prince Monalulu, who was coal black and an expert on the horses. The street was fascinated by him. Barefooted children followed him down the road, a mystery Pied Piper from foreign lands. 'Aah got a horse,' he'd begin and then write out little betting slips and give a rundown of horses he claimed would win races.

That would tickle my grandmother. She was a terrible gambler. She'd have betting slips in every available vase. 'Just for reference,' she'd say. Granny Foreman was born Stacy Flynn, of good Irish stock. She was a real scrapper, and would regularly fight with her neighbours on Saturday nights after leaving The Flag pub.

Almost everything imaginable was offered for sale in our street. From goats' milk to stolen motorbikes, huge blocks of salt, accumulators for radios – if you were lucky enough to own one – and vinegar by the pint. As a kid, you were amazed and fascinated at the polished brass of the gypsy caravans at the bottom of the road. Those caravans were spotlessly clean inside and out.

Sometimes, for a treat, you'd be sent with a tray to the local butcher and return with specially cooked pease pudding and faggots with saveloys on the side. It was a lovely meal consisting of mashed peas made into a thick paste with brains, herbs and saveloys. You can still get it today in Bermondsey. Other than that, we'd eat a lot of bread pudding. Meat was a luxury for Sundays only and for afters my favourite was rhubarb and custard; we'd fight over who licked clean the custard basin.

Our heroes were the faces on cards given away with cigarettes. They were usually boxers like Welshman Tommy Farr (British and Empire champion), the German Walter Neusel, Ben Foord (South African champion) and Jack Doyle (Irish champion). We'd swap these with other kids as you would swap stamps. I remember listening to the Tommy Farr/Joe Louis fight in America in August 1937, when I was five. I still vividly remember us being gathered around our crystal set and excitedly awaiting the verdict. We all felt that Tommy Farr had won on points but it was a home-town decision.

All the entertainment was in pubs and you might be lucky enough to see singers and vaudeville acts at the Grand, Clapham Junction and the Princess Head in Battersea (where the army had nicked my old man). The famous blind jazz pianist George Shearing lived in Alfred Street, near The Flag pub, and used to walk past our house with his mother on the way to school for the blind.

Although we were Church of England, my father never believed in religion. He had a strict code of morals that he stuck to all his life, though. He was a proud man who would not accept charity: if he was down to his last penny, he'd stay out of the pub rather than accept drinks he couldn't afford.

At home, he would never curse, and moral issues were spelled out in black and white. You would never steal from neighbours or your own, or from people as badly off as yourself. And a cardinal rule was that you never trusted a policeman or told them anything. I stuck to that code throughout my career as a villain. My targets were always large financial organisations or stores. I never broke into houses or mugged people. In spite of the poverty in our road, doors were left open because most people respected these unwritten rules – unlike today.

My biggest treat during those early years was to persuade my mum to allow my brother Bert to take me to a Bela Lugosi film. For weeks afterwards I paid a terrible price for this indulgence by having nightmares about zombies.

As one of the older boys, Herbie was always going to the pawn shop with something of my father's and then retrieving it a week or so later. The old man's suit used to get hocked as regular as clockwork. One day a woman stopped Herbie and asked him a favour. She asked him to buy her five Woodbine cigarettes, giving him the money. 'That shopkeeper doesn't like me,' she said. 'I'll hold your brown-paper parcel,' she continued, pointing to the suit tied up with string. When he came out of the shop with the cigarettes, however, there was no woman and no parcel. She'd done a runner with the suit!

Looking back on it, I realise how impoverished my parents were in those times. Thankfully, that era came to an end when us boys were old enough to work. From then on, we started to live reasonably well.

Herbie used to work at the Eccentric Club in Ryder Street, St James. He started off as a lift boy, and graduated to the billiard room as billiard marker. He got Wally a job replacing him on the lifts, while George worked at Whitehall Court, an exclusive apartment block on the Embankment next to the National Liberal Club.

Many famous names used the flats at Whitehall Court during the week, before returning to their country bases at weekends. Among them were George Bernard Shaw, Mr John Dewar (of the whisky family), Sir David Llewellyn and Sir Ernest Tate from the Tate and Lyle sugar family. Sir Ernest was a mean old boy and George, whose wages were then 10 shillings a week, was never tipped by him for shepherding his girlfriends into the lift up to his apartment. Most of the other gents were always generous to the hired help. Lord Wakefield, from Wakefield Oil, used to give half-crown tips every week – enormous money for those times – and John Dewar generously arranged for a whole lamb, turkeys, boxes of shortcakes and hampers to be delivered at Christmastime, along with a white £5 note. What a good old man he was. Always smiling – even though he only had one leg...

One day my father took me to a boxing match at Blackfriars Ring, near The Cut on the south bank of the Thames, to see 'Kid Chocolat' fight (there weren't many black fighters in those days, and he was very famous). At around the same time, just before the war started, my brother Herbie was doing a bit of amateur boxing himself. There were pictures of him in the local newspaper when 'Erbie and Albert Bessel fought to raise money for the International Brigade, who were fighting against Franco in Spain in 1937. The Germans backed Franco with Stuker bombers and arms for Franco's fascist army. It was a rehearsal for them before they started invading Europe. Kid Bessel from Bristol used to come and stay at our house and they'd frequently go down to Blackfriars Ring to watch the big fights and they'd tell me all about them. I had been fascinated by the sport from an early age, when I had watched the bare-knuckle contests outside The Flag pub.

CHAPTER 2
HARD TIMES

I was a product of the war years. We learned to be street smart, to survive without food and to take care of ourselves in a fight. We lived just for the day. Tomorrow we could be blown to bits.

We grew up with a strong sense of loyalty, bravery and honour instilled into our psyche – even at the risk of death. Although I was too young to fight in the war, the lesson was drummed in: if you were captured by the Gestapo, you would never reveal information, no matter what the outcome. The public were continually brainwashed. Everywhere you looked, on trains and buses, were slogans like: 'Be like Dad, keep Mum', 'Careless talk costs lives' and 'Walls have ears'.

As kids, we practised our reading on these public propaganda signs, which were not exclusively directed against the enemy. They also advised on the nation's health: 'Coughs and sneezes spread diseases. Trap the germs in your handkerchief and help to keep the nation fighting fit.'

In the struggle to survive within our own little world, the 'enemy' became the authorities and the lessons from all that propaganda brainwashing we received as children applied to them too. Cossers in particular: my father's refusal to talk to police, let alone acknowledge them, was virtually inborn in the family.

The English are a barbaric and warrior-like race, although the public only recognises this attribute during wars. Young men in particular need to let off steam and prisons would have far fewer inmates if the authorities helped youths channel their energies in positive ways.

I am a warrior. I would defend England to the death if need be, and I admire the fighting spirit for which we have been recognised throughout the ages. I remember reading a Roman soldier's account of the bravery of a British warrior fighting with Queen Boudicca when she rose against the Romans. The soldier sliced the British warrior through the jaw with an axe. A lesser man would have fallen but not the Briton. He tucked his beard into his mouth, holding it with clenched teeth and came back on the attack with his jaw wide open.

Nothing has changed since then. We proved it during the First and Second World Wars and in the Falklands. We are a fighting nation and I'm proud of the fact. Even Hitler said, 'Give me the British soldier and a German officer and I'll conquer the world.' That inbred loyalty, which wins battles and keeps alive national pride, is also evident in prisons. The men I served time with would sacrifice their liberty to stay solid with you.

Looking back, I have learned to understand some of the forces that dictated my actions. Being brought up in a violent era was one factor; obviously, I went over the top on a number of occasions and I would put that down to the madness of youth. Although young men at the time never considered the implications, if someone died as a result of a fight you could very easily find yourself facing a murder charge. And in the 1950s and 1960s, the death penalty was still in force. In spite of that, you continued to risk life and liberty by doing violent battle with others.

As young men, we had no fear. Nobody wanted to lose their freedom or their life, but there was literally nothing that could frighten us. Physical pain was something you accepted as inevitable and confidence inspired by youth made you think you were infallible. If you took part in a serious fight and someone got hurt, you would take every precaution to avoid arrest, but, at the crucial point of battle, nothing could deter you, particularly if your foe was a liberty-taker.

In 1939 when I was seven, Sheepcote Lane was pulled down and we moved to a brand-new block of flats at 32 Croxteth House, Union Street, Wandsworth Road. This was luxury compared to before. Our new home was a three-bedroom council flat that had electricity and a bathroom and wash basin – thank God, no more tin baths.

The only downside – which became obvious to us a couple of months after moving in – was the location. Opposite us was a projectile-munitions factory identified to the enemy by Fifth Columnists. As a result, the factory – and the surrounding area – became a target for German bombers. Next to the factory was a foundry and we would watch a small train carrying the white-hot, glowing shells for storage on a concrete base across the road. In the winter, we kids stood close to the shells for warmth. The factory was targeted many times during the war, but only hit twice. Most streets in the area were wiped out by bombs missing their mark, though.

War was part of our lives. My first memory of it was watching an aerial dogfight high above London on a clear summer's day. The sky became a spaghetti junction of vapour trails from Spitfires and Messerschmitts. At first, nobody took any notice. It was only when the blackout sirens sounded that we were warned to get under cover to avoid fallout from shrapnel.

From our first-floor window at Croxteth House, I would watch the WAAF girls practise putting up barrage balloons filled with helium gas to deter bombers from flying too low. We lived in daily fear of bombs. Other than being killed outright by a direct hit, windows and doors represented the greatest threat of injury: flying glass could be a killer, and so could a door ripped off its hinges and sent flying through the room. We were advised to cover the glass to stop it shattering or, if the windows were blown out, to staple translucent material in their place until workmen could be sent to make repairs.

There were six concrete shelters at the back of our flats, with bunk beds littered around them. When the bombing started, people would pour into them, bringing their bedding and food. There were no toilets, just tin buckets behind a tarpaulin sheet for about 40 people. Even back then I thought it was quite degrading to hear the sound of adults urinating all through the night. The refuge the shelters provided was awful. There was no privacy. From a dark corner you would hear couples carrying on their sex lives, grunting and groaning: 'Ooh, you're hurting me, Joe!' Through half-closed eyes, I would be trying to see what was going on, but I couldn't work out why two people should be lying on top of each other facing the same way...

All my older brothers joined up and fought in the war. Watching them go was a stirring experience. Young men dressed in uniform with kitbags and rifles making their way down to Parliament Square, Westminster, under the gaze of Big Ben. Their first steps to war began with a march across Westminster Bridge amid the fanfare of brass bands and cheering crowds; but they didn't know what they were letting themselves in for. The younger kids followed them all the way to Waterloo Station. Later, the young servicemen were to say it was safer being with the Forces than facing the Blitz in London.

I still find it hard to believe that some people are alive today who have not been properly educated about what happened to England, and in particular Londoners, during the Blitz. The word Blitz comes from the German *Blitzkrieg*, which literally means 'lightning war'. The attacks would happen so quickly – and so devastatingly. By the end of May 1941, over 43,000 civilians had been killed and more than a million houses destroyed or damaged. When the Germans invented the pilotless V1 and V2 bombs, they raised the death toll to 51,509 in 1944 – an astonishing figure when you compare it to the 2,819 that died in the 11 September 2001 terrorist attacks in New York. Another common misconception is that the Blitz lasted only between 7 September 1940 and 16 May 1941 in World War II. Oh, no. We lived in fear every day until 1944, and even then the V2 rockets had only just started to fall.

Before the war began in 1939, Wally was in the Territorials, awaiting a posting abroad, but he immediately joined the Royal Artillery, when battle commenced. Herbie had already joined the King's Royal Rifles (my father's old regiment) in 1939 and George was in the navy. When the bombing got too bad, I was evacuated with my brother Bert (and 650,000 other children). The people who billeted kids got about 50 pence a week per child – quite a decent amount of money. But it was horrible for me.

The first time I was sent away I was given an apple, an orange, a bar of chocolate and a gas mask in a cardboard box with a string around it. You never went anywhere without that. My name tag was attached by safety pin to my coat, and we said a tearful goodbye to my parents at Waterloo Station.

Bert and I arrived at Woking and were taken to a church hall. We sat on the floor while people walked about, picking children out like cattle. Some stopped in front of Bert and me: 'I'll take him, not that one...'

An official replied, 'You can't separate them, they're brothers.' But they did.

Bert was chosen by a nice family. They had a lovely home and later wanted to adopt him. I was left on my own, feeling totally rejected. Out of a church hall full of young kids, I had endured the pain of watching each of the others being chosen by a host family, wondering when my turn would come. When they took my brother away, my heart sank. How could they leave me? Why not take me? What was wrong with me? I was heartbroken.

Evacuees were generally looked down on. Eventually, an awful woman with five children of her own picked me out. Now that Bert had been taken away from me, I felt completely alone. I was as miserable as arseholes. The woman's place was dirty. We all had to pile in the same bed with her sons. One morning I woke to find myself and the sheets covered in blood. This kid I was sleeping with had TB and had been coughing up blood throughout the night.

To wash me, this woman would try to get me to stand in the sink with no clothes on. I didn't like it. There was no relationship within that family. The old man never acknowledged us. There was no conversation and very little to eat. At least at home in London there was love, cleanliness and food. I was billeted for only one reason: to supplement the family income by 50 pence.

My mother visited me there to see if I was all right. Hoping she'd come to collect me, I ran over to her expectantly and she leaned over the fence at the school playground saying, 'Look at the state of you, Fred.' And then, to my embarrassment, in front of the other kids, she spat on her handkerchief and tried to clean me up, washing my face and my ears. She even came back to the house with me and I remember thinking, as she viewed the dirt and squalor, 'She's bound to take me home!' But she didn't. The bombing in London was still too heavy.

Now I was really miserable again. My mother had left me a second time. Then, a month or two later, I was walking home from school and looked up the country road to see my father standing there. I ran up to him, he put his arms out and I grabbed him round the waist. 'Come on, Freddie,' he said gently. 'I'm taking you home. If the Germans bomb us, we'll all go together.' He came back to the house, collected my bits and pieces and we went home to London – I was overjoyed.

Unfortunately, the pleasure of returning was short-lived. London was still being heavily bombed, so I was evacuated for a second time, to Irthlingborough, in Northamptonshire. Herbie arranged it for me.

While on leave from the army, he had met a girl called Judy who was to become his wife, and he'd asked her parents to billet me. I'll never forget the journey to King's Cross Station. I sat silently on the bus, my heart breaking at having to leave my home and family and live once again with strangers.

I liked Judy's father, but her mother was not that keen on having me stay. They were middle class and owned a shoe shop. A south-London Cockney kid was not really their cup of tea. Next door to them lived a nice young lad with whom I got on really well, but when his parents noticed that he started talking like me, a true cockney, they stopped us playing together. That's the kind of neighbourhood it was.

I worked in the shop putting eyelets in the boots for laces, and doing a bit of cleaning. One day, I was cleaning the upstairs windows and fell out, rolled down the shutter blinds and into the road! A bus was heading straight for me, but luckily saw me in time. I broke my arm, but at least it kept me out of school for a few weeks.

I was grateful to move away from them to a family called York, who were bakers. I spent the summer sat in Mr York's delivery van, saving his cakes and tarts from hungry wasps as he did his rounds. It was a new freedom. While I was staying there, Herbie arrived in a Bren gun carrier, chewing up the street and leaving deep marks in the bitumen. Then Wally came to visit. He was an army despatch rider, wearing trousers with leather inside legs, big brown boots and a .45 gun in his belt. Their visits were the highlights of my stay. I was so proud, especially when all the neighbours came out to admire them in their full army regalia.

The Yorks were upset when I left. Although they had a son and daughter of their own, they had grown quite attached to me. The curious thing is that I always kept myself apart. In winter, the family would gather around the fire and invite me to join them, but I would sit on a hard-backed chair on the opposite side of the room, listening to the radio, thinking how pleased I would be to get back to my own family. I hated being sent away and missed my parents and brothers. Nobody could take their place.

After Northampton, I was evacuated twice more, to Hove, Brighton. The house where I stayed was on a hill facing down to the sea. One day, I saw several dray horses shed their load as they bolted down the hill and crossed the main road, crashing through the window of the David

Greg grocery shop. The whole episode was very messy but I watched, fascinated, as police held down the horses while a man in a suit put a metal frame on each horse's head, with a hole in the forehead. He then killed them with a spike and one blow with a club hammer to the brain. I was close enough to look into the horse's eyes, and held its stare as the man clinically struck the fatal blow. I saw the pity in the horse's eyes, then nothing, just emptiness. It was a mercy killing. The man showed no emotion as he carried out this macabre task. I remember the blood was so thick it stuck my shoes to the street. Those images stay with you for life. For a boy of 10, I saw far too much blood and guts.

Mrs Freeland, my Hove billet, was quite a fat lady who sold her body as a sideline. She used to tart herself up with rouge and bright-red lipstick, then march out to the seafront in her white strappy sandals to earn a bit extra while her husband was away on nightshift. She always made sure she was back before he returned.

Mrs Freeland's son and I once nicked a whole tin of chocolate biscuits and sat in bed eating them until we felt really sick. We did quite a bit of nicking and I became a dab hand at it. I remember, during one air raid in London, a blast blew out the window of a grocery shop in Wandsworth Road. We loaded up an old battered pram – which I used to fetch coal from Nine Elms coal yard for my mother and her two neighbours – with Australian canned fruit that we'd been salivating over through the window for days, and made a dash back to our flats. My parents would not have approved of us nicking, so me and my mates gorged ourselves on it in secret in the bomb shelter till we made ourselves ill again. Kids never learn, do they?

After Brighton I returned to London, determined not to be sent away again. There had been a lull in the bombing, due to the Germans having lost most of their planes. But new and more dangerous missiles were imminent – the V1 and V2 rockets. After we had gone through those terrible doodlebugs (V1s), we thought it was over. Our armies were at the gates of Berlin, for fuck's sake, yet 84 V2 rockets fell on the borough of Wandsworth alone between September and November 1944, not to mention the rest of London. At first, the government misled people about the V2 bombings. To avoid panic, propaganda was spread throughout the media, putting the blasts down to gas explosions rather than the rockets, which were killing thousands in central London.

As frightening as the bombing was, it was also fascinating. I will never forget the sight of a young woman caught in a V2 bomb blast under an arch. When I noticed her, she was picking herself up off the middle of the road, her clothes had been blown away and her stockings were in shreds. I watched as she tried to hide her modesty. For a 12-year-old, it was a very erotic scene and the first time that I had laid eyes on a semi-naked woman.

Large numbers of civilians were killed by doodlebugs and rockets and you would see young children whose limbs had been torn from their bodies, and rows of dead people laid out on the pavements, some killed in shelters, others pulled out of their wrecked houses. Tragically, a bomb scored a direct hit on the King's Arms one night, killing nearly all the customers, including several of our neighbours who were in there having a pint.

My parents were lucky to have four boys survive the war, although there were moments when they feared the worst. I can remember Lord Haw-Haw's propaganda programmes on the radio. (He was hanged in January 1946. Amazingly, many years later, I would get to stand on his grave inside Pentonville Prison.) In spite of the fact that he was a Nazi propagandist, he pulled a large audience. One particular night we heard him say, 'Germany calling, Germany calling. This is Lord Haw-Haw speaking… The Führer's navy today sunk the minesweeper *Fitzroy* in the English Channel. All hands were lost…' George was on that boat and we were all convinced he was dead. My mother burst into tears. My father was visibly distressed but kept a stiff upper lip. I sensed their tremendous sadness. Over the next day or two, we waited with anguish for the knock on the door and the official telegram that would confirm the bad news.

Days later, I was leaning over the balcony, deep in thought and looking down at the square when I saw a figure coming into the housing estate in a boiler suit and a sailor hat. As it loomed larger, I couldn't believe what I was seeing. It was George! My George! He was alive. I couldn't contain my excitement. I could hear my mother washing up in the kitchen and shouted to her, 'Quick, Mum, it's our George. He's alive!'

Mum rushed out, disbelieving me, but wiping her hands on her apron as she joined me to look over the balcony into the square. 'Georgie!' she cried out.

George, a big grin on his face, waved his arm cheerfully and my mother rushed along the balcony to the top of the stairs to greet him. She hugged him and cried with joy. The old man got out the hard stuff and that night it was down to the local Portland Arms for a good session.

George told us the story of how his ship had struck a mine and went down in four minutes. He had just finished his duty watch in the stoke hole. The ship had capsized and he crawled out hand over fist, upside down along an escape ladder and jumped into the North Sea. He'd managed to get into a life raft, but had to go back in the water again to make way for a petty officer with an injured back. He was in the water for two hours before they were rescued by HMS *Elgin*, another minesweeper, and taken to Great Yarmouth. All his possessions were lost and he and the other seamen were given fresh clothes and two weeks' compassionate leave. But they were recalled after only a week because they were concerned they might leg it, so they sent him off to Mombasa, East Africa, on the *Stirling Castle* troop carrier. While he was out there, George joined the cruiser HMS *Mauritius*. It was a notorious ship. They had more arrests on that ship than on any other in the British fleet, because of disquiet onboard. The crew of the Mauritius were in the thick of the action for 18 months during the invasion of North Africa, Sicily, Italy and the Greek islands, having just one break of leave in Malta, so they had the right hump. The crew were also unhappy with the ship's number one over an incident that occurred during a swimming break off the coats of Italy. Many of the crew were allowed overboard to have a swim, but, when German bombers attacked and the alarms raised, the captain simply took off, to become a moving target. The men had to swim like Tarzan to reach the rope ladders in time! When my George eventually arrived home on leave it was the first time he'd laid his eyes on Georgina his baby daughter, who was 18 months old.

A book could be written about my brother Herbie, who fought in 11 different countries for King and Country and escaped death on a number of occasions. He was one of only 22 of his battalion of 600 to survive a drop into Arnhem, an event that inspired the movie *A Bridge Too Far*. To any folk who have served their country, Herbie's records from the Ministry of Defence are nothing short of tremendous. From 1939, he fought for the Parachute Battalion and in countries from North Africa, to India to Singapore, winning a host of medals. Sadly, he passed away last year, but I will always remember his smiley little face. When Herbie met Prince Charles on the commemoration of Arnhem in Holland, he instantly recognised him because he was so small. 'Erbie was five-foot five – and I'm giving him an inch there. Charles looked at his medals and said, 'You got about a bit!' and 'Erbie replied, 'I must have been a hard target to hit!'

As I said, we're a fighting family, the Foremans. George himself was awarded six campaign stars, clasps and medals during his service, including the Atlantic Star, Africa Star, Italy Star and the War Medal 1939–45. I'm so very proud of all of my brothers. I'm afraid there is simply not room enough in this chapter for me to list their military achievements and bravery in full.

Whenever the boys returned home, we kept an open house to whoever was a friend of theirs. They would come to Mum's and stay on their short home leave. When friends of my brothers came on leave to stay with us, I would lead them to the local pub during blackouts. I knew my way there blindfolded. One was Bertie Chapman, a pal of George's who would end up working for the Inland Revenue – and chasing me for tax evasion!

One inevitable problem arising from the war was the amount of armoury entering the country. My brother Herbie brought home Lee Enfield bolt-action .303 rifles, and his mates would bring back pistols and knives as souvenirs. My brothers presented me with German bayonets and daggers, which I proudly showed to my friends. Herbie and Wally, both paratroopers in the First Airborne Division, had access to all kinds of weapons, including knuckle-dusters. They even had dyed-blue wooden bullets, which had been used to save on metal. Everywhere you went in the less gentrified areas of London, metal railings had been pulled out to help the war effort – though the middle and upper classes living in areas such as Belgravia and Knightsbridge were spared this inconvenience. Schooling was regularly interrupted by bombing raids too.

The bombsites around us were ideal for fighting. All around were tunnels and wasteland, where mock battles would be fought. Fireworks represented live ammunition, although, on some days, real bullets were used. I broke into a shed next to the temporary school and nicked all the smoke bombs and crackers belonging to the army and let them off in the girls' lavatory. The school notified the police and three of us responsible for this outrage were dragged to the front of assembly and given a terrible dressing down by the headmistress. 'You are nothing but Nazi children! Hitler's children! Nazi youth!' she told us venomously.

This was too much. I protested, 'I've got four brothers fighting the Germans. I'm not a Nazi!'

One of the problems with school was that, by the time I was 14, and showing an interest in learning and developed a thirst for knowledge, it was time to leave. But, even so, they could have encouraged my natural ability in art, the only subject in which I excelled.

My art reflected my environment. I drew battle scenes, tanks, artillery, aircraft and scenes of carnage. I had an artist's eye for detail: I could tell a Wellington bomber from a Lancaster, a Hurricane from a Spitfire, a Heinkel from a Messerschmitt and could identify enemy tanks. I drew gory fights in which death came at the point of a bayonet or a bullet.

Those images were true to life. I was getting the violence down on paper. My reputation began to spread. Schoolkids went out of their way to see what I had drawn and offered to swap their comics for my art. I started to take this further and drew my own action comics. This led to a fight between two pupils who argued over what I was drawing one day.

One of the kids punched the other in the face, and a pencil he was holding went right through the victim's rosy cheek. I got the blame for that and it alerted the teacher to my art. He took my drawing and examined it in detail. I probably had about a hundred figures on it: Germans and British troops, action scenes involving tanks and aircraft, buildings being blown up, barbed wire, killings. A lot of work had gone into it. The teacher summoned his colleagues and examined it, showing a lot of interest. I thought I'd get just one word of praise, but no, instead they said, 'This is one sick little bastard.'

But it was a comment on the times. There were always guns in the house, German Lugers, old service revolvers, Japanese swords, crudely made scabbards and Arab daggers. I used to love playing with them.

In spite of my bad school record, I had a grudging respect for Mr Nye, even though he regularly beat me with the cane. He had a withered arm and had this amazing robotic capacity to administer six of the best while speaking to the rest of the class at the same time. Unlike other teachers, however, he would pay me compliments for my sporting abilities. I won all the races at school and he would tell everyone, 'That boy's got shoulders on him like a horse.'

At one point I remember seeing a parachute come down. Men ran to it, prepared to lynch the German pilot who'd dropped these bombs on us. But, instead of a German, there was a landmine attached to it and a couple of streets were blown up.

Towards the end of the war, my father was on warden duty when a doodlebug hit us late at night. My mother and I were in the shelter and my father came down, his face covered in brick-dust and blood trickling from his forehead. 'I'm all right, Lou,' he told my mother. 'But we've lost everything.'

Croxteth House was reduced to rubble and we were moved first to a two-roomed temporary accommodation in Wickersley Road, Battersea, and then to Usk Road, at the top of Clapham Junction West Hill. Our balcony overlooked the railway. Bertie arrived home on leave once in his navy outfit, all nice and white, and whenever one of the boys came home they'd be cooked a special breakfast of bacon and eggs. But, while Mum was preparing this treat for Bertie, there was a terrific explosion.

As Mum walked to the kitchen the blast lifted up the thick lino from the floor, stopping the door, which had been blown off its hinges, from hitting her in the face. Soot blackened the flat and all you could see of Bert was his white teeth and eyes, looking like a Kentucky minstrel. 'Oh, Bert, look at your eggs and bacon!' said Mum. She was more concerned about the pile of soot over his eggs and bacon than the fact the front of the flat had been blown away! It turned out a V2 had dropped on the other side of the railway embankment, shielding us from a blast that had killed 42 others.

Eventually, Croxteth House was rebuilt and we moved back again. Most of our personal belongings and family 'treasures' were lost, though. We had to make do with very few possessions. Furniture was non-existent. You had to improvise tables and chairs from tea chests.

Understand: these were *really* hard times.

CHAPTER 3

YOUR COUNTRY NEEDS YOU

The slogan before and during the war was: Your Country Needs You. Now that the war was over, *you* needed the country; I was young enough not to be disillusioned with the way the system worked and old enough to be aware that those with nothing got nothing. My four brothers, and our father before them in WWI, had been willing to lay down their lives for their country. When the war was over, though, they got very little in return. On being demobbed, you had the choice of either a Prince of Wales checked suit or a blue pin-striped suit and a gratuity of about £60 to £80.

Everybody you saw those days was dressed in the checked suit and I could sense some of the bitterness and resentment that accompanied their paltry reward. My brothers George, Wally, 'Erbie and Bert were only skilled at killing the enemy, so the jobs they were offered were quite lowly: digging trenches at the top of Northcote Road and building prefabricated houses, mostly made of asbestos. The boss didn't like them, so they got the sack after two weeks.

My brothers Wally and George then put their money together and, with a little extra from my father's meagre savings, bought a stall, and a horse and cart. They parked it on the corner of Princess Head, Battersea, and sold fruit and vegetables with a sideline in logging. I helped them, although I was still at school, and we went scavenging on bombsites, dragging out old rail sleepers, cutting them up with large cross-saws, then chopping them up into bundles to sell as firewood. I was in my element working with my brothers.

But a freezing winter and an impoverished neighbourhood did not make for good business, so George went back to work doing what he was used to in the navy. He shovelled coal off barges on to a conveyor belt in the Thames for Nine Elms power station. That was a terrible job, breathing in all the grime and dust in a hold full of coal, and the tough existence was etching lines into his face. He was a good-looking chap, with fair skin and blond hair, but he was ageing prematurely. There must have been a couple of kilos of coal dust in his lungs and he still suffers with his chest today.

The war had done nothing to dispel people's mistrust of uniforms – those of coppers and authority in general. You trusted no one. Officers shot you in the First World War if you lost your nerve or were slow getting out of the trench and they, in turn, were executed by the soldiers. Shot in the back. My father told me about that. So, if someone came out of the army and saw someone thieving, they would look the other way as long as the victim wasn't one of their own. That attitude was very prominent in the period after the war.

We had lived on the edge. A German bomb could have ended our existence at any moment, but in our youth we felt we were invincible. We were too busy enjoying the excitement and exhilaration of discovery – and Milky.

Milky Big Tits was a good sort. Big busted, with blonde hair down to her waist and nice long legs. Just the type of girl I always fancied. I was 14 and a virgin when I met her. Milky (her real name was Olive) was a couple of years older than me. She was brazen and adventurous. Nobody could wish for a better introduction to manhood than spending some sticky moments with a girl as eager to please as she was. 'Catch me and I'm yours,' she'd say. From time to time she would allow one or two other boys to catch her but she was physically able to resist our advances if she didn't fancy the outcome.

Milky went beyond the call of duty. The more we indulged, the more she enjoyed it. It was a lot like the film *Once Upon A Time In America*! The backdrop to this nonsense was anything but romantic. We had a kiss and cuddle ending in a knee trembler against a brick wall within the compounds of a bombed-out school at Larkhall Lane, just around the corner from our old council flat in Wandsworth Road, which was being rebuilt.

Sharing these sexual encounters with mates extended Milky's horizons even further. After I'd had my wicked way, I would talk her into letting a pal have a go. Without too much persuasion, she would say, 'All right, but just this once.'

Then they would start queuing up: Johnny Brindle, Ronnie Mitchell and the Long brothers – George, Teddy, Tommy and Jimmy. Jimmy was only a little kid at the time, probably about nine or ten. When it came to his turn, the big boys would shove him to the end of the queue and Milky would snort, 'He's too little. He can't do it!'

But little Jimmy was determined. 'Yes I can, yes I can,' he'd insist. Every time he was pushed out of the queue he'd race to the end and wait patiently for another chance.

Taking pity, we'd plead, 'Come on, let him have a go. At least he'll shut up.' Eventually she'd relent but it was all over in a wink and none of us ever discovered whether Jimmy had made it, or not, or whether Milky was aware of the fact.

Milky, like the rest of us, had experienced the ravages of war. Two years earlier, sharpnel had smashed through a brick and grazed her breast, so perhaps enjoying life meant that much more to her.

With the war, very few schools were left standing and I left mine at the age of 14, with few qualifications, and got a job with South Western Railways as a driver's mate delivering goods in London and all over southern England. We started off with an old Iron Horse, a three-wheeler petrol-driven truck that you would hook up to a horse-box and use to take the horses to different stables. We then graduated to a Bedford truck, which had tarpaulin sheets on the back and could hook up to trailers, some with containers already loaded. The jobs were diverse. We could be delivering fruit to Covent Garden one day, and gold to the Bank of England the next. Sometimes we'd take a load of metal drums filled with coins to the Royal Mint. When delivering bullion, we were paid an extra £2 on top of our £5-a-week wages for the heavy work involved.

Alfie, my driver, was not backward when it came to nicking loads of fruit from the market. We'd take luxury items like lovely Cape grapes and peaches and fruit. In those days, you never saw anything like that at local shops, and down it would go under the seat in the front cabin of the truck, hidden by a blanket. Alternatively, we'd deliver a load and damage some of the parcels, pulling out some of the contents, like shirts perhaps, from the middle. Everybody was doing it: crane drivers in the docklands would always drop a load on purpose. If it was a crate of whisky, they would nick a few bottles of Scotch that had remained intact and write off the whole load.

Never had my senses been as aroused as by the sight of all the gold we had volunteered to collect from King's Cross when I was still a lad of 14. We backed the Southern Railway Iron Horse – with tarpaulin sides and a sheet at the back with leather straps to close it from prying eyes – right up to the railway carriage. Inside was a fortune in wedge-shaped gold bars, two on the bottom, two across, one on top, neatly packed so you could get your fingers underneath each precious bar. All together, the load would have been worth several million pounds.

And all we had guarding this lot was a 14-year-old boy (me), two coppers and a government official next to Alfie, the driver, who was one of a family of well-known greengrocers in those parts. We would drive from King's Cross to the Bank of England in Threadneedle Street or, if we had coins, we took them to the Royal Mint on the north side of Tower Bridge. Snatching the gold would have been the easiest bit of work ever for anyone with a little bit of enterprise. I fantasised even then about nicking it: at today's prices, each bar would have fetched £100,000, and I lovingly cradled those bars like I would a child. The deliveries were made on a fairly regular basis and because of the heavy work were unpopular, and word quickly got around because everyone was asked to volunteer. It would have been easy for us to tell someone where it was coming from, but, those days, people weren't that way inclined. They didn't think of thieving big lumps of money. For me, though, a seed was sown.

My next job was at Pannet and Eden, as a warehouseman. They were based in Wandsworth and did herbs and stuffing as well as hair cream and associated products. One job involved carrying hundredweight sacks full of breadcrumbs up ladders and stairs, which built up my strength. Another part of the job was handling 56lb boxes of lard or fat intended for the stuffing – so, needless to say, my mother's family and friends were never short of hair oil, mint sauce, stuffing or lard. Nor were many of the women working in Pannet and Eden. I would wrap chunks of lard in greaseproof paper and slip it into their open handbags. I never charged them a penny for this, although a number showed their appreciation in different ways – usually among the empty sacks in the loft above the storage rooms. We were still on ration books shortly after the war and limited to only about an ounce of lard per person, per week, so I became the most popular young male among 45 women workers.

People always go on about men on building sites, but you have to see it to believe what women get up to in factories. The old ones were the worst. They'd grab your dick and get a little too excited. If you gave them a playful kiss, you'd get a tongue down your throat.

With a wage of £4.50 a week, I'd nick anything to make up for the hard work I had to do. A good line was women's make-up, which would get you a few quid on top of your wages. I stayed at Pannet's for about a year, the longest I've had in any job, and eventually got sacked when someone grassed me up for giving cooking lard to one of the women. The sack came out of the blue, but it didn't worry me very much and I went to work for Stevens and Carter, a scaffolding firm. Onwards and upwards!

The only person to be really upset at my abrupt departure from Pannet's was a lovely spinster of about 40 called Gladys. She cried when she heard I'd been dismissed. Gladys lived with another, more elderly woman. She was tall and thin with dark hair swept back and wore glasses. While she was no beauty, her nature made her a lovely person. She didn't have a bad word for anyone and was always kind and laughing. Gladys had a lovely little twinkle in her eye and I think she got quite attached to me – not sexually, you understand, but in a maternal way, like an affectionate aunt. I used to chat to her quite a lot, and we got on well together. I would help her tie parcels and lift them off the bench after she'd packed them up. She talked to me about life in general and liked to see me enjoying myself.

Gladys was well aware of what I was up to with some of the young girls working on the factory floor. In fact, she became my accomplice and would leave me in the warehouse with the girls, shut the door, and say, 'You two stay there...'

I last saw Gladys when I was 15 and was very upset some years later to learn that she had committed suicide. I was too sad to ask the details, but she must have been a troubled soul, or very ill, to do that.

Years later, a very strange set of events involving her took place. Gladys made what I can only describe as psychic contact with me during moments of great stress. I was 37 years old and in the depths of despair after being charged with the murder of Frank Mitchell – of which more later – when Gladys 'spoke' to me. I swear I could hear her voice saying, 'It's all right, Fred. Calm down. Take it easy. It's going to be all right.'

Gladys came to me again when I was kidnapped and brought back to England from Spain and I know she is always there to help me in times of crisis. She's lovely, my Gladys. A guardian angel sent to comfort me in times of need. I hope and pray she is now at peace and that I won't need her services any more.

Her death, like the death of my parents, possibly affected me more than it might otherwise have done, because I was never able to mourn for them. I was unable to attend the funerals of my father, mother and sister-in-law Nellie because harsh prison rules would not allow me out. The same thing happened to Tommy Wisbey after he was jailed for the Great Train Robbery. While he was doing his 30 years he lost his teenage daughter, Lorraine, in a car accident, but was not allowed out to attend her funeral. I was godfather to his other daughter, Marilyn, and he was godfather to my son Gregory. At that time I was unable to grieve their loss with the rest of the family and, somehow, your mind doesn't accept they are dead if you don't go through the ritual of a funeral service. I still wake up at times and, just for a moment, think I must go round and see if the old man and Mum are all right. And then it slowly dawns on me that they are no longer here...

But back to my youth.

Scaffolding was considered a macho job and attracted strong young men, including ex-soldiers. We were all south-London men working on a site at Hatfield College, near the Armstrong Siddeley aircraft factory in Hertfordshire. The college had received deliveries of a large amount of sheet copper in packs of one-hundredweight rolls. These were stored under lock and key in a large metal bunker at the back of the site next to some woods accessible only by a dirt road, and I immediately saw the potential of nicking them.

To help me with this enterprise, I engaged the services of an elderly man called Fat Joe and his partner Claude, an evil-looking bastard with dark, slitty eyes. Fat Joe weighed about 20 stone and he and his partner owned the right vehicles to get the load away. They told me they would be able to sell the metal in Croydon.

The ex-guardsman who was supposed to be minding the site was more often than not in the village pub with his big bastard of an Alsatian dog. The man was a bully and very unpopular with the locals and some of our lads who had already had punch-ups with him. Naturally, I timed the robbery for when he was at the pub. We drove up the dirt road and knocked off the paddy (padlock) to the steel shed; then, we loaded up two big old cars, a Ford V8 shooting brake and a Chrysler. It was all dense weight, but we cleaned most of it out. The operation was a success and proved to be a nice little earner.

Next day, when I returned to work, enquiries about the theft were already up and running. Stevens and Carter scaffolders didn't suspect me but, as I was sitting eating in the canteen, the guard's Alsatian walked up to me and started sniffing me out. As if that was not enough, he then plonked himself down in front of me and sat staring at me. Never suspecting anything, my workmates made a joke of it: 'Are you sure you never nicked it, Fred?' they asked and then jokingly added, 'Look at the dog watching you!'

The bloody animal looked as if he was about to spring on me! This went on for a few days but, thank God, only the dog sussed me out.

While working as a scaffolder, I had a relationship with a little firecracker called Joyce who was separated from her husband. There were other girls too who were quite saucy, nearly one in every block on my estate, and I used to cop for quite a few of them. But Joyce was a bit special. I'd met her at a party and took her outside for a drink on the balcony: She was more forward than I expected. She took off her knickers, put them in her handbag and, without waiting, undid my trousers and jumped on me, wrapping her legs around my waist and clinging to my neck. Then she started bouncing up and down like a bloody rabbit. It had never happened to me like that before. My mother poked her head around the door and caught us at it while I was banging away like a good 'un. Later she warned me to stay away from that girl. But I found her a sexy little thing and she knew a lot more than I did; she taught me a thing or two. (Today, my wife Janice says this is an understatement!)

Joyce was a little bit on the tarty side – very attractive, with a nice body and cheeky eyes. I used to take her down a dark alleyway and she was quite as happy having it there as anywhere. She used to work at the button factory on the Wandsworth Road, where quite a lot of the young girls used to work. One of Joyce's workmates I copped for once had acquired a strange reputation in the factory: she was always the first in at work and the last to leave. It was subsequently discovered that she liked to lean on a certain part of the machinery, which vibrated like hell, so that she could enjoy multiple orgasms all day long! But she was too much for me. As some might have said back then, I was like Superman: faster than a speeding bullet – and no match for the girl at the button factory!

Anyway, my relationship with Joyce thrived until I saw her with another guy walking down the same alleyway that I'd thought was 'special' only to us. Obviously I was wrong. She was not true to me, but I was infatuated with her. I was with Lennie Sunbourne, a relation of mine, when she walked past. I hadn't seen her at first because I was buying a cup of tea and a hotdog sandwich at a stall. Then Lennie pointed her out and I pretended I didn't care. But, of course, I did.

I went down there just as they were coming out of the alley again and chinned the geezer. He went spark out. I then gave her a backhander and called her a fucking slag. My ring had sliced open the geezer's cheek and Joyce got down on her knees to help him. 'Look what you've done!' she cried.

I told Joyce not to come near me any more and walked back to the flats.

A short time afterwards, I heard an ambulance siren and then a worried Lennie tapped on my door. 'Did you do him with a brick, Fred?' he asked. 'He's in a hell of a state, hasn't regained consciousness.'

I had a right dodgy night worrying about the cossers coming round. But it had only been one punch, a right hander. Anyway, the guy never grassed me to the police so I was OK.

Later, Joyce came to my local and tried to make up. I was nearly tempted but in the end I simply blanked her. I was hurt and felt she had done the dirty on me. In fact, looking back, she was just a lively and lovely girl who worked in the button factory. A good little jiver, too.

Anyway, there were always plenty of other girls about. I had quite a lot of romantic little flings, as you can imagine, and I know that there are one or two little Freddies about, but I can't go into details as I don't want to embarrass anyone who may be married with a family. The last thing I want is to cause any problems. I often feel that I would like to hire a hall and get all my old friends and family together for a big nosh- and drink-up and chat about old times and see the kids who have grown up.

I retired from scaffolding after falling from a second-floor level. Although I landed on my feet, I got pinned to a plank of wood with this rusty old nail. It went right through the sole of my shoe and into my foot. I was taken to Hatfield Hospital and given antibiotic injections. My leg felt like a war was going on inside. It throbbed like fuck for about a week. In fact, it was a good time to leave the scaffolding job: winter was coming on and scaffolding wasn't much fun in lousy weather. I went to see George, who was still shovelling coal, and told him he had to stop that and do a bit of work with me.

We met a guy who said we could earn good money for a few months' work pile driving. We needed two extra men to make up the work team, a steel fixer and another to control the pile driver and change the sections over as the holes for building foundations got deeper. It was a bit like drilling for oil. A big crane smashed down these metal and concrete tubes deep into the ground, some 25 feet or so, till it hit rock bottom. Then I would slip the steel cage that I had fixed and that fell to the bottom and the steel rods would stick out of the top, ready for the concrete. Once that was poured in and set, the foundations would be solid enough for blocks of flats, or flyovers. I suppose that's how the stories of Ginger Marks's disappearance came about – the speculation that he had been buried under a flyover. Mind you, if you did stick someone down one of those holes, they would have to pull the whole building down to find anything, so it's not a bad idea, and it did cross my mind on one or two occasions years later...

On most Saturday nights, we'd go to the dances, for the big-band sounds. All the town halls put on English bands like Vic Lewis, Ted Heath and Ivor Kerchin, playing American big-band music. I remember seeing Ted and Barbara Andrews and their daughter Julie singing on stage at the Grand, Clapham Junction. Most of the upcoming stars would appear there too, including the Goons Peter Sellers, Harry Secombe and Michael Bentine. Harry Secombe's farmyard imitations would bring the house down, as would Sellers's impersonations of film stars. The Grand would also put on boxing exhibitions with the likes of Freddie Mills and Frankie Hough. The entertainment industry had started up again in a big way because during the war large numbers of people were prevented from congregating in one place in case they were bombed. Needless to say, manpower was at a premium.

We enjoyed the sounds of Ted Heath and his orchestra, the Squadronairs, Vic Lewis, and the Ray Ellington quartet. My mates at the time included Patsy Toomey, Lennie White, Jimmy Turner, Tommy Wisbey, Tony Reuter, Jacky Cramer, Arthur and Teddy Suttie, Billy Adams, Freddy and Dinny Powell, whom we called Nosher, because his father was a horse trader at the arches behind the Elephant and Castle. The name Nosher came from the 'nosh-bag' that hung around a horse's neck containing food.

At the time, I was a member of the Battersea Boxing Club, run by a Mr Hall. One of his trainers was old Billy Whitely, who used to come to parties at my parents' house and load me up with pennies. I introduced the gang to the club because they were all pretty keen to learn, as we often fought with other gangs in the streets.

One time, I had problems with a gang down the Wandsworth Road, so we got together to sort them out. During one street fight, a guy jumped out of an upstairs window on to my back while I was battling with his brother. He was a lot older than me, and in the navy, and he looked well muscled in his white vest. But I think he must have regretted coming home on leave from the navy, because some of us beat the shit out of him. We really fancied ourselves at the fight game. Patsy Toomey would ask, 'Who's the best fighter around here? Go and fetch him and I'll have a straightener.'

On one occasion, we were at a stall down the World's End in Chelsea. Patsy challenged this guy and I held their coats. There were five of us and about 30 of the other gang. Everyone crowded around to watch the fight with cups of tea in their hands. 'Patsy, you better win this one,' I said to myself. But he came unstuck: the guy he was fighting had him pinned down and sat on his chest punching his head in. I couldn't stand seeing my pal hurt, so I interfered. I pulled the guy off and smashed his head against the kerb and the next thing I heard was running feet followed by blow after blow smashing down on me. They were laying into me with their boots. I rolled under a parked lorry and got up on the other side. 'All right,' I said, 'let's make this one-to-one.'

One stepped forward and said, 'I'll have him.'

We started to fight and, being a strong kid, I held my own for a long time until, exhausted, we both ended up on our knees facing each other, still punching it out. By mutual agreement, whispered in each other's ears, we'd had enough. That signalled an honourable tie-breaker. We stood up and shook hands and everybody went back to have another cup of tea. In a way, it was like history repeating itself: we began where our fathers left off.

The dance halls and pubs also became a major venue for our brawling. We'd go into the pubs and bars, get tanked up and, if anyone tried to chat up any one of our girls, you would have a row and the place would degenerate into a free-for-all. Going to dance halls in different parts of London was like going to a football match and meeting the other team's supporters. If it was the Lyceum, you took a pitch in the corner and no one else was allowed there apart from us south-London and Elephant and Castle boys.

Before the end of the night, there'd be a row and the girls would get excited and want to go home with you afterwards. It was all very macho stuff. The next day, we'd dissect the fight, revel in our victory and relive the finer moments. Sometimes the fights would turn quite serious and tools like starting handles would be brought out. But, then again, you'd also end up respecting one or two of the opposition and get pally with them in the future.

One of our gang had been to a wedding in Dulwich and a crowd of lads had bashed him up and taken liberties with him. He asked for a bit of help and, as we were prepared to travel anywhere for a good row, we offered to sort things out for him. It was the done thing back then.

With our adrenaline flowing, we descended on the other gang at a youth club. A few got injured and the club was wrecked, but that was as much the fault of the other gang as it was ours. The main principals in this fracas, including me, got away while some of the lesser fry got nicked and stuck up all our names. A couple of days later, though, I was dragged off to the nick, charged with assault, GBH (grievous bodily harm) and affray.

The police found a few coshes, made from steel rungs from a barber's shop chair, and a thick woollen sand-weighted sock belonging to a friend called Francis. I was too young to be put in Wormwood Scrubs Prison so they put me into Stamford House Remand Centre, where a few of the warders were nonces: they were into young boys and at the same time were sadistic bastards who wanted to beat the shit out of you with canes.

Police raised such a hue and cry over this case that it went to the Number One Court of the Old Bailey. It was my first time at the famous court, but little did I know I would be back there six times in total in the years to come – and always to the Number One Court. It should never have come to trial, let alone been heard in the Central Criminal Court. What a ridiculous waste of public money and police time. I was only 16 years old and already I was in the most famous court in the land! Such treatment served only to elevate me in the eyes of my peers. The trial in 1948, heard by Sir Gerald Dodson, the Recorder, was full of comic moments. The prosecutor ran through a list of weapons and then held out Francis's smelly sand-filled sock at arm's length, turning his head away from it as he spoke.

Each time he used the phrase 'and one sand-weighted sock', we lads in the dock – there were 11 of us – all repeated the phrase with our heads down, whispering the words with the QC: 'and one sand-weighted sock'. Then we went redder and redder, exchanging looks and stifling giggles and fits of laughter.

The judge bound us over and fined us £5 each. We were also ordered to be taken down to the cells at the Old Bailey to experience 'the feel of life behind bars'. 'This experience should serve as a lifelong lesson,' Sir Gerald told us. 'When you come out, look up to the sky and be thankful you can see it.'

I wonder if he was aware that we had already spent time in prisons and remand centres awaiting this trial as well as many hours in the cells under the Old Bailey awaiting His Lordship.

With all the practice we were getting inside and outside of the ring, our little firm got quite skilled in the art of fighting. Eventually, I took Nosher's brother, Freddie Powell, down to the Battersea Boxing Club; having a heavyweight champion from the army join your local club was a feather in your cap. He had several fights for the club and then turned professional.

The club officials got the horn when they saw Freddie, who was a big sun-tanned six-foot-three heavyweight. He was a real crowd-pleaser. Nobody left a show until they had seen him fight. The promoters always put him on last to keep the crowd and atmosphere alive. Nosher and Fred are still friends of mine today.

In my teens, I was a light welterweight at 10st 3lb. Patsy was two or three pounds lighter and Lenny White was only 9st 9lb. We all gave our best in bouts but did very little training: a couple of times a week at most. The rest of the time we'd go to the big bands, drink beer and go out with the girls. We would also train at a number of different centres: the Budekai Club, where I learned a bit of jujitsu, the Battersea Boxing Club (Latchmere) and Joe Jones's gym in Islington.

On Sunday mornings, we'd go to Jack Solomon's gym in Windmill Street, Soho. He ran a nursery for a few young amateur boxers. And what an experience it was. Nat Sellers was the trainer then and Jack Solomon the fight promoter. Jack was a lovely man who was never without a big cigar in his mouth. Apart from American pros, we had people like Freddie Mills, George and Tommy Daley, Joe Carter, Tommy McGovern and Alby Hollister and the Barnham brothers from Fulham. Most of the active fighters in London worked out at Jack Solomon's gym at one time or another. Exhibition matches were put on about once a month between ourselves, and they could turn nasty if you got hurt and sought revenge on your sparring partner.

Stewart Granger often came to Jack Solomon's. He was then a budding young actor in the Gainsborough films with Margaret Lockwood and would often comment on our fights. He said of me, 'Young Freddie Foreman is similar to Freddie Mills in his line of attack,' and once handed out a prize of dressing gown and shorts. My father and brothers would proudly watch the proceedings from small wooden benches.

We kids were all protégés of Bud Flanagan of the Flanagan and Allen comedy duo. Bud was famous in those days and his voice is still heard on TV today – if you watch *Dad's Army*, he sang the theme tune. Bud was a nice old boy: he used to give us free tickets for his West End shows and treat us to slap-up meals in Victoria before taking us to see his Crazy Gang show at Victoria Palace. (Today, the Leukaemia Foundation that Bud Flanagan set up is still running, and my son Jamie and I support it by attending various fundraising functions.)

Anyway, we had some tough contests when we did the rounds at the 'bath fights' – boxing matches arranged at venues like town halls and local baths. Our opponents were from other clubs and the three Armed Forces and we fought all over London. I must have had about 30 fights in all at venues, which included Nine Elms (lots of times), Tooting Bec,

Manor Place, Victoria Park, Bermondsey baths, Seymour Place baths, Shoreditch Town Hall and Grange Road baths. Fights were held nearly every week in those days. I had a few wars with opponents much older than myself, old timers who had been around for years. I was only in my mid-teens and they were in their late twenties and early thirties.

It was quite hard work some nights, because you could end up fighting three different opponents. You might arrive for a novices competition at 6.30pm, fight an hour later, then go in the ring with the second opponent at 8.30pm and, if you got through the first two, then go on to the final at about 11pm. During all those excruciating hours, your black eyes would puff up more and your swollen nose become sorer and sorer. I had a couple of nights like those, only to get beaten in the final. I was so disappointed. I had set my heart on a beautiful cup and lost it to a guy I should have beaten.

At one fight in Nine Elms baths, two MPs (military police) had to bring an Army champ to fight me (apparently he was doing some chokey [imprisonment] in the stockades). He was all tattooed up, muscles everywhere. A right hard bastard. It was only a three-round fight in the welterweight division. A great but damaging fight: I really felt the pain afterwards. The girls we knew from the dance halls were there and they screamed the place down. It was the best fight of the night and they loved it. I gave as good as I got, but he edged it on points.

Some years later, during a prison spell in Wandsworth, I ended up in the same cell with Joey Carter, whom I had seen at Jack Solomon's. He was featherweight champion of south London and had fought Ronnie Clayton for the British featherweight title but lost in four rounds. Then Tommy McGovern got nicked for receiving and was sentenced to six months, and I wound up with the two of them in my cell! I felt sorry for Tom, as he was basically a very straight person and couldn't handle prison life. It seemed like the end of the world to him.

Tommy was an ex-lightweight champion of Great Britain. All he and Joey talked about was boxing and as I was quite well up on the subject it renewed my urge to do a bit of training and fighting again when I got out. After being locked up with these two I decided that on my release from prison I would become a professional boxer. Soon after my release, I turned professional under the experienced eye of Tommy Daly, training at the Thomas A'Becket in Old Kent Road, south-east

London. (Tommy Daly's son, John, was later to become a well-known film producer and formed Hemdale Productions with the actor David Hemmings.) Tommy got me fit with plenty of sparring and road work: I would run around Brockwell Park, Herne Hill, down to Camberwell Green, along to Loughborough Junction, under the arch and up Shakespeare Road and finish off in the park again. Then I'd run up Milton Road with my knees up to my chin for the last 10, as fighters call it, get indoors and do my mat work. Sit-ups, elbows to knees, all stomach work, wrap up and sweat it out. I got really fit. Tom used to put me in with a light heavyweight for three rounds, then a middleweight and a welterweight to speed me up. I was really banging hard, even with the big sparring gloves. I caught the light-heavy a shot and wobbled him after two rounds one day and they said 'enough': I didn't take liberties in sparring, because we were in there to help and learn from each other.

When I had my medical, the doctor held his stethoscope to my chest and kept looking up at me making 'um, ah' sounds. He got me doing press-ups and listened to my heart again, saying, 'Very strange, very strange.' I wondered what the problem was. Perhaps there was something wrong with me and he was frightened to tell me? Just goes to show how ignorant we were in those days. My mother suffered with angina all her life. When I was a little boy, she used to collapse into an armchair, and say to me, 'Quick! Can you fetch my bottle of salvelity?' And I'd give her a spoonful of that until the pulse in her neck would go away. You could see it I her neck trying to pump the blood to her heart.

Years later, when I was in Full Sutton Prison, I was told what it was: I have a very slow heartbeat: the average beat for a person is 70 and mine is only 45 – and that is very much in my favour. Thank God, I've got something going for me.

All the local fighters from south London trained at the Thomas A'Becket: Henry Cooper, George Cooper, Freddie Reardon, Dave Charnley and Charlie Tucker, to mention just a few. Dave Charnley wound up British champion. Peter Waterman, Eddie Hughes, the Auld twins from Bermondsey and Fred and Dinny Powell also trained there.

Tommy had fixed me up with a guy from Croydon called Del Breen for my first professional fight at Manor Place baths. Del was experienced. He'd had about 20 pro fights, winning the last four on knockout, so I was cannon fodder. Stan Baker was the promoter.

Topping the bill were Henry and George Cooper, Dave Charnley, Freddie Reardon and Charlie Tucker. Then there was Del Breen and little old me on the undercard.

It was a Tuesday evening, 23 November 1954. Normally, boys were given a few easy ones to get their confidence up and not get too hurt for about six or so fights. That's the general rule of a manager. Tom may have had second thoughts about pitting me against Del, but, even if he had wanted me to pull out, it was too late, because I had sold so many tickets. I was quite well known and already had a bit of a reputation as a street fighter.

The place was packed: I looked at Del. You could see every muscle in his body. He was a fit man. The first two rounds were all Del's. I couldn't match his experience. In the third, he caught me with a good shot. I fell back on the ropes and the crowd went wild. I came back strong at the end of the third, though, and caught him with a left and right hook, bang on the chin. I felt it go right up my arm to my shoulder. He went down right in his corner.

The crowd went wild. I was the underdog of all underdogs and I'd knocked him out, I thought. But just then the bell went and he sat in his corner, his seconds feverishly working on him. They lifted him up and pushed him out for the fourth round. The baths were buzzing. He boxed his way out of trouble in the fourth and I couldn't get a good shot in. His head cleared and his experience came to his aid. We both gave it our all for the rest of the fight. It was a war. Toe-to-toe stuff that the boxing crowd love to see. The final bell went and it was all over. Del won on points. If the bell hadn't gone in the third, I would have won. That's the luck of the game. The money started to pour into the ring. The seconds picked it up in a towel. I got £12 for the fight and Del and I shared £25 in nobbins (tips thrown in by an appreciative crowd).

Ernie Derfield, a promoter, was on the phone to Tommy: 'We want your man on our next show; he's a good ticket-seller and crowd-pleaser.' So that was my moment of glory in the fight game. All the fighters up and down the country have had similar fights to mine. I hold out my hand to them for their courage and heart, because it takes a lot just to step into a ring.

My rating in the *Boxing News* went into the six stars, so now I would never have an easy fight, only wars with experienced fighters. Their report on my match noted, 'Promoter Stan Baker can have every reason to be satisfied with the attendance and crowd-pleasing bill of fare in his first venture at Manor Place baths. Three former ABA champions Freddie Reardon, Henry Cooper and Dave Charnley all won their bouts and gave promise of great things in the future ... "Nobbins" were showered into the ring after the first bout of the evening, in which Del Breen, Croydon (10–11), outpointed Freddie Foreman, Walworth (10–11 3/4), over six rounds. It was Foreman's first pro bout...'

Stan Baker was asked about his best undercard fight and he mentioned mine. In the book *Down Memory Lane With Stan Baker*, he said of the fight, 'It was right at the end of 1954 when I put on my first bill there. I had three ABA champions on the undercard, Freddie Reardon, Henry Cooper and Dave Charnley. Henry's brother Jim boxed in one of the six-rounders and Charlie Tucker topped the show against Hanley's Tommy Higgins. The entire bill cost me £300. Do you know what I paid Cooper? – 20 quid!

'One guy who deserved to be paid 100 notes was Freddie Foreman, who had his one and only pro fight, against Del Breen. Best supporting scrap I ever saw! They hit each other with everything but the corner buckets. Nobbins were still coming in five minutes after the fight ended. After such a fistic baptism Freddie never again drew on a glove.'

As it happened, I did go back into training intending to carry on with the fight game but fate had other ideas in mind. The promoters wanted me on the next bill. I fought as a middleweight and was in really good shape, so much so that my trainer, Tommy Daly, made me a sparring partner to top fighters. I sparred with Peter Waterman, who was British welterweight champion, and even got into the ring with cruiserweights, whom I was bowling over with big gloves. Unfortunately, I had no sponsors to pay my bills and I still had to put food on the table for my wife and son. So, to support my boxing career I had to continue thieving. Then I got nicked and another stretch in prison ended my pro career – at least in the ring.

I sometimes wonder whether things might have turned out differently if I had done National Service. My brothers talked me out of joining up; the war in Malaya and Korea was beginning and they thought that, although the four of them had survived WWII, this time the family might not be so lucky. The problem was how to get out of it when I was in such peak physical condition. We decided I would become mentally deficient, and my brother George organised a medical certificate requesting a deferment on the grounds of my 'schizophrenia'.

We went down to Chelsea Barracks, George leading me by the hand and complaining that he had to take the day off work to accompany me. My mum, who was not party to the proceedings, asked incredulously if I was going out of the house in my present state. My hair was unkempt, I had Bert's clothes on (he was much smaller than me), which were tight-fitting with bits of wool hanging out of an old blue jumper, and some sticking plaster on my face. I had deliberately cut myself while shaving and was a complete mess. On top of what I was wearing, I'd donned an old air-raid warden's overcoat. When we got to the barracks, I meekly did as I was told by George, not taking any interest in the surroundings but staring, open-mouthed, through the window. George bullied me: 'Get over there and sit down. Get your socks off and hurry up, don't take all day.'

Watched by the Army personnel, he then took my socks off himself. They must have thought, 'We've got a right nut here.'

George never let up for a moment: 'All he does is sit watching out the window seeing them trams run by. He won't do anything. He just sits staring.'

The Army doctor said they would give me a deferment for four months before making a final decision.

George had a go at them: 'I've got kids to support,' he complained. 'I can't spend all my fucking days here. He's a fit boy. He did a lot of boxing and sparring but fucked up his brain; he's a bit scrambled.'

After going through my acting performance of being a nut-nut, I was getting dressed in a cubicle when the curtain pulled open and George's head popped in. He told me he'd heard the panel of doctors talking about me.

'What did they say, George?' I asked.

'They're going to make you a fighter pilot!'

I creased up – it made it very difficult for me to keep a straight face back in front of the panel.

We had to come back a second time. Following George's excellent tuition, I again sat on the edge of the seat, gaping open-mouthed, and the medical board obviously thought I needed help. 'This young man needs some treatment,' they told George. They assessed me as Grade 4, which exempted me from doing National Service, and recommended that I attend Cane Hill mental institution in Surrey for electric-shock treatment! Maybe they were right.

In some ways, I regretted not doing National Service with my mates. Lots of my friends were sent all over the world – like Micky Regan, who went to Suez, and Freddie Puttnam, who went to Malaya. Patsy Toomey and Lenny White joined the Army and became PTIs and fought in the Army Boxing Championships so, in a way, I later felt that I had missed out.

Money was in short supply back then, and most of my friends had secure jobs in Smithfield meat market, Spitalfields, Billingsgate or Covent Garden. Being a market porter was quite the 'in thing' to be those days, and I did it myself for a short time. I had bigger ambitions, though.

At around the age of 18, I teamed up with a load of girls known as the Forty Thieves. You virtually had to be born into it to become a member of this gang. All the girls were hoisters, and followed their mothers' footsteps in professional shoplifting. (They used to call shoplifting 'clouting', which was Old English for 'drawers'. The amount of goods those girls could stash away in bloomers under their dresses was unbelievable...)

My job was to graft with girls like Mae Mae Cooper, Annie Revel and Nellie Donovan, and make sure they got away after shoplifting from top stores like Harrods. You would bump into the guy who was going to give them a pull, or give him a right-hander if he got too clever. We met the girls in the local pubs. Their mothers, all from the Elephant and Kennington, were the original Forty Thieves. Though they had cockney accents, they knew how to talk lah-di-dah, putting on the upper-crust voice whenever the situation demanded. They wore their clothes better than titled ladies and really looked the part. They were stunning girls, well known throughout London.

When they got nicked, they got it hard. Some of these girls were sent to Holloway for two to three years, even though they were mothers with children. They were not treated gently but they were tough and did their lump of bird. Like fellas, they risked their liberty every day of the week to get a pound note.

A lot of them were scarred up, because they could also be vicious bastards and were often in fights and rows, cutting each other up.

When they let their hair down, they were totally outrageous. Sexually, some of them were hot stuff. People who live on the edge can be – as I've said before, they lived life to the full and knew how to make a man happy. When they tired of their man, they'd kick him out and move on to the next one. They were real characters. I still see a few of these lovely ladies, beautifully turned out and probably still grafting. It's in their blood.

Working with the girls was only a part-time activity. It was fun to do and I enjoyed the company of these larger-than-life ladies, each of them a colourful character in her own right. But there were bigger prizes to be had.

CHAPTER 4
THE JUMP-UP

I'm moving on too quickly here. Let me go back and tell you of my teenage years at Wandsworth Road, which were amongst the happiest of my life. At 18, while still living at my mum's, I became a full-time thief. My social life was exciting and fulfilling and I was fit and ready to take on the world.

My mates Lennie and Patsy loved staying at my place, mainly because my house was the general meeting place and also local girls joined us for sexual adventures in the drying rooms at the top of the block. We used to hang around the entrance to the flats late at night while Rosie, one of the girls I fancied, would come by. I'd greet her and offer to escort her home. Of course, there was a diversion. A gentle tug on the arm would be enough to change direction and I'd lead her up to the drying rooms. Her protests were never meant to carry much weight and we'd soon be at it with a knee-trembler against the wall. Lennie used to tail me off minutes afterwards. The routine was: handkerchief out of the pocket, wave it so Lennie could see, and give a little cough to signal the changeover. Rosie would act startled: 'Who's that?' I'd tell her it was my mate Lennie and, a little indignantly, she'd threaten to go home. But the thrill of a further sexual adventure was too strong and she stayed. Lennie would slip up behind and take over from where I'd left off. This became a right regular occurrence.

On another note, I was still worried about my George's health shovelling coal and breathing in all that dust in the barges. Even though he was older than me, I suggested he pack the job in and join my little firm. 'You'll be dead in five years if you don't,' I warned him. The pollution outside the power station was bad enough. A fine layer of coal dust covered the roads and footpaths, so when you walked down Nine Elms Lane to the power station you left a trail of footprints. I couldn't bear to think what this did to my George's lungs and reckoned his chances of survival would be better with me. In those days these was no social security, so you only had two choices: to work or to thieve. I thought thieving was the lesser of two evils.

After working with the Forty Thieves, I progressed to the jump-up. This involved stealing the goods from a commercial traveller's car or from a lorry and driving them to an arranged meet where they were loaded into another van and sold on my behalf. I bought a five-hundredweight Ford van and, through trial and error, taught myself to drive it. Driving licences were provided by a friend in County Hall.

Just after the war there was good money to be made from the black market in rationed goods. The profits were better still if you didn't have to pay for the rations in the first place. The canteen at George's power station catered for hundreds of people and was given a large allocation of tea, which was very much in demand. Every three or four months they would get eight or nine chests, some of which would probably go to other canteens. You could get double the price for it on the black market, so I decided we had to have it and asked Lennie and George to help. We broke into the building one night, made our way to the canteen and got the tea chests out without any problem. It was a good night's work.

The night watchman was alerted to us, but it was nothing to tie him up, the work of only a few minutes. Much better than battering him unconscious. People are normally so surprised and shocked by a sudden hold-up or threat that they freeze and are easily subdued. George said he earned more from that night than working for several months at the gasworks, and that convinced him to turn his job in and join me. Soon we had organised people in different factories to sell our bits of gear to their large workforces, and people began approaching us with orders for items in demand. I was always being asked for spare lorry wheels with plenty of meat on the tyres. They came to between

£10 and £20 each, which was a lot of money then. We stored the tyres in George's house in Wickersley Road – until we broke the floorboards bouncing tyres into the backyard. The final straw came when we broke the staircase. George's Rita was not amused.

We used to nick anything and everything. We'd follow a travelling salesman and, as soon as he went into the house selling goods on the never-never, the jump-up would happen. You'd use a screwdriver to open the quarterlight window of his motor, up went the catch, open the door, start the car up with a flat key and drive off. Lenny or George would follow in our van to a quiet street, preferably a cul-de-sac with a wall on either side, load up the gear and leave the salesman's motor there.

We got plenty of Twining's vans loaded with tea chests and a couple of drivers even let us have all their goods by parking up outside a café. While they were having a cup of tea we'd jump up and drive it away. Some drivers would even approach us and ask if we'd rob them for a percentage of the take. One of my relations offered to let us have his truck, which we 'nicked' from him at the Lyons Corner House by the Tower of London. Offers were coming our way all the time.

If we sold our goods at factories, we'd have to wait until the end of the week before we got our money. This became a bit of a hassle, so we found a buyer in Chelsea who stored the gear in a garage adjoining a vicarage. We first met Fatty Sid the Yid in the local pub and he gave us an address to deliver our goods. We said we would bring a van full of clothing the next day at about 2pm. 'I'll be on the corner waiting for you,' he told us.

We drove there as arranged, only to see the old vicar standing on the corner. I went around the block again hoping he'd go away, but he was still standing there with Sid the Yid at his side, gesticulating and mouthing, 'Come on!' I refused to drop off the clothes, pointing at the vicar. 'Don't worry about him, it's the vicar's garage! He'll be in for a pair of grey flannels in a minute.' After that, Fatty bought all our gear from us in bulk.

The jump-ups improved as time went on. You progressed to lorryloads of tea, cigarettes and cloth, and buyers from all over London started to spring up. You could sell anything then, and people would place orders for the next time you got a load. Nobody grassed you up in those days – they would rather buy something cheap.

Mum was getting a little worried about my activities, though. Even when I was working for Pannet and Eden I would tell her to help herself to my wage packets if ever she was in need of money. She would open the wardrobe and find £50 in notes and all my wage packets unopened. Once she found a .45 revolver stuffed at the back of the drawer: 'Oh, you do worry me, Fred,' she told me once, though she never brought the subject up again.

My father knew I was thieving, but never talked about it. He was grafting as a taxi driver by then. He'd done his 'knowledge' – on a bicycle, learning all the shortcuts along the back streets of London. The hansom cab he drove had no sides or protection from the weather and, like many drivers, he finished up with rheumatism in the elbows and joints. Years later, in his late seventies, he had to have plastic replacement elbow joints fitted. He'd suffered badly.

George and I would take our goods to various markets where we had contacts. But, with a busy schedule, I was seeing less and less of Patsy Toomey, who worked in Covent Garden. Patsy had always been very possessive of our friendship and was now becoming unreasonably jealous. He wanted to be in on the action and felt he wasn't, even though we'd given him gear to off-load on our behalf. Patsy's personality was undergoing a change – his moods became excessively brooding and violent. I was soon to find out what that entailed.

I had gone with George to the Nell Gwynne Café in Covent Garden. It was packed to capacity. You got very good food there, and George and I and a couple of porters sat at a table for four in an L-shaped section of the café. I was about to get stuck into my baby's head and two veg (meat pudding – a speciality of the house) when Patsy walked in. I looked up and greeted him, 'Hiya, Patsy.' He didn't reply. Instead, he smashed me full in the face with a left hook. I crashed backwards over the table behind me and rolled on to the floor. I was up on my feet like a shot and steamed straight into him with blood pouring from my nose. We'd been the best of pals, stood together, fought together, protected each other. We'd been like brothers. Now he was laying into me – and Patsy could have a fight.

All the customers cleared the area and became spectators. People outside hearing the commotion came in and stood on tables and chairs to get a better view. As we battled, everything around us got wrecked: mirrors, pictures on walls and chairs. We really went at it. I finished up getting him in a stranglehold on the floor. His face was in my stomach and he was kicking his legs like a man struggling to stay alive.

'Fred, don't choke him, he's gonna be dead. You're killing him,' someone warned me.

But I wouldn't let go and still had a cross-collar hold. My old judo was coming in handy and he was gasping away, going blue in the face. They pulled me off him – not a moment too soon. He was already semi-conscious and closer to death than I'd realised. By now the police had been called and just before they arrived we were hustled out to the pub next door. We used to drink in there and the governor let us use the toilets to clean up.

While we were washing, George and some of the porters came down and told us we were silly boys to fight like that when we'd been such good friends. I gestured at Patsy: 'Talk to him about it.'

Any thoughts of a reconciliation were abandoned when, shortly afterwards, George picked up a leather cobbler's knife with a curved blade and wooden handle. They were a common – and lethal – tool for cutting people in those days. Sharp as a razor. When I saw that, my blood boiled. The blade had been meant for me. I went to do Patsy there and then in the toilet, with his own knife. I turned to him: 'You'd fucking use this on me?'

With that, he broke down and started to cry, saying he was sorry but thought I had dropped him out and that I didn't look on him as a best friend any more. He was convinced I'd blown him out and replaced him with my brother George.

My anger gave way to pity. I felt really sorry for him. It became obvious to me he was mentally ill. Afterwards, though, I could never feel the same about him again. What can you do with people like this? He was paranoid. Psychotic. All that we'd been through together and the close friendship we'd had destroyed on that day. And, although he'd never used the knife on me, I knew the intention had been there. From then on, we went our separate ways.

Patsy was always getting into fights and rows. As he got older, he became bigger and heavier. He once had a row with a taxi driver taking him to a pub in Covent Garden after he'd been drinking in the West End. The cabbie stopped outside Bow Street police station, sounding his horn. When police came running out, Patsy knocked two of them out, but was then overpowered and dragged into the cells. He finished up with a 12-month sentence and was sent to Wandsworth.

Patsy was always being carted off to the nuthouse for one reason or another. One time it was for trying to strangle his wife, Margie (a lovely girl). Some years later, he came to my pub, the Prince of Wales, when he knew I'd had a bit of aggravation. 'I'm with you, Fred,' he said, brandishing a shooter, which he'd pulled from his pocket. 'I want to sign on the Firm again.'

I told him to put his gun away. There was no way I'd have a loose cannon like him about me. It was all very sad. Patsy was a lovely guy but, as I say, he was a sick man who needed help and never got it. In 1983, Patsy died of lung cancer in St Thomas's Hospital. I often think of him and feel sad.

When I was 18 going on 19, I was introduced to my future wife, Maureen Puttnam, on a blind date arranged by my friends Sammy Osterman and his girlfriend, Joanie Winters. Sammy worked in the print and he and future Great Train robber Tommy Wisbey were old mates. Tommy worked for his dad, who had a bottle factory in Cook's Road, Camberwell. His girlfriend, Renee Hill, whom he later married, was related to Joanie who was also a good friend of Maureen's.

The girls aroused Maureen's interest in me. They said I was always spending money like water and treated my women well. I wasn't such a bad-looking chap either. We got on fine together and she was an absolutely straight girl. No funny business at all. It was ages before we made love, and in my way I respected her for that.

At my age, I didn't feel ready for marriage but all my pals had girlfriends and were getting married so you just seemed to follow suit. Maureen must have had marriage in mind. I let her down two or three times on dates and once she came around to my house demanding to know why I hadn't shown up. She was a strong girl. Our courtship, like our marriage, was volatile. She was very possessive and jealous and I couldn't look at another girl without upsetting her. We were always rowing, sometimes even in the street.

There was a reason though: she had a very unhappy childhood and needed a lot of security, love and affection. She lived with her aunt Lizzy, who had a heart of gold. Whenever Lizzy was out of the house, Maureen and I would have a kiss and cuddle in the front room. We did all our courting there and also in the back row of the Kennington Odeon cinema.

Inevitably, Maureen fell pregnant with my Gregory and we got married at a church in Walworth Road on a Monday, which was the most convenient day for market and street traders. The wedding party was an all-day affair held at Tommy Wisbey's sister-in-law Janie Shaw's place, a four-storey home on the Walworth Road. It was a good day out and everyone enjoyed it. Maureen was given away by her uncle Joe; her father had been killed falling off the back of a lorry crossing Waterloo Bridge. (He had worked the smudge – camera – in Trafalgar Square, taking pictures of tourists until given that fateful lift by a grocer friend.)

We set up home in Milton Road, a wide tree-lined street in a very desirable part of Herne Hill, south London. Maureen gave up her job as a presser once we got married, but she always pulled her weight. I used to joke that she believed manual labour was a Spanish wrestler, but she was never frightened of hard work. When I got nicked, she went straight back to work at Waterloo Station on the tea and buffet cars. The job was handed down to members of the families and it kept her going while I was in the nick. She was also very protective of me and never frightened to weigh in physically on my behalf.

In the past, I've had to do a bit of ducking from Maureen myself. When we had the Prince of Wales pub in Lant Street and a flat on the Brandon Estate, Kennington, she once threw flowerpots at me from the 14th floor after a row. Another time, I'd been out with George, Bertie Blake, Buster and Tommy Wisbey and got home late – having popped out for a quiet drink, we finished up in Brighton! Maureen steamed into me and I legged it back to my car – a brand-new Citroën DS 19, painted in racing green – dodging a hail of stones, bricks and small change from her handbag, which dented the car roof. From the 14th floor, these missiles were as dangerous and deadly as bullets, causing sparks to fly off the pavement, nearly penetrating the roof of my new car. (I hate to think what they'd have done to my skull.)

But I could be just as angry towards her. On one occasion I was several hours late for Sunday lunch. When I arrived home from drinking after hours with the chaps, the roast smelled wonderful, but Maureen had retired to her bedroom with the Sunday papers. 'That smells lovely,' I complimented her, and went to the dining room, expecting her to serve up the food. Maureen came into the kitchen and without a word to me, opened the oven, took out the roast and went straight out the back door to the yard while I sat expectantly with my knife and fork at the ready. Instead of a steaming hot roast being delivered on my plate, I heard the sound of a knife scraping the serving plate as she emptied the lunch into the dustbin. She then trotted back in, disdainfully looking past me, and went straight back to the bedroom and her newspapers.

I was incensed. I went to the yard, picked up the dustbin, carried it to the bedroom and emptied the contents over her as she sat fully clothed on the bed. I then walked out of the house and returned to my cronies and carried on drinking. When I returned home a couple of days later, we were sweet as pie to one another. Childish really, but that was typical of our early days together.

Even before we married, Maureen had witnessed gang fights involving me and our friends. It was all part of life in those days. The Harrises picked on Sammy Osteruran outside a pub in Camberwell New Road one Sunday morning. Sammy got a glass in his face as a result of this feud with the Harris family. A terrible fight followed – in fact, the feud went on for several years. Tommy ended up working with them after the feud and one of the brothers, with whom I had a straightener, even came to my wedding. Later in our careers, we'd drink together and help each other out if there were any problems. Many of my early rivals have over the years become solid friends and we still drink together sometimes.

On one occasion, there was a row between the Harris family and Tommy Shaw, a bookmaker, involving bets and street pitches. Tommy was a generous man with a charming personality and was very successful. If you were short of a tenner, he'd give it to you. Curiously enough, when bookmaking became legal in Britain, licences were only given to those people who could prove they were in the business. So, for some, the only acceptable proof entitling them to those much-sought-after licences was to prove they had broken the law and had convictions for betting!

One of my mates at around this time was Horace 'Horry' Dance. He was an old friend from Battersea and lived in a nice respectable street just off Clapham Common. His mother was one of those well-spoken ladies who would proudly show you a photograph of her Horry immaculately turned out in his cricket whites surrounded by the rest of the team. The bit she didn't reveal was that the photograph was taken in Borstal.

Horry was a well-known face and married a beautiful girl called Barbara. But he was a right handful – always in trouble and getting nicked for assaults on police. He had a powerful BSA Thunderflash motorbike on which we rode to work. I would do a snatch on a night safe while he would wait down an alleyway or round a corner. We'd make sure the numberplates were covered up and we disguised ourselves with pilot helmets and goggles. (There weren't any crash helmets in those days.) After the snatch, we'd roar off. There were rich pickings to be had. We robbed furniture stores such as Times Furnishings, where the day's takings might be left in a drawer minded only by an office girl. The money piled up from people bringing in their monthly instalments for goods that they'd bought on the drip (hire purchase).

Later on, we nicked a Vincent Black Shadow motorbike (the fastest motorbike on the roads) and used that to snatch money off managers and cashiers as they went to put cash in night safes. Indirectly, I gave some of it back later when I bought a Times Furnishings bedroom suite – for cash.

There was nothing Horace wouldn't do for you. He was once in hospital with peritonitis when he heard that I'd been nicked. He pulled out the tubes connected to his stomach, got out of bed immediately and went to the police station to bail me out at Catford Magistrates' Court. That's the sort of chap Horry was.

And there was nothing he wouldn't steal. Wherever he went, he carried a screwdriver and nicked everything he could take home. He bought three houses and built a fourth one entirely from stolen materials. There was a violent streak in the family too, though. His wife Barbara, who helped him build the house, was involved in a hilarious brawl with Horry's mum and dad. The argument began inside the house and spilled out into the garden of their lovely suburban street, with neighbours peeping through curtains at the commotion. The garden became a battlefield. Both sides picked up stones, bricks and gardening tools – anything they could lay their hands on. They used metal dustbin lids as shields to protect themselves against the missiles. You can imagine the din.

For all that, they were lovely people and good friends. I didn't see Horry for years and then learned the sad news that he'd taken his own life with an overdose.

In the early days, Horry had introduced me to some heavier people who were into bigger paydays than we were getting. For me, it was like serving an apprenticeship. I was continually progressing up the scale with more experienced people to whom Horry had sung my praises.

One of Horry's past acquaintances was 'Mad' Mo Jones. When Mo came out of Wandsworth Prison after serving five years for cutting up a copper's face, he called on Horry's mother. We reckoned there might be a problem, because he and Horry had a fight some time previously, and so we tooled up. Thankfully, the meeting was amiable. Mo was with another chap I knew, Lennie Morgan, so we all shook hands.

This was a relief, as Mo Jones was a fearsome man. He was built like a brick shithouse and had a nasty temper with it. Mo was always tooled up and had a terrible reputation in and out of the nick. Once, I was invited to work with him and Lennie and another chap called Bertie Blake. We did a few post offices, tie-ups and pay snatches. In those days there were still trams and trolleybuses and one evening Mad Mo actually did a raid on a tram! Believe me, this was a one-off in the annals of crime. We had been waiting for the cashier of the Super Palace Cinema at Clapham Junction to leave the building with the day's takings. We missed him and someone pointed out that he was getting on a tram. Mad Mo jumped on the same tram and we followed. He walked down the gangway, looking from left to right for someone holding a cash bag. When he found him, he asked the chap if he was the cashier.

The geezer confirmed he was and Mo grabbed him out of his seat and said, 'Give me the fucking money!' The poor chap handed it over without hesitation. Mo had that effect on people.

Something was bound to give eventually, and it happened in an unexpected way. Mo raped Lennie's girlfriend Rose, a good-looker with a voluptuous body. He went around to her place, threatened her with a knife to her throat and then raped her. She came screaming and crying to Lennie and told him what had happened. Bertie Blake and I were unaware of this when Lennie called us for a meeting at the Prince's Head pub.

When I got to the pub, Mo Jones was already there. He bought me a drink and I sat down with him. Mo and I waited an hour for Lennie and Bert to arrive, while having several drinks together. Then, Bert put his head through the door of the pub and waved me outside. He said Lennie wanted to show Mo something on his own and that we would meet back here later. Bert took Mo to meet him as arranged. I didn't think any more about it and waited for them to return. As far as the customers and publican were concerned, though, I was the only identifiable person with Mo that night.

Our fashion in those days was to wear gabardine raincoats with epaulettes. It was the Robert Mitchum look – given currency by the film *Build My Gallows High*. Your hair was slicked back with gel, meeting in a duck's arse at the back of your nut – the DA haircut. The look was big and baggy and, worst of all, easily identifiable. And Lennie was wearing an identical gabardine raincoat to mine.

Bert returned to the pub and again beckoned me outside. Lennie Morgan was there, with his coat collar turned up. 'What's going on?' I asked.

'I've done Mo! I've killed him,' Lennie replied. He opened his coat and I could see he was smothered in blood.

'Fuck me!' I said. 'That's naughty.'

Lennie kept talking: 'He's gone to my home while I was out and fucking raped my Rosie with a knife to her throat. She was in a right state. She's still in bed and can't talk.'

I commiserated with him: 'The bastard deserved it,' I said. 'Rosie's a lovely girl.'

Rosie had the voice of an opera singer and could sing songs from all the shows, specialising in Ivor Novello tunes. Lennie was one of the chaps and well respected. He was then about 30 and I was still in my teens. He asked me if I thought Horry's mother would give us a change of clothes. At that time, Horry was away doing nine months in Wandsworth for GBH on a copper. (It seemed all of our friends or acquaintances were in and out of Wandsworth at the time.) I went around to see Mrs Dance and she was a good old girl about it. She had a big fire going in the grate and we burned all of Lennie's clothes. Then she gave us a fresh set belonging to Horry. We then cleaned out all the ashes and left.

But, later, I began thinking about the implications. If Mo was dead, I would have been the last person to be seen with him. I'd been sitting with him in the pub for several hours having a drink and had then gone out with him, although I had come back afterwards. It would still not look good if people recognised me, though. I started to visualise reports about me: 'Young man with slicked-back hair, Latin looks, wearing gabardine coat. Wanted for murder…'

Later, Lennie told us what he'd done. He'd taken Mo to Spencer Park, which is close to Wandsworth nick. It was pitch black and was bordered by a row of large fashionable houses. Apparently, Lennie pointed to a house. 'That's the one we're going to screw,' he said. Then he stepped behind Mo, pulled out an iron bar and smashed him over the head several times. Mo held up his hands for protection but Lennie kept bashing away. He left him in a crumpled heap with his head split open and bleeding profusely. Nobody could survive an onslaught like that. Or so Lennie thought.

For two days, there was no mention of Mo. We had been looking in the newspapers for a murder report and were understandably concerned, since we risked getting hung for a lady's honour. Then we read a report that screams had been heard in the park and police had discovered a considerable amount of blood, indicating that someone had been seriously injured. But no body.

A bit later, Bert got a message from Mo's sister to call around to her house in Garratt Lane, Wandsworth High Street, about a mile from Spencer Park. Bertie was shitting himself when he went to see her. He pretended to be shocked to find Mo lying in bed with towels around his head. Mo was not to be fooled. His piggy eyes were alert. He told Bert that he had been led into a trap.

Mo's look said that he would kill him if he had the strength. Then he took the towel away from his head and Bert said the wound was like looking into an open mouth. They had to take Mo to hospital then, or he would have died. He had two or three brain operations and several hundred stitches in his nut and hands. All his fingers had been crushed and broken during the attack.

Amazingly, he had crawled away from the spot to his sister's house, leaving a trail of blood. But he wouldn't let her call the police. He said nothing. That was the way it was then and always will be in our world.

Years later, Lennie was doing nine months in Wandsworth when who should come into the metal shop but Mo Jones. They looked at each other and immediately ran around the shop searching for tools. They were ready to kill each other. But they missed their chance. A screw saw what was happening and rang the alarm bell. They weren't given the chance for a return contest and both were dragged down the block.

About four months after Lennie's attack on Mo, we were out with Bert, Lennie's girl Rose and Sylvester, a stallholder, and a lovely old guy who was a street bookmaker called Jack the Pie. We started out on a pub crawl and ended up at The Surprise in Vauxhall Bridge Road. We were in high spirits. The pub was packed and Rosie was sweetly chirping away some Noël Coward tunes at a grand piano in the corner.

We boys were near the door laughing and playing around with Jack Pie, riling him about all the money we had lost to him over the years.

He took it all in good fun. But then we took it a step further: we grabbed Jack, tied him to a chair with our scarves and sat him on the tramlines in the middle of the road. It was about 10pm and trams used to come up there at speed. Poor Jack suddenly got scared, but we were close by, ready to drag him away as a tram approached. 'This is what you get for taking our money,' we shouted to him. The tram driver was frantically trying to slow down, winding the brake handles at a furious speed and donging the warning bell with his foot. He was convinced he would run over Jack. We dashed out and scooped Jack away with only seconds to spare. It was all boys' stuff. Highly spirited antics inspired by plenty of gin-and-tonic and Scotch on the rocks.

Excitement over, we went back into the pub to hear Rose finishing her number and giving it the big one (she always finished her songs on a high note) when a load of coppers arrived from Peel House, a section house for training police, which was only two streets away. A fight started and spilled out into the street. One copper had a stranglehold on Lennie from behind. I pulled him off and cracked him one on the chin. The copper staggered back on his heels, right across the pavement. His back hit the railings gate and he disappeared down the basement steps. Oops! Very nasty.

Now all hell broke loose and everyone headed in different directions. I had three coppers chasing me up Vauxhall Bridge Road, intent to kill. I was running out of puff at the foot of Vauxhall Bridge and just made it on to a departing tram. My legs were gone. I couldn't step up off the platform. I looked around gasping for breath. The coppers were straddled in a long blue line a short distance away. One determined bastard, bent on getting his man, was closing up on me as the tram stood waiting to go.

The tram conductor came down the stairs, sized up the situation at a glance and without a moment's hesitation gave the word for the tram to continue: 'Dong dong, fares please.' Magic words! He looked at me and winked.

'Thanks, mate,' I said, as I flopped down on the seat. The tram left the coppers labouring for breath and kicking the air in anger and frustration.

Unfortunately, Lennie, Bert, Jack and Sylvester were all arrested and received time for assault on the police. Lennie told me afterwards that, when they were arrested, they were taken down to the nick and all of them were pressed (a polite word for it) to reveal my name. But they all stood up – strong men, solid men – and wouldn't tell the police anything. At the magistrates' court, the coppers came to give evidence swathed head to toe in bandages. Lennie got nine months, the others three and four months.

As each of them was released, we had another piss-up and a good laugh. Lennie, like me, also had a brother called George, who had some good contacts in the car business. George was keen to get some muscle on his firm and wanted to include me in everything. He told me that he had a man in County Hall who could get brand-new car log books and stamps. Would I like to go into business with him? I jumped at the chance: 'When do we start?' I pulled my brother George in on the action and got myself a set of twelves (keys). They would open most of the cars we had targeted for nicking: Ford Prefects and Austin A40s. If the key didn't fit, then two screwdrivers were all you needed to break in through the small quarter-light side window with very little damage done.

My job was to nick the cars, then drive them to Tunbridge Wells and park them up. My George would follow and take me back to London. A car dealer he knew in town would put them in his showroom furnished with a log book and all the right details. They started to go like hot cakes. George and I were doing very well. In fact, the lock-up garages were full and I was told not to nick any more for a while. But all good things come to an end.

The showroom sold a Ford to a man who was very knowledgeable and he spotted a number behind the sun visor that shouldn't have been on that particular year and model. He called the police and the dealer was arrested. They traced the log books back to County Hall, but nobody grassed on our firm. The wartime propaganda – that golden rule that insisted on silence – still held good.

Georgie Morgan's next scheme was counterfeiting and we had a load of white fivers printed up. But that one was short-lived. One of his relations, who did a bit of work for him, nicked a parcel of the dodgies and went to Wandsworth dog track, where he got himself nicked. Then, on top of that, George Morgan got nicked and it all blew up in our faces.

It was clearly time for me to move further up the ladder and try something new.

CHAPTER 5
FIRM FRIENDS

Villainy relies as much on sound business practice as any other enterprise does. When our profitable car-stealing scam came to an abrupt end, we had to switch operations and find new products to market. Luxury items, such as washing machines, spin dryers, television sets and radiograms, were very much in demand in the early 1950s, but their high cost put them out of the reach of many people.

A little market research showed it was a business that couldn't fail. All I needed was a small Ford van, a white dust coat, a pencil in one ear, papers in my top pocket and a lot of front. Dressed to deceive, I would then walk into shops, target a fridge or washing machine, which would often be just inside the door, and walk out with it. If a salesman was standing there, George would act as a decoy and lead him away to the back of the store to look at carpets or other goods. With one lift – a deep knee bend is all it took – I'd have the object of my choice up and out of the shop and into the van. The back of the van would be padded with a mattress covered by a blanket to avoid damaging or scratching the goods. Once I was out of the shop, George would be minutes or seconds behind me. It worked like a charm.

It was only later, when you were delivering the goods to customers, that you realised how heavy they really were and wondered, 'How the fuck did I lift that on my own?' But, during the robbery, your adrenaline worked like a wonder drug and provided extra strength.

We sold the goods at just one-third of their shop price and consequently couldn't get enough to satisfy all our customers. Client families even gave us orders for their married daughters and sons. The list was endless. It gave us a lot of pleasure to see how happy we made people when they got something new. The Foreman brothers were doing very nicely: there was no violence, nobody got hurt and we were giving pleasure to people who couldn't otherwise afford these luxuries. I'm a saint, ain't I?

While this was going on, though, I was continually on the lookout for more ambitious projects. On one of our shopping expeditions shortly before Christmas, we found a store in Clapham Junction that could easily be burgled by tampering with its steel shutters. It was an ideal night for the robbery, because a thick fog had blanketed London. I had already borrowed a large van from a market guy in Covent Garden and told him to scream if anything went wrong; otherwise we'd return the van the following day.

Everything went to plan. We got to the store at night, up came the shutters and in we went while the night watchman was fast asleep in his office. In no time at all, we took what we wanted and had the pick of each department: washing machines, carpets, Hoovers, curtains. We began loading up the van. Just as we'd finished, however, a guy walked by out of the fog. We decided to move away very fast, and George went to get the back-up motor parked around the corner. Meanwhile, I finished packing and locked the van doors. I stayed in the van and waited for George.

All of a sudden, a Wolseley police car screeched around the corner and stopped bang in front of me. Three cossers piled out of it and jumped on me. 'Gotcha! You're nicked!' they said, pinning me to the shutters.

'Not if I can help it,' I muttered and struggled as they tried to hold me down. In the skirmish that followed, I came clean out of my jacket, leaving them wondering where I was. They were still holding the sleeves, which had been turned inside out, as I legged it into the peasouper.

I could hear them coming after me and looked desperately around for a hiding place. Near by was a car with a tarpaulin over it. I got underneath the canvas, slid on to the bonnet and lay across the windscreen. The Wolseley drove round and round the block in pursuit. They were obviously quite upset with me!

I was thankful they had no dogs with them. I stayed hidden for more than an hour and by the time I made a move it was getting light, although the fog had not fully cleared. I had to get to the nearest and safest port of call because I was very noticeable in just a shirt on that cold winter morning. Who could help me out? I almost spoke the answer out loud: Jack Pie, the bookmaker. The one we'd tied up and put in front of a speeding tram. He lived near by.

I made my way there and knocked him up. 'Jack, Jack, open the door, let me in. Hurry up I'm freezing my balls off out here!' Jack was as good as gold. I cleaned up and borrowed some fresh clothes and then caught the bus home to Maureen, who had been worried out of her mind. George had been inside my house, telling her that he couldn't find me. He didn't know what had happened: As I arrived, he was just leaving and about to get in his car. The police, in the meantime, had gone around to the Covent Garden man, who owned the van, and held up my jacket to ask him if he knew who I was. He told them nothing, but later joked, 'I could see you standing there, Fred. It was your shape.'

You can get away with an awful lot when you're fit and young. I remember one time when George and I were desperate for a bit of money and targeted the cashier's box at a Dorothy Perkins store. The ladies kept putting the big £5 notes into a wooden box, but it was one of those boxes where you couldn't pull your hand out if your fist was clenched. A bit like the monkey-and-coconut syndrome.

I boldly walked up to the cashier and shoved my hand inside this box, but couldn't get it out because I'd grabbed a load of notes. Exasperated, I pulled so hard the whole top came off so I just stuffed my pockets full and legged it to George, who was waiting in the getaway car. (Desperate times call for desperate measures.)

I wasn't so lucky, though, when I was grassed by a pal of Horry Dance. As I said earlier, Horry had been ill in hospital with peritonitis and suggested I continue working with a pal of his who was really a plumber and had a big motorbike with a sidecar. He was basically a straight man but had sold lots of gear for us. Horry had assured me he was OK, so we went to Catford and heisted loads of gear into the sidecar, which he took back to his place. But we'd been sussed and the next morning proved disastrous for me.

At the time, I had an Armstrong Siddeley car, which I parked in the next turning to my home in Milton Road because I'd lost my licence and didn't want people to see me driving it. The Armstrong was a beautiful car. Coach-built and fast. An ideal car for our sort of work, as people never suspected it was driven by villains.

On the morning after the robbery, I was in bed and heard a knock on the door. It was the police. I didn't even have time to get dressed. Annie Revel of the Forty Thieves lived next to us and I raced out the back, over the wall and up the side of her house, vaulted the gate and took off down the road. The cossers were still standing at my door and saw me go by like a flash in my underwear.

I got to the Armstrong Siddeley and lay down on the front seat, but someone spilled the beans and told the police they'd seen me get in there. The cossers opened the door, gave me a few whacks with their sticks and got me out. I ended up getting nine months at Greenwich Magistrates' Court.

By this time, Maureen and I had our first child, my Gregory, who was born in the St Thomas's Annex. Our home in Milton Road was nice and comfy. Everything had been paid for. But, with me away, Maureen went to work at the tea bar at Waterloo Station, where she met June, Buster Edwards's wife. Buster – later to become known as one of the Great Train Robbers, of course – was godfather to my second son, Jamie.

Prisons were a much tougher regime in the 1950s. While I was in Wandsworth, I was sent to work in the woodshed. There were all manner of particles floating in the air, lit up by sunbeams. Concerned for my health, I told the screws I wasn't going to injure myself breathing in all these impurities. Working there was like being on a production line: there were big electric bandsaws and rows of guys chopping up wood on a conveyor-belt system.

To make my point a little more effectively, I went to the screw sitting on a platform overseeing the work and buried my chopper into his desk. He got frightened and I told him to put me down the block: 'I don't care where I go. Just get me out of here. I can't stand the saws any longer.'

They gave me a job in the hospital, which suited me for a little while until I realised what that involved. There was shit everywhere, on straitjackets, mattresses, floors and all over the walls. You couldn't clean the place. The 'patients' had blocked the toilet cisterns with books and the place was covered in excreta. Even their porridge bowls were filled with the stuff. This was the first time I had seen people so mentally deranged and disturbed. (I never doubted my own sanity after that experience!)

I requested a cleaning job on the wing. A screw was approached on my behalf and I was given the 'number one' job on the landing, which meant you were in charge of the cleaners, handed out the razorblades every morning and took them back after they'd been used.

Other privileges followed: I was given extra food. The best grub was goulash, which you could make into a nice sandwich – although it was a bit greasy and looked like bread pudding. You were always starving in those places and couldn't wait for the next meal. People who came out of prison in those days were instantly recognisable by their prison pallor: a grey sallow look.

I was in Wandsworth with Georgie Cornell and Jackie Cramer. They put you three in a cell – safety in numbers, in case of rapes and assaults. Prison was clean back then, not like today. Cells were inspected, everything had to be correctly hung up, and sheets folded like in the army. It was all very regimental.

But there were always fights. I got put down in the block over a fight with a gypsy kid and his brother. Each landing had its own food orderlies and they used to come around with buckets of tea and soup. Each prisoner had his metal plate, tin mug and cutlery made from cheap tin. The knife's serrated edge had been folded over and beaten with a hammer and probably would have failed every hygiene test in the country. Now they issue them in plastic.

The tea orderlies would come along past your cell. Three of us would hold out our tin mugs and then quickly produce a water jug for a top-up. Other orderlies would give you a cob of bread and dinner. They would be followed by the screw, who would come up behind and bang you up for the night. This all happened at breakneck speed because it meant the screws could go off duty as soon as it was done.

This gypsy kid wouldn't top me up, saying he didn't have enough tea, but he still had enough to give a second helping to his mates. Next time he came around, I told him to go to the next cell and I'd get my tea from the guy following. He refused to move on, so I whacked him and knocked him out (a hungry man's an angry man). The tea went all over the landing floor as I sent him sprawling. I then dragged him into the cell by his ankles, but was stopped by Stevens the screw, a hard-faced bastard, from inflicting more damage.

The screws told me I was nicked and marched me straight down to the block. In the morning, the governor gave me nine days' bread and water: three days on, three days off. The diet was a jug of water and a cob of bread. You were left in the block without belt, shoes, tie or braces, and made to sleep in an empty cell on a wooden bed. You could only take your bedding in at 5.30 at night and it was freezing. To keep warm, you had to lie down by a hot pipe. You were allowed library books, but they were crap. To pass the time, you did press-ups and walked round and round the cell like a caged animal. Warders kept looking at you through the door and all the time you got hungrier and hungrier and angrier and angrier!

The first three days are the worst. After nine days, your stomach shrinks so much that you lose your hunger and feel light-headed.

My battle with the gypsies was not yet done, though. After I'd been down the block, I was out in the exercise yard. The two brothers sniggered and took the piss. Although we had to be three paces behind each other, I got close to the gypsy and at a blind spot I did him again. This time, he ended up flat on his back in a shrub. That livened him up a little and let him know it was not all over. But the screws found out and I was sent back down to the block again. They really had it in for me. Nevertheless, they couldn't prevent the clock from going round.

On my release, although my Greg was only a little boy, he looked at me as if to say, 'Where have you been? Why did you desert me?' And I felt I had, as these were the most important months of a child's life.

While Maureen worked at Waterloo Station during the day, a cousin, Renee Darling, looked after Gregory in Baylis Road. The road was named after Lillian Baylis who founded the Old Vic Theatre, which was at the end of the road where Buster worked. On his demob from the RAF, he'd found it hard to get a living, so he went to work as a florist. (He worked for Adie Warner, a gay chap who lived with his mum and always wore a trilby hat.) That's when Buster and I became friends.

After my release, Maureen suggested to me that I might try going straight. I considered it, but not for long. In fact, I went straight back to grafting with Joe Carter, my old cellmate. He was an ex-pro-fighter, who even fought Ronnie Clayton for the British lightweight title, but got stopped in the fourth round. Joey and I used to do the windows: smash them and grab all the gear in the early hours of the morning. You'd either reverse the car into the window or you smashed it with a heavy object. But my partnership with Joe Carter ended abruptly. One terrible night, we were involved in a police chase around Streatham. There were about three patrol cars in front and another three behind when police cordoned off the road and made us stop. As they approached the car, we took off again like something out of Brands Hatch, crashing patrol cars as we escaped. They gave chase because they knew we had been grafting in the area and had been waiting for us at around five in the morning while we were on our way to Wallington. We were eventually cornered for a second time when Joe drove into a cul-de-sac after being rammed in the back by a police car. We both ran off in different directions. Unfortunately, Joe climbed over a garden wall and fell through the roof of a chicken coop, where he was arrested. I managed to escape over several garden fences and made my way home. Joe wound up with nine months for stealing a car, resisting arrest and driving without due care and attention.

One thing that came of selling all this crooked gear was that I met my pal Charlie Kray. Charlie was connected with Stan Davis, a big buyer of our goods. Stan would take the lot from us and collect it from a garage or safe house and pay cash on the nose so we would take a little less but eliminate the risk of putting it about. Charlie was a good man to do business with, and safe. We acquired a lock-up over his manor in Old Ford Road as well as our own in south London, so we didn't have too far to travel after each bit of work. It was good money for a year or so.

As we got to know each other better, I used to go over and drink with Charlie and the Twins. Over the years, I'd seen Charlie and the Twins at boxing shows and gyms and they had quite a reputation in the amateur-fight world. Charlie and I hit it off straight away. He brought his wife Dolly over to my place because he liked the way we had decorated it and wanted to show her. She also got on well with Maureen and, while we had little Gregory, they had their son Gary. Dolly was always given first choice of any kiddies' clothes we'd nicked before they went to the rest of the punters. They were frequent visitors and, when everything came on top for me and I had to go on my toes, Charlie and the Twins helped me out.

Charlie always tried to talk a bit of sense into his brothers, but they wouldn't listen. They were ambitious and wanted to go places fast. They had an aura about them that people recognised. I always found them polite and well mannered. You could take anybody into their company and they wouldn't embarrass you.

Violet Kray, their mother, was lovely. She'd make cups of tea and sandwiches and loved the kids when you took them around – a really nice lady. She wasn't a bit like they portrayed her in the film *The Krays*, where she was played by Billie Whitelaw. She'd never say she wanted to cut someone's throat. That wasn't her style. She was a very gentle woman and, of course, she loved the boys to death.

Their old man couldn't handle them at all, though. There was nothing he could do when they went out in the yard and beat the shit out of each other. In the end, he took no notice of them.

Their home was a typical east London, cockney house. Violet kept it immaculately clean and extended a warm welcome to visitors. The Twins were just like other young kids when they were growing up, except for their overpowering ambition. Charlie had a kind of calming influence and encouraged them in the gym.

The Twins initially helped their father out by buying and selling gold in the street, but they didn't really like that. They'd knock on doors, and if anyone had anything to sell their old man would weigh it on a small pair of scales and make an offer on it. The Twins wanted more out of life, though. You didn't need a lot of money to start little businesses then, and they moved on to the Double R Club, which also had a gym above it, and the pool hall.

It was after Ronnie had been to Wandsworth for GBH that the Twins seemed to become more violent in their dealings. While he was inside, Ronnie chinned a couple of screws and they moved him to Epsom, where they could keep him indefinitely in the nut-house.

I was invited a couple of times to join the Twins when they were being wooed by Billy Hill and Jack Spot. Both of them wanted the Twins on their side because they had an army of heavies around them. Had they wanted to, they could easily have mustered an army of about 20 to 30 guys. If there was trouble or they needed to intimidate somebody, they could arrive mob-handed with these ugly-looking bastards with big Mars bars down their faces. Some were massive – 20 to 24 stone in weight. Tommy Brown was known as the Bear and tipped the scales at nearly 25 stone. All were streetwise guys who knew how to handle themselves.

The Nash brothers were also coming up at this time and the Krays were friendly with Johnny and Jimmy. Billy Hill was trying to coax them over as well. Billy Hill would ask the Twins and their friends to show some strength at race meetings and pay them money. They asked me to do a bit of growling at race meetings – because arguments often arose over the best pitches – but I was a thief and this sort of work was not really my scene.

It was different with Charlie. He and I went to Billy Hill's spiels (gambling dens) as minders. You could eat and drink from a really terrific buffet – smoked salmon, vol-au-vents, things you'd take for granted today, but back then it was a real luxury. The people who went to these spiels very rarely got violent if they knew who was minding the business. Clients included people from Mayfair and Kensington. In those days, gaming was illegal but people loved to gamble, and some very posh people would turn up. There was a naval commander, titled people, including baronets, lords and ladies and other top-ranking members of Her Majesty's Services. The naval commander, despite owning a Rolls-Royce, welched on a gambling debt. His was visited by the Twins' firm, who dispensed summary justice by embedding two pickaxes into the door panels of his Roller.

Around this time, my George got grassed up and was sent down for three years in Wandsworth. During his sentence, he was approached and asked if he would help Bruce Reynolds get an automatic pistol into Wandsworth Prison. Bruce was doing three-and-a-half years and was concerned about his family. He wanted to get out as quickly as possible and George thought he was helping in an escape attempt. But Bruce had a different plan in mind. He wanted time off for good behaviour and his plan was to hand in the gun to the authorities and earn special remission. He was going to say he found it in the brush shop.

They got George the gun through an outside working party, who were supervised by a screw called 'Yogi Bear'. The prisoner with Yogi was Speeby, a one-time friend of Joe Carter. He was on the same wing as George and came into his cell at afternoon tea, gave him the automatic, and legged it. George put the gun under his pillow. Where else could he hide it? And he says to this day his bottle has never been the same since. Every time someone walked past his cell door, his bum was making buttons. And they were coming by every few minutes: screws, and other prisoners returning from labour. You can imagine how little sleep poor George had that night. The next morning after slop-out and breakfast, when the prisoners were assembled on the 'Wandsworth centre' (this was the centre of the prison block where warders scrutinised and counted all the assembled inmates before sending them off on work parties – standing there was an ordeal for every prisoner), George stood there with the gun in his back trousers feeling like John Wayne. He was never so glad to get to work in his life. He hid the gun in the storeroom until they came to pick it up two days later. Bruce's scheme didn't work, as he'd already approached a screw previously about getting a gun in but this screw had thought better of it. Some people obviously didn't like what he'd done and he paid dearly for it.

On his weekly visit to the bath house, Mad Frank Mitchell stabbed Bruce in the back, puncturing his lung. He was found slumped in a bath full of water that was slowly turning red. Frank Mitchell was nicked and sent to appear at Marylebone Magistrates' Court, on a charge of attempted murder. Bruce never grassed on him and Mitchell was acquitted. It took 13 coppers to get Mitchell out of the dock when he remonstrated with them at the magistrates' court.

Once George was released, we still did a bit of work together if he put something up, or I'd got to work with anyone else I knew and trusted, like my brother-in-law, Freddie Puttnam. Freddie worked for a gown firm and told me he was due to collect the Firm's wages, with another fella. Our plan was to snatch the money and I would clump Fred in the process so he wouldn't be a suspect. It had to be done right, so I gave him a few whacks and he had to have a couple of stitches. Obviously, there was someone with him, so we had to make it look realistic. He was a bit overzealous and grabbed my leg as I made my getaway. Hence the stitches.

You had to laugh. Later, he put his share of the hold-up money into a home fish tank, which had a decorative treasure chest and diver. Freddie wrapped the money in waterproof packets and stuffed it underneath the treasure chest in the gravel on the bottom of the tank. I had warned him not to buy anything new, as he would be suspected of helping in the raid. Sure enough, two months after the snatch police came around unexpectedly and asked him about his new radiogram. 'Where did you get that, Fred?' they asked.

He was able to pull out a payment book showing he was buying it on the never-never. Freddie got married and was able to pay for the wedding out of our little touch. After that, there were no more visits from the police.

George and I were always open to fresh opportunities, like the one that presented itself at George's own workplace. Geo Harding and Co. had converted an old prison in the Borough into a large warehouse on different levels. George got friendly with the night watchman, a lovely old rogue George falsely introduced to everyone as Digby Morton. George has a good sense of humour and was always giving people nicknames. The real Digby Morton was one of the top fashion designers of the time and this old watchman was the complete opposite. He resembled a tramp. He had the face of a tired hound dog, a bulbous nose mapped with blue veins that looked ready to burst, and a knobbly head on which he balanced a battered trilby. Wrapped around his body, and held together by a belt, was an ageing and stained raincoat and, to complete the picture, he shuffled around in boots that were several sizes too large. You would expect to see him on a park bench rather than in an office with a bunch of keys rattling at his side. So this was Geo Harding and Co.'s night security officer. His wage was a pittance. It was a case of who is going to watch the night watchman?

We used to meet Digby at the pub about half-past nine at night. You had to get him pissed so that he'd go back to the warehouse and leave the back door open for you to sneak on to the premises. But our timing with regard to his drinking had to be more precise than our thieving. If you got him to the pub too early, he would get too drunk to do anything. If we left it too late, he wouldn't be pissed enough to do as we said.

When it came to drink, he was a sly old fox. He used to draw it out to the last minute. 'I think we can have another Guinness now,' he'd say, just as it was coming to closing time. Then he'd add, 'Can I have a drop of Scotch, George?'

Anxiously looking around, George would respond, 'How many times do I have to tell you, Digby, not to come into the pub rattling those fucking keys?' People knew he was a night watchman and he'd stand out a mile drinking with two rascals like ourselves.

Eventually, he'd make a move and we'd follow. He'd unlock the door and leave it an inch ajar. He'd then walk off to his cubbyhole, where he had a primus stove for making tea. We knew what time the police came around to check the back door. Once inside, we'd be selective about the goods we took. We made parcels with cardboard boxes and filled them up. You could get away with up to £500 worth of gear – a lot of money then. We did it once or twice a week, but you had to be careful. If they'd caught us filling up the car round the back, the night watchman would have been nicked and, even if we'd managed to escape, we didn't want that to happen because he would probably have talked. We treated him quite well. Digby always got his booze paid for and a nice bit of money on top.

With the amount of goods we were getting, we decided to get our own outlet rather than selling the goods through others. George was the driving force in this enterprise.

One night, Freddie Puttnam asked us to a party, but we'd already made a meet with Digby to get another load at the warehouse. Not wanting to miss either opportunity, we seized both. By the time we met Digby, we'd already been to the party and got pissed. Nevertheless, we filled up the car with the stolen goods and returned to the party once more, after parking the motor in a square by the block of flats near Lambeth Walk. In our inebriated state, we left one of the back doors unlocked, although we'd put a blanket over the gear. While we enjoyed a nice drink, someone who came to the party told us that two cossers were examining the car with a torch.

One of the policemen went to Kennington Road nick for reinforcements, while the other kept guard under a porch near by. We had to get rid of the car lively. George and I strolled over to it, unlocked the door and were about to drive off when the cosser came up. 'Excuse me, sir, is this your car?' he asked.

'Oh fuck off! Leave us alone.' We went to drive off, but the copper bravely threw himself over the bonnet of the car and as we drove off he was desperately trying to smash our windscreen with his truncheon.

We roared through the square from Lambeth Walk into Kennington Road, dodging a load of metal posts on which people strung their washing-lines. We drove through this obstacle course until the copper was shaken off. The gear was then taken to a lock-up in Herne Hill and we returned to the party for another drinking session. It had been a nice bit of work, regardless of the slight hiccup.

As was to be expected, Digby became less reliable as time went by. On one occasion, he had one too many and was so paralytic that he passed out in the warehouse without leaving the door ajar. There was nothing we could do to wake him up from his drunken stupor. All you could see of him through a crack in the door was his pair of boots, turned up at the toes like a clowns, lying halfway up the passageway. It was a wasted night.

All good things come to an end and Digby finally got sacked for being drunk on duty. He came by to see George a few months later and said he had a job in the City. George gave him a few quid and we went for a meet outside St Paul's Cathedral. He gave us another fanny about being a night watchman again and hit us for £20 or more. Of course, he was unemployed and had us right over.

George said, 'I bet I know where that bastard is. At the Elephant and Castle kip-house!' And that's just where he'd gone.

He was sauntering his way to the kip-house, but we made sure we were waiting for him. I grabbed him and threw him in the doorway. We let him go because he said he had no money and was desperate. He was too old and sick for me to batter, so I just kicked him up the arse and sent him on his way. The last we heard of him was that he'd died from the booze. Well, it was only a matter of time.

Eventually, George took over this shop in Larkhall Lane, Clapham. It was an old fishmonger's, complete with living accommodation above, and situated not far from Union Road, where we had lived during the war. We called it the 'Larkin's store' – all the goods for sale were down to 'larking' (that meant they cost nothing). George recruited an unusual storeman for the Larkin's store – a housing-estate caretaker called Bert. The man looked after the goods and stored them all over the flats and cupboards of the housing estate in Lambeth. Even an old air-raid shelter in the grounds was full of Larkin's goods. The Larkin's store was doing well and Bert, a stocky man with pebble-glasses, a fat gut, an angry disposition and a know-all attitude, was now on the Firm.

The kids on the estate thought he was a tyrant as Bert wouldn't allow them to play or enjoy themselves, 'Keep off the grass,' he'd yell, 'no playing football!' But my Greg and Jamie were used to him, and would say, 'Don't worry, it's only Bert the caretaker.' They'd seen him at our parties and at Nell and Johnny Fitz's place, which was on the same housing estate. Now that Bert had substantially increased his income, he was getting pissed more often. He was a real know-all handyman and had every tool that was ever made – all down to the council.

We got a bit flippant, in a way. The shop had a yard containing a brick smoke-hole; we wanted to pull the smoke-hole down to make more room so we could drive a stolen lorry and trailer into the yard. To assess the job, all three of us – George, Bert, and myself – got up on a high wall at the back of the sloping roof, which was a little dodgy after years of smoking haddocks and kippers.

Bert the know-all loudmouth said, 'Now look, fellas, don't walk across the roof any old how, step on the main beam that supports the roof here, and here.' He stamped on the roof to emphasise his point. At that precise moment, there was a loud crack and the sound of splintering wood and clattering tiles. Bert made a partial disappearance through a hole in the roof, leaving only the upper half of his body visible. The know-all expression had changed to a look of terror. We heard a further crack and the rest of Bert followed through the hole, crashing 20 feet to the floor below; a cloud of black soot rose up and mushroomed like a mini Hiroshima. All went quiet. George and I had been comfortably and safely perched on the wall and had to bite our lips to stop ourselves laughing in case he was seriously hurt.

We got down to Bert, who was moaning and groaning with pain and lying in a crumpled heap, looking for all the world like one of the black-and-white minstrels. He was white-eyed, red-mouthed and groaning for an ambulance. George leaned over to him: 'What's the number, Bert? Do I ring 999? Is that it?'

Bert was outraged. 'Stop fucking about, George! I've busted me ribs, ring 999!'

Later, George made to get in the ambulance with him when it arrived but Bert refused. 'He'll only try and make me laugh and it fucking hurts like hell.' Afterwards, he wouldn't speak to us for months and sulked something rotten. Know-all bastard! As if it was our fault he fell through the roof!

But even working with George, I had no full-timers on the Firm, especially with Joe Carter away. Pressure was put on me again to go straight and get a job, so I spoke with Tommy McGovern, who fixed me up with a porter's job at Smithfield meat market. I used to collect Tommy at about 4am on my way from Herne Hill. He had a flat at 'The Horns', Kennington. Although I tried not to, it wasn't too long before I strayed off the straight and narrow again. The wages at the meat market were so poor I had to have a little extra, so I saw a pal who had a fiddle going with a big cosmetics firm. I took gear from him on credit and sold it at a good profit. It helped supplement my wages. Once, I even had a vanload of nicked policemen's boots and sold the lot to the market porters. They went down a treat and all the porters were running around in nice soft coppers' boots.

There were some great guys working there, but ultimately Smithfield was not for me. I had been my own boss since my job as a scaffolder and couldn't stick working for someone else. That's when I decided to start up my own firm.

CHAPTER 6
EAST ENDERS

My firm of Buster Edwards, Tommy Wisbey and Billy Hart was formed in 1956. Tommy, Billy and I had been friends since our teens, when we had gone to pubs and dance halls together. Buster used to sell my gear at his florist's in Waterloo and, when we became friendlier, he asked me if he could come in on the action. So I took him out to work and he became a thief. In a way, I corrupted him. He'd been a straight bloke. He had worked as a cook in the air force and, on being demobbed, started his own window-cleaning business. That went belly-up, so then he worked as a florist until finally he became a criminal with me.

Billy came from the Elephant, Walworth. There were a lot of thieves from there and neighbouring Bermondsey, which was part of the docklands. Although people from those areas may have been a poorer class on the social scale, their fathers earned good money in the docks. Every docker had a radiogram, TV and fitted carpets in his front room. They lived a good life because they earned that extra bit of money. When the docks folded, all the families of the younger men were used to a bit of luxury and inclined to go out and get big money, so you found that most of the armed robbers were from that area. Unfortunately, the prisons are full of those men, now serving long sentences because they got a taste of the good life.

Our firm had made good contacts throughout London, so we were always being told about little bits of work that would keep us busy. The core enterprise now included using skeleton keys to break into shops and emptying the premises, but had extended to snatching wages if the opportunity presented itself. The skeleton keys that we had specifically made up would open most shop doors and not many businesses had alarms fitted in those days. It was all trial and error. We'd pull up outside the shop in a transit van and try the key in the lock. If it didn't fit, you'd blacken the key by smoking it up with a lighted match, reinsert it into the lock and wiggle it about to see where it needed filing. Then you'd go back to the van and file it down. Normally that would do the trick and, flop, over the lock would go.

We would then return to the store and walk around inside the shop, trying to set off hidden alarms. You'd then lock up again and keep observation from a safe distance. If the police arrived, you knew it was belled to the local nick.

We did shops all over London, the best ones being Greys and Stones electrical stores, though fashion shops were also a good touch. We even robbed the first of the Mothercare chain of shops, which probably helped set them up. Not only did they receive publicity, but they were also able to claim insurance on losing all their stock. Privately, someone from their firm admitted it was the best thing that could have happened to them. With the money to buy fresh stock, it gave them a good start and they opened up further branches. (So you see how we helped people in those days!)

We always did our research. Generally, we'd watch the shop one week and return the next. We'd find out how many employees there were and when the last one was due to leave the premises. You'd see him or her come out and lock up the premises. Then, you'd follow to make sure the person got on a bus or in a car. We'd go back, pull up in front of the shop as bold as brass, and go inside. I'd usually wear a pin-stripe suit to make it look as though I was the manager, and the others would be dressed in overalls or white dust coats.

You never faltered, even if the cossers walked by, which they occasionally did. You just carried on not taking a blind bit of notice. Then we'd fill up the van and drive off to my lock-up in Herne Hill. We always had a high-speed back-up car, such as a Zephyr, Ford Zodiac or Consul.

One bit of business in the East End, recommended over a drink, was a menswear shop. We fitted it up and went to work, getting all the gear into large sacks. Having cleared the shop out, Billy went to fetch the van. But, while we were waiting for him, Tom, Buster and I heard this tap-tapping sound coming from a stairway.

The noise came in stops and starts and was disconcerting because we had watched the staff leave and had been in there for at least half an hour getting everything packed up by the door. We just had to find out what the noise was and crept upstairs to investigate. Peeping through a crack in a door we had gently opened, we were astonished to see an old Jewish boy with his back to us, sewing away on a machine. He must have been stone deaf.

We closed the door again and tried to stifle a laugh. Tommy was a notorious giggler. For a second, we were going to slam the door on the way out, but thought better of it. We often wondered what happened when the owner came back and found the shop empty but the old boy still machining away in his own little world.

Charlie Kray's partner Stan the Fence did quite a lot of business with my brother George and he would also buy things back off Stan – until he got nicked with Stan's goods. He'd bought a load of Prestige knives from the man and, without warning, his flat was raided by coppers.

We figured it must have been Stan who grassed him, because, the next thing I knew, they were raiding one of my lock-ups and certain things the copper said could only have come from Stan. Inside the garage, they found one of my vans full of stolen gear and I went up for trial at the London Sessions. Fortunately, I had a friend called Albert Connell, a local bookmaker, who acted as an intermediary between me and the police. Albert associated with them, but there was never any harm in it. He was a solid man and, if he could help you in any way, he would. I asked for his help and he arranged for us to have a meet with them in a Streatham club owned by Edie Clements. It was nice food and we had a good time. At the trial I was found not guilty. It was a good result, but quite expensive.

After that episode, Charlie split up with Stan.

Like Mothercare, most of the shops we robbed were probably very grateful to us for the insurance they could claim – though I don't say this in mitigation of what we did. We had no regrets.

We had a good run with our robberies, but London was getting too warm so we ventured out into the sticks. It took longer to get home with the goods, but the work was the same.

Until we went down to Southampton, most of our jobs went smoothly. I had some relatives on the coast and found a couple of nice shops to do. On one particular occasion, we stayed overnight and did the shop early in the morning. There were four of us: Tommy, Billy Hart, Buster and myself. We got there bright and early. The doors had two deadlocks, top and bottom. In the middle there was a Yale lock, which had to be knocked off with a heavy screwdriver. We went to work and all went well. I must mention here that, when carrying out the TVs and other goods, you couldn't wear gloves. It would have looked very suspicious, all four of us wearing black-leather gloves. So, every item we touched had to come out with us, and that had to be the rule. At the back of the shop was a warehouse full of goods packed in boxes, which made it easier for us to get more goods on to the van. There was no wasted space.

On show in the shop was a lovely Decca walnut radiogram, a type we'd had before and which we knew was a very popular seller. As we liked keeping our customers satisfied, Tommy said, 'We got to take that one, Fred. I know someone for it.' We filled the van to the brim, locked up the shop and drove away, sweet as a nut.

About five miles down the road, we could hear the Zephyr hooting the Ford van and then drawing alongside to stop us. It was Tommy. He said we had left the radiogram behind, with his prints all over it. It had been moved right next to the doorway and they were bound to print it up. I told him, 'OK, jump up here and I'll go back with Buster and pick it up. You carry on and we'll catch up with you on the road.' Leaving a print behind was like leaving your name and address.

Buster and I went back to the shop. One guy was already setting up his paper stall next door and another was cleaning the shop's windows. We went straight to the front door, spun the locks off and snapped the Yale back with the screwdriver as quick as a flash. We then got the radiogram into the boot of the Zephyr. I stood in the entrance, held up my trade board and wrote down bollocks for the benefit of the window cleaner and the paper man. We drove away feeling OK about it, put our foot down once we got out of Southampton and even caught up with the van, overtaking it and giving a relieved Tommy the thumbs-up sign.

We got back safely, changed the plates of our transport, and set about selling the gear.

A few days later, Tommy asked to borrow my new five-hundredweight Ford van, a nice little motor for business and running about. He had to deliver some of our goods to one or two customers who had ordered items.

Apart from working with us, Tommy still used to stand out on his father's pitch and collect racing bets. His old man was an SP (Starting Price) bookie and had a sideline running a bottle-washing business with Tommy's brother. The bottle factory was in a yard down an alleyway and Tommy would stand at the entrance so that if police came he could run down the back and escape over five or six back gardens of adjoining houses.

The police were always trying to nick you for illegal betting and it became a sort of game with lookouts down each end of the street to give a good whistle if anyone came along who looked suss. The cossers would use every ploy imaginable to catch people. They came disguised as dustmen, milkmen, postmen, tramps and even old ladies. Once they jumped on you, they held on and a police Wolseley would come tearing round the corner. Other police would emerge from hideouts, whistles blowing and causing mayhem in the neighbourhood.

And, after all that fuss, Lambeth court would fine the offender £2.50 – or, if you had six or seven previous, it would double to £5. Anyway, Tommy had my van with some of the gear from Southampton parked outside the gate when police sprang to arrest him for gambling. After he got nicked, they searched the van and found the stolen goods that they traced to the Southampton robbery. He was then further charged with handling stolen goods: they had put Tommy on an ID parade, but neither the window cleaner nor the newspaper seller could pick him out because fortunately it was me and Buster who went back.

The van, however, was traced back to me. Now, there was no way I could afford to be nicked and go to Southampton – they would have put me away for a five-year stretch – so that's when I went on my toes over the water to the East End. Charlie Kray and the Twins found me a nice little flat in Adeline Grove, right opposite the Blind Beggar pub run by Jimmy and Patsy Quill in the sixties – lovely people, who were later to go on to bigger and better things. Patsy has sadly since died, but I still go and see Jimmy and Chris for a meal.

The local greengrocery was owned by Laurie O'Leary. O'Leary was one of the pallbearers with me at Ron's funeral and had been manager to Doris Stokes, the clairvoyant, and to various pop groups. He also ran a club in Swallow Street, Piccadilly, in which Beatle George Harrison, TV personality Alan Freeman and Sir William Pigott-Brown (the former two-times amateur champion National Hunt jockey) had an interest. It was called Sibylla's after society girl Sibylla Edmonstone of Duntreath Castle, Scotland, who was also involved in the venture. Although it was an exclusive club with a restricted membership of only 800, I was always welcome at the club.

Laurie did me a great favour years ago. Like many friends from the past, he gave my son Gregory a job at the Exhibition Club while I was in prison. Laurie was a loyal and trusted friend of the Krays and myself. Sadly Laurie has died now. I still miss him.

Charlie's wife Dolly was a marvellous help in getting Maureen over to join me from south London when I was on my toes in Adeline Grove. She really helped a friend in need. All wives and mothers in our circle are like that. Adeline Grove was just around the corner from Sidney Street – made famous by Churchill when, as the Home Secretary, he led troops to the famous siege of Sidney Street. It was there that they shot 'Peter the Painter', a terrorist who had threatened to bomb the Royal Family and Houses of Parliament.

It was quite a wrench leaving Milton Road. My Jamie was only a little boy and Gregory was in Oakfield School and it was a shame having to pull them out of a familiar environment and family home to follow me to the East End. Gregory had to start a new school, although he was getting on fine at Dulwich. But what could I do? It was too dangerous to stay across the water, where I could be spotted by local police, who knew me on sight. It had to be done. I couldn't be without my kids.

So, anyway, I was on my toes for a couple of years. The kids went to local schools, and Buster and June from south London and Dolly used to come over nearly every day. We had a very good social life with all of our East End friends, but Maureen was a bit homesick for south London. It didn't matter much to me, though, because I was in a new environment that I liked. Crossing over the Thames was like going to another country in those days.

My Greg also must have had a hard time in the East End school because he couldn't help but speak posh so he got into lots of fights, poor kid. Jamie was too young to really know the score. Ronnie, Reg and Charlie used to pop around and I would go to the Double R Club, the pool hall, the Blind Beggar and many other pubs in the area. It was mostly Jewish food over there and you got all these characters like Sammy the Yid, Nobby Clarke, Bill Ackerman, Limehouse Willy and Leslie Berman. They were all part of the organisation, working at the local spielers. I used to pop in there to pass the time, though I never played cards.

I became a regular at Bloom's, and Kossoff's the bakers for my fresh bread and bagels on Sundays. It was a new way of life for me, coming from the south side, and it was to be a turning point in my career because I met up with some other chaps I'd previously known but had not worked with: Alf, Ron and Big George.

The flat in Adeline Grove was the same flat the Twins had used when Reggie and Ron traded places at Epsom Prison and Ron went on his toes. I had it decorated out by John Doland, a very artistic fellow who had a well-paid job as floor manager of a large commercial enterprise by day and sometimes worked as a barman by night. He was gay and had a part-time job as barman at the Double R Club; years later he came to work for me at the Prince of Wales. But really he should have been an interior designer.

I asked Ronnie King, an ex-ABA middleweight champion and old friend, to come and look after my home in Milton Road, Herne Hill, until I returned. Things always worked out better if you allowed as much time as possible between the offence and getting nicked. One advantage with time is that IDs wouldn't stand up so well and, with any luck, witnesses may have moved. Time is a great healer – as was proved when they finally caught up with me over the Southampton job.

I was nicked at an illegal spiel in Limehouse. Maureen had been in the car waiting for me while I walked inside for a few moments and all of a sudden the place was surrounded by police vans and cossers. Everybody got nicked, including me. Apart from being a police station, Arbour Square was also a magistrates' court, where small fines were given.

But then they started fingerprinting everybody and that was a different story. I had already given a moody (false) name of Freddie Puttnam. They insisted on keeping me there, so finally I gave in and thought I might have a chance to get away before they checked my prints.

In court the next morning, I went up and got my fine in the name of Puttnam, together with 30 to 40 others out of the spieler. My George also came to court in case I needed to come away a bit lively. As I walked out of the dock, there were two coppers waiting for me at the back of the court. I recognised them. 'Hullo, Fred, we've been looking for you for a long time. Come on, it ain't going to be too bad.'

Fortunately, but unbeknown to me, Maureen had done the sensible thing and had got in touch with Albert Connell, the bookmaker go-between, to do whatever he could. We were all sensible that way. We knew the routine and were usually one step ahead.

I went along with the coppers to the car park and as we got around the corner, instead of three of us, there were suddenly four. George had fallen into step and was marching alongside, his hand in his jacket ready to pull out a big cosh that was down his trousers. Looking sideways at me and then George, the coppers asked, 'Who the fuck is he?'

I turned to George and told him we were going to the nick and I'd be OK.

Now, George had been willing to have a row with the coppers, put the cosh about and spring me. He said, 'You sure, mate?'

I replied, 'See you later, George,' and he reluctantly walked away.

At the nick I was kept in the cells for a couple of hours and then one of the guvnors called me into an office.

'Where've you fucking been, Fred? We been looking everywhere for you. You been in the East End? That's a bad manor to be in, Fred. You're a south-London boy.' The copper told me that he'd see whether they wanted me in Southampton and would play it by ear.

He got on the phone and his conversation went like this: 'You know the guy we're looking for, I got him in custody. Freddie Foreman. Are those witnesses still available? But how are they going to deal with it after two years? Do you want me to deal with it or do you want to be fucked about with it down there? I've got him for receiving. All right, leave it to me, I'll deal with it then.' He put the phone down and said that was that: did I want to put my hands up to receiving? To me that was a good result. I got three months, and being sent back to Wandsworth Prison was like going back to a mother's womb. Good old Albert had done the trick again!

The Firm were upset by my departure, because we had business to do and work to complete. Now that I was no longer on my toes,

Maureen wanted to return to south London to be near her sister Nellie and Johnny Fitz. Buster and June and Renee and Tommy Wisbey were on the other side of the water, so we took a flat in Vauxhall Walk, a council estate, right next to Lambeth Walk. John Doland came over and made the place look presentable and Maureen spent far too much on it for a council flat, but it did look nice. Now that I was back in south London, I could get involved again with George and Buster, although I was still working with the other firm.

But the East End had marked a new stage in my career, a graduation. Banks, post offices, bullion, wages and payrolls were now the target. I had progressed to a bigger and heavier firm.

Buster Edwards was still grafting with the shops and a bank firm known as the Bowler Hat mob. Tommy Wisbey was in prison over the Southampton job. The new firm liked the way I worked. I was a hard grafter and could drive any sort of car or lorry and handle myself if there was any trouble. If any of the Firm got into difficulties, each one of us was 100 per cent loyal and dependable. You wouldn't leave anyone behind. If we got nicked, we got nicked together.

This was no job for weaklings. You had to be powerful to pick up oxyacetylene bottles, heave them on your shoulder and carry them up fire escapes, over rooftops and lower them into the well of a building. We would have to cut our way into banks and other buildings by sawing through iron bars, knocking down walls, or cutting through joists above a ceiling. We had a few disappointments, but the paydays were very good.

We planned our operations carefully, paying close attention to detail. While our inside information was usually spot-on, we never totally relied on it. We would sit in the back of a van outside a bank, factory or post office, and observe the target premises from holes drilled into the sides of our vehicle. If the windows of the target building were high, we'd come back with a furniture van to get a better vantage point. We did things then that police do in surveillance today. I lost count of the number of places we robbed. During some months, it seemed to run at about one a week.

Like everybody else, you wanted to own your own home and car and to have money in the bank and provide a good education for your kids – something I never had. Whichever way I earned my money, my sole aim was to provide for my family. I sent my Greg and Jamie to Oakfield

College in Dulwich. Later, when we returned from the East End, the boys attended Christ College, Blackheath, and Jamie, who got the acting bug, went with Danielle, my daughter, to the Italia Conti Academy of Theatre Arts.

I never robbed poor people or broke into homes. We robbed only businesses and factories and did jump-ups with lorries. We considered that respectable and honest thieving. Not like today's mugging of old ladies and young girls. We treated and looked after women and paid good money for presents and clothes for our friends and family. We never nicked cars to go joyriding; we nicked them to go to work and get a living. We stole money to live well but, ultimately, our intention was to earn enough to go into business, go legit – and stop having to risk our liberty. It was a business and no one felt ashamed of what we did.

CHAPTER 7
THE PERFECT TEAM

It didn't take long for me to progress to a much more serious firm. I'd met Alfie Gerrard, Ron and Big George on other occasions at Paddy Onions's and Alf's car site at the Elephant and Castle a year or so before. I told them to keep in touch as I had plans for a bit of work later if they were interested. I knew Big George was good with the old fizzer, cutting open safes, and that there would be some big prizes. Later, as we became more successful, we recruited two more chaps.

Micky Regan and Patsy O'Mara were experienced, courageous and reliable. With Mick's arrival, the team was now complete and there was no stopping us. An added bonus was that he became a lifelong friend. We were fearless, loyal, skilled and determined to win. We'd met through introductions from others and got to know each other better through having a drink. You always get the belly of a man by having a drink and watching how he behaves. Whatever shortcomings there were in any of us, you'd find out over a drink. But we'd served our apprenticeship in villainy and now you couldn't have wished for a better, more reliable group of men.

Each one of these men was strongly individual with a colourful history. Big Ronnie was never into clubs or gambling – he was far more interested in family life and being with his children. He's a lovely man who I've been very proud to know. Big George was from Canning Town. A big lump of a man and as tall as Micky Regan, he was very muscular with a granite face and carried oxyacetylene bottles as if they were light as a feather. He was a good-natured man and a very good worker. He had a curious habit of stretching his arms out to shorten his jacket sleeves every time he sat down. His size and bearing contributed to his frightening appearance. What a formidable team! Big Mick, Big Ron and Big George – all the same size. Then wild Patsy, me, and Neanderthal Alf.

Big Ronnie was an excellent grafter as well as a good coach. He could drive anything. He knew all about cars and lorries and could repair them if they broke down. Although he had fingers like bananas, he could deftly pick up the smallest screw without fumbling or dropping it.

Alf Gerrard was also from Canning Town. He and I got on like a house on fire. Alf once got into a row with a load of fellas and was heavily outnumbered. They had surrounded him and were closing in to do him. He copped for one and got his head under his armpit and dug his two fingers into the socket of the geezer's eye, threatening to pop it out on to his cheek. He growled, 'Are you going to fuck off all of you or do I blind him?' So that finished that one-sided row. If you were fighting him, it was all or nothing. Alf would rip your jugular out, as Stan Thompson found out in the nick. Alf was always going to win any way he could.

Neither of us feared any man or any thing. You just didn't give a shit, you knew what your capabilities were. You would know, if there was any heavy work that needed to be done, you were quite capable of doing it. There was no limit to what you would do. People knew that, so you held that bit of fear and respect and it was true of the situation at that time.

Alf was a Neanderthal with a heart, though. He'd lay down his life for you, but if someone got on his wrong side they'd be in trouble. He was built like a brick shithouse, as wide as he was tall. He loved his food, too. He once told me how he swallowed a chicken bone while devouring the whole bird. 'Fuck me, Fred,' he'd say, 'I've swallowed this chicken bone and had to fish it out of my arse.'

His other love in life, apart from food, was his dogs. Alf ran a scrap-metal yard in some arches with a big smelter to melt down gear and had a couple of dogs guarding the place, one a mangy longhaired Alsatian. A young guy of about 30 worked for him at the yard and tried to emulate Alf by acting tough and doing a bit of growling around the place. He was a bit of a bully really, although Alf found him a good worker, and strong. There were a lot of rats in the arches and Alf's worker was trying to poison them, although he was told not to do so if the dogs were around. Defying Alf, he put the poison down and the next morning Alf came in to find the Alsatian dead. 'What did I tell you!' Alf said, brokenheartedly, to the young geezer.

'Well, he was only a mangy old dog anyway,' replied the young bully.

Well, first off Alf got hold of his dog and shoved him into the furnace. He then turned on the young guy and said, 'Mangy old dog, was he?' Crash! He punched him straight in the forehead with the club hammer. The bruise ballooned immediately and he then grabbed this fella off the floor and made to throw him into the furnace after the dog, but he was restrained.

While Alf loved dogs, he only respected them if they had a bit of spirit. I went around to his house in Green Lanes, north London, on one occasion, and found a hell of a commotion going on. I had just walked into the large entrance hall, which led to stairs and a first-floor gallery, when his wife Margie screamed out at me, 'Stop him, Fred, stop him! He's killing Tiger!'

As she pleaded with me, Tiger, a vicious boxer with the build of a bull mastiff, came flying over the gallery rail and crashed down on his back on the tiled floor below. Growling ferociously, his legs slipping on the marble floor as he raced to scramble back upstairs, Tiger shot up to the bedroom. I followed to find the dog in a crouched position on the bed snarling at Alf and waiting for an opportunity to spring on him.

Alf was in a rage. He held a four-by-two timber high above his head, ready to bring it down on the dog's head. 'That fucking dog, Fred, he won't do as he's told. I told him not to get on that fucking bed and the bastard still gets on it.' Whack! Whack! Whack! He brought the stick down on Tiger. After that, he couldn't handle the dog any more, so we had to ship him out to the country.

About six months later, we had cause to visit the farm late at night in pitch-black conditions and, as we got out of the car into the yard, we could hear growling in the darkness. A heavy, deep growling. Understandably, I hesitated before getting out of the car – I didn't fancy getting my nuts chewed off! – and Alf started laughing, saying, 'It's that fucking Tiger, he thinks I'm coming to take him back.'

I exercised caution, staying in the car until the new owner put him away.

Whenever we went to the pub in Alf's Jaguar, there'd be a scramble to get in the back seat when we came out. Alf was a terrible driver. He couldn't drive slowly if he'd wanted to. He even knocked his uncle down in the garage once. When they pulled him out, slightly stunned, he had the Jaguar marque emblazoned on his forehead from being hit with the bumper!

Nothing in the world rattled Alf. We were on a bank job in Manchester once and had to sneak through a mortuary. Bits and pieces of bodies from accident victims were slung into metal coffins. I tried not to look, but Alf would say, 'Come over here and have a look at this one, Fred.' He'd have been quite happy to sit down alongside a coffin and eat a roast dinner. But for all that he had a heart of gold and he'd never let you down.

Together, we must have created a menacing presence. If we ever walked in anywhere, people would draw in their breath and say, 'Mind how you go with them two.' You didn't fuck with Alf. But, for all that, he had a sense of humour. We once kept watch on a security van while Alf was parked outside a butcher's shop window. He was drooling over sides of beef and legs of lamb in this butcher's shop as two young girls walked past. 'Lovely bit of a leg!' said Alf, talking about the meat, but they thought he was drooling over them and shot back: 'Drop dead, granddad!' Alf saw the joke and fell about laughing.

With his enormous appetite, Alf would eat six to eight pies and mash at Cooks' Pie and Eel shop in The Cut next door to the Young Vic. They had the best pie and mash in London. He was always interested in food, more than sex, and ended up owning the Blue Plaice fish restaurant, employing as his assistant chef Eddy Watkins, whom I'll mention again later. I took Maureen to his restaurant on one occasion and we got there before opening time. Maureen, as always, was dressed to the nines – she always was when she went out with me. Alf popped his head around the door of the kitchen and said he'd be with us in a minute. He came out wearing his white cook's outfit covered in blood, a knife in one hand and a big conger eel with its head half hanging off in the other. It was like a scene from the *Texas Chainsaw Massacre* and put Maureen right off her food. 'I think I'd prefer a Chinese meal, Fred,' she whispered.

'What's the fucking matter with her?' he growled as we slipped out of his restaurant.

'See you later, Alf,' I replied, chuckling to myself.

Alf was intuitive: he always had a sixth sense about people and jobs and was a good judge of character. Like Big Ronnie, if he got bad vibes on a job, we'd pull off. Both of them were proven right on many occasions. Ron, particularly, was our eyes. He'd weigh up a situation and if he didn't fancy it, he'd drop it. No questions asked.

Sadly, I was away in America in 1980 when Alf died. He was on his toes in Brighton, wanted again for some robbery or other. Unfortunately, he ate something that caused internal bleeding. His stomach slowly filled up with blood but he didn't want to go to hospital as he was on the run. By the time he agreed to see a doctor, it was too late. He collapsed in the hospital lift and died from an internal haemorrhage. It was a sad way for him to go, and ironic that he died because of his own passion in life: food.

After that, his son Nicky followed in his father's footsteps but was not up to it. He was a bit of a lump like Alf and had a few rows with people. He shot a few people, cut a few people and did all the usual stuff growing up. In June 1982, his killers lured him to a party and blasted him with a shotgun through the windscreen of his car. (This would not have happened if Alf had still been alive or if I'd been around.) Afterwards, apparently they threw up with nerves in their getaway car, so it wasn't the mark of professional assassins.

I've digressed a little, so I'll continue by describing the rest of the chaps. Patsy O'Mara was a true-blooded Irishman, even though he spoke with a cockney accent and came from Finsbury Park, north London. Patsy was about six feet tall, but of nondescript appearance. Slim and dressed conservatively, he had this great advantage of looking like a bank clerk or an office worker. No one would ever take him for a pavement artist or a thief like the rest of us. As a result, he was a right asset because he could walk into places or stand outside a hit and not draw any attention to himself. The rest of us would be hiding in the van and, on his signal, usually a tap on the side of the van, we would spring out and do the business. His job was to always make sure he got the moneybags. He and Mick Regan used to do safes together, knocking off the rivets with a hammer and chisel. Patsy was well read, intelligent and argumentative – but really good company with it. It was Patsy who first coined my nickname, 'Brown Bread Fred'. Of course, 'Brown Bread' was the cockney rhyming slang for dead, and, when Patsy used to ring up and ask for me, he'd simply say, 'Is Brown Bread there?' It was partly a joke, and partly to fool any coppers who might overhear him.

If he was in a row, Patsy could handle himself and he was game for anything, even pulling the trigger if need be. He also liked his drink. One night, he had a bit of an argument with some people at a party. He got mad and took his shotgun and blew out all the windows in the house. Patsy didn't give a fuck about anyone.

I once took Patsy to see Fred Coffey, the Firm's GP. He was another lovely Irishman – as were most of the Firm's GPs. Patsy had a ruptured belly button, it was like a golf ball and Fred Coffey told me to bring him into the surgery at Paddington. I was sitting with him when Dr Fred told him to drop his strides and get on the couch. He lay there chatting away – Patsy was a good conversationalist – while Dr Fred slipped on his rubber gloves and spread Vaseline on his finger. He gave me a wink and told Patsy to put his knees up. 'This won't hurt a bit,' he said.

And all of a sudden, Patsy was doing a wrestler's bridge raising himself by his head, catapulting his stomach into the air and shouting, 'NITTO! FRED! NITTO!'

Dr Fred had inserted two fingers into Patsy's arse. Patsy screamed with surprise at this unexpected intrusion. 'Hold on, Patsy,' Dr Fred said, seeing Patsy's eyes watering. Apparently, this rupture was caused by his excessive drinking – and poor Patsy needed an operation.

I knew he was a big drinker but didn't realise how badly it had got to him. Patsy, me and Ronnie Everett had all bought caravans in Hastings and during the school holidays I would send Johnny Fitz and Nellie with their kids and my sons to the caravan for the summer. Patsy would start drinking with Johnny at about 9.30am and continue throughout the day. But he never let drink interfere with his work. Fitzy was a good drinker too and popular because he could sing all the old music-hall songs. Patsy sang Irish songs and the pair would get paralytic together.

Sometimes he went a little over the top, though. He and I were in a bar in the Tin Pan Alley Club (owned by Jimmy and young Frank

Fraser – our families go back over 40 years) once, when Patsy picked an argument with two geezers in the corner. On this occasion, he had his arm in plaster so it was left to me to sort them out. He was such an argumentative bastard, but I loved him.

Whenever we did a bank or vault job, I never did the burning open – that was left to Ron and Big George and Mick. Me and Alf used to cop for anyone who came back to check us out. We'd wrap them up and make sure it was safe to carry on.

Sometimes you had to work between security shifts, so you did things like pin-up the door – put a matchstick in the door so you would know when it was opened and, if possible, time the openings. That had to coincide with cracking the safe. We could tell from the make of the safe exactly how long it was going to take to open it.

We varied our operations so that there was never a definite pattern and we'd go up and down the country, cutting and burning open vaults, wrapping up staff and snatching payrolls. Other firms were working at the same time as us and our democratic organisation would allow any of us to join them on specific jobs. Buster and my friend Lennie were still with the Bowler Hat gang. Ronnie Scrutton and Micky Kehoe had their own firms. From time to time, I would also work with other pals, like Billy Ambrose, Jerry Callaghan and Big Tommy Sullivan, who also had his own firm but was always available if an extra man was needed.

Our success was incredible, and I earned enough dough from the pavement work to get premises in Lambeth Walk and turn it into a drinking club with entertainment and live music. We called the place the Walk Inn, after the song from *Me and My Girl*.

The club opened in 1958 and was an instant success. Johnny Fitz was one of the barmen, Ronnie King was on the door and George and Buster helped run it. Jock the piano player was at the keys most nights and Bertie Blake did the cabaret. The building was long and narrow – and a potential death-trap, because we only had one window halfway down the club. Before it was inspected for fire regulations, we knocked a hole through the back wall and put in a door leading to a supposed fire exit. In fact, it led straight into Sainsbury's private goods depot. This did the trick, but as soon as the inspection was over, we had to brick it up again, leaving the door on show complete with Emergency Exit sign. Thank God, we never had to use it.

The premises were licensed and luxuriously fitted out. The place was cracking away but it also drew a lot of attention when people left late at night. They made a lot of noise, laughing and joking and waking up neighbours, so we knew it was only a matter of time before police raided us. We got nicked a couple of times for after-hours drinking and that's when I got to know Frank Williams, a detective inspector from across the road at Kennington police station. Albert Connell knew him well and arranged a meet. He became a good contact and helped me out on a number of occasions.

Upstairs at the club, Joe Carter ran an SP office, so that was another string to our bow. It was a good little earner. Even so, we were only one of many clubs in the area: the Richardsons had their club in Camberwell, there was the Bungalow Club in Brixton and Ronnie Scrutton ran the Chase Club at the Angel.

You could go from one club to another and see the same faces. We could easily tell which pavement firm had a touch on a particular day by the way they were celebrating in the afternoon. They'd be walking around with bottles of vodka or Scotch. Money just flowed. There were always loads of tarts and birds on week nights. Friday was chaps' night and wives were only allowed on Saturday and Sunday nights. (We were only being fair!)

We had terrific times. All the women would dress up as flapper girls on Roaring Twenties nights. On other nights, we'd have fancy-dress parties and lots of music and drink. Like all club owners, you had plenty of trouble indoors with wives and girlfriends. I worked hard on the pavements by day and played hard in the club most nights.

Johnny Fitz's wife, Nellie, was a lovely lady but a real little firecracker. She'd come down to the club and drag him home if he was drunk and stayed out late. Apart from her being mad at him for drinking, though, she was as good as gold most of the time.

While Joe Carter had an SP office above our premises, Micky Regan ran one upstairs above the Chi Chi drinking club at the Angel. All the chaps used to use the club, which was respectably run by two women, so nobody took liberties. People from all over London drank there. Mick's offices were run by his sister Pat, a lovely person, his brother Maurice, a cousin Danny and Nobby Clarke, his board man. Mick would help out on the phones when we were not doing other business.

We never knew the reason for it, but Mick's premises were attacked by a gang led by Peter Langton, a local face who was making a name for himself on the manor. But he only got as far as the stairs. He charged up to Mick's SP office with six or seven of his gang, looking for trouble. A violent row followed. They'd come tooled up with a few bayonets, so at the end of the fight there were several broken arms, cuts and bruises shared out on both sides.

As Mick was one of the Firm, I got tooled up when I heard about the trouble, went over there to him straight away and slept on his settee that night to offer him support. Afterwards, our firm went for a cruise and toured all the little pubs to find those responsible.

Late one night, I had one of the gang responsible in my sights and we stalked him through the back streets of Islington. Fortunately for him, he got to his street door just in time. Years later, I met him under different circumstances and found him one of the nicest chaps you could meet. But that's the way it was in those days. You couldn't sit on the fence, you had to declare who you were with, friend or foe, and I was with Micky Regan, come what may.

We drove around for weeks in two cars looking for other members of the gang. We had spies and finger men out visiting all the pubs and clubs with orders to report to us immediately if they spotted any of them. Several weeks went by and I was in the corner of the Walk Inn having a drink with Ronnie Kray. The club was packed out on this particular night. Ronnie said to me, 'Don't look now Freddie, but there's that geezer Langton at the corner of the bar. I'm with you if you want to sort it out.' Langton was with two of his friends. I told Ronnie I'd sort it out myself another time, I didn't want to involve the Twins – it was the Firm's row – but then Buster, who was behind the bar, said Langton wanted a word with me.

He offered me a lorry load of booze he'd nicked and I said I might be interested if he gave me a breakdown of what he had and came back to see me the next day. I got in touch with Mick immediately and let him know that we were going to get a visit from someone he badly wanted to meet again.

Langton arrived for the meet with two of his guys and I had Alf Gerrard, Big Ronnie, Big George, my George and Buster with me. I stalled for a bit and told him a buyer was coming over who'd probably have the lot off him.

About half an hour and a few drinks later, Mick walked in and the blood drained from Langton's face. The two guys with him didn't know what was going on, as they hadn't been part of the row. Langton looked around. There was only one way out: the window. Alf warned him that if he made a move he'd be a dead man. 'Don't even think about it,' Alf told him.

Langton looked at me: 'You too, Fred?'

'I'm afraid so,' I replied.

One of Mick's people backed a van to the club door and I said, 'Whichever way you want to go out of here, you're going now.' The other two guys were crapping themselves. I told them it had nothing to do with them and told them to sit down in the corner with my George and Buster while the rest of us dealt with Langton. I then gave Langton the choice of walking out or going out feet first.

'Will it be bad?' he asked. I told him he would have to wait and see and that it was up to Mick. He walked to the van and we roped him up and blindfolded him. The place we were taking him to was our flop – a farmhouse a couple of hours' drive away in the country, and by the time we got there he was starting to talk gibberish and was obviously in a state of shock.

I asked Mick what he was going to do. Mick had an iron bar and said that he would just do his legs. I said, 'I'll anaesthetise him and put him out of his fucking misery.' It was more out of mercy than anything else. I hit him on the chin and knocked him out, breaking his jaw. Mick sat him up against the wall, propped his knees up to his chin and gave him a few good whacks with the iron bar.

Langton started to come round and began pulling down his blindfold. 'Pull that fucking blindfold down and you're not going to leave here!' I warned him. We put him in the van and on the way back he was talking gibberish again.

We got back to Myddelton Square at the Angel and pulled him out. I stuck a tenner in his top pocket for a cab fare and left him on the pavement. He couldn't walk or do anything. Both his legs were busted. It was no surprise he just disappeared off the scene. Everyone knew he'd been taken for a ride, but he never came to the front again or tried to be a name. The other people involved with him went to ground and didn't surface for six to twelve months. On one or two occasions we got the motor out and went looking for them, but they had vanished.

Twenty or so years later, I went to the A and R Club for a drink.

Mick and Ronnie Knight owned it, and Mick told me I'd never believe who was drinking there that night. It was Peter Langton – who he said turned out to be a really nice guy. Langton told Mick that his trip to our flop was the best thing that could have happened to him. It set him on the straight and narrow and he'd never done a day's bird since. He bought us drinks and said we had treated him right and taught him a lesson. We all shook hands and that was the end of that episode. It shows that the short, sharp lesson sometimes works!

The Walk Inn was taking too much of a toll on our lives by now, and we were considering giving it up. As I said before, we were continually in the doghouse with our wives and families, so we thought we'd have an insurance coup. I had a word with a friend of the family who worked as an assessor and on inspection of the premises he said there was too much concrete and brick for a good fire so we had to think of other solutions. In the end, the problem solved itself.

Buster, who was getting drunk all the time at the time, drove into about six cars one evening, writing off his own in the process and leaving a gaping wound in his head. The blood just poured out. He came into the club and we thought this was the final straw. He was getting into too much trouble through the Walk Inn. I had just had a touch and money was no problem, so we thought we'd smash the fuck out of the bar, smash all the mirrors, the chairs and juke box, all the stage lighting and plants. We literally wrecked the place. We then got Buster to go around and flick his head up and down, leaving huge streaks of blood splattered across the walls. He was a bit masochistic in this way, but I thought the world of Buster and sadly miss him to this day. I only wish I could turn the clock back.

Anyway, having smashed the place up, we called the police and Buster sat there with the gaping wound still oozing blood. Frank Williams, the station DI, came over and we said we'd had a bit of trouble from a gang across the water.

He looked at Buster and said, 'I know who that is. It's Porky Bennett's gang.'

I'd never heard of him at that time, although he came from Bethnal Green, which was the Twins' territory. I later found out they'd had a few rows in clubs over the East End.

So I told DI Williams, 'I don't know who the fuck it was. I just got here. We've had enough of this, Mr Williams, we're going to call it a day!'

He said we were going to lose our licence anyway so we put in a claim and my insurance man got us a nice few grand, plus loss of profits. We had turned defeat into victory. Now we could concentrate on other projects.

One such offshoot to our main business involved Paddy Onions, Alf, Brian and Peter Loughran, who organised a smuggling enterprise bringing in watches from Switzerland. It got so lucrative we had our own special brand made up called 'Moodoo' watches (a play on 'moody' watches), which were gaudy and garish. The chunky ones with lots of gold, bangles and stones in them, were sold in Brixton. The ladies loved them. For gentlemen, we had a 'slimline' watch, which was quite plain-looking. They were genuine Swiss watches, made to order but shipped in without paying tax and duty. We had good contacts with some fishermen and smuggled them in on a fishing boat at Newhaven. The captain would pick up the gear off the coast of Belgium and then Paddy would sail out to meet him in a dinghy and bring the watches into Newhaven in a holdall. Small fortunes were made and some of us bought houses with cash from the profits.

On one particular day, the Customs were waiting to smash this enterprise. Brian was the coach, Alf was there minding and Paddy had the gear. Customs men had disguised themselves as fishermen and they had an attractive undercover lady officer who chatted up Paddy on a train journey to Switzerland, showing off her legs and putting him in promise land. He'd already taken her out for dinner and she'd intimated that next time they met he'd get his leg over. But the next time he saw her, he was a million miles from getting his leg over. He was in the dock in the Old Bailey and she was giving evidence for the prosecution.

When Paddy sailed into Newhaven, the fishermen asked what was in his bag, as they were talking downstairs over a cup of tea in a harbour canteen. Paddy's reply was: 'Cock-a-doodle-doo, it's got nothing to do with you.' That expression was later repeated at his trial, provoking great laughter.

In those days, Customs were quite gentlemanly in their business and were used to people responding in like manner. But not our team. The officers confronted our lot with the words: 'Good morning, gentlemen, we're Customs officers. You're under arrest!'

'Bollocks!' came the reply as the three rushed out to their Jaguar getaway car and took off. A Customs officer stood in front of the car for a brief second but thought better of it when he realised they would not stop.

A chase ensued and, unfortunately, the Jaguar's accelerator cable broke. That didn't stop our men, though. Alf opened the bonnet and lay across the engine, bringing the bonnet back down on top of him, and held the broken accelerator arm together so they could escape. They threw all the bags containing the watches – approximately £40,000 worth – into a farmer's ditch and covered them over as best they could. Unfortunately, the next day the farmer decided to clear his ditches and found the watches, which he handed in to the police. When the three appeared before the magistrate at committal proceedings in Lewes Magistrates' Court, we watched the prosecution's car arrive and followed it at lunchtime to the local pub. While they were having a bit of lunch and a few jars, we stole their briefcases containing the evidence. We got all the prosecution's phone numbers and found out how they had done their investigation. Amazingly, they had gone as far as bugging a public phone booth outside my flat in Kennington. This was 1960, so you can imagine what they get up to today.

When Alf was tried, the jury got him off the more serious charges because they all lived in the Isle of Dogs and were sympathetic to an East Ender. He went down for nine months. Paddy got five years.

Back then, you had no privileges like today. There were no phone calls home to your wife, visits were only allowed once a month and then you could only shout through thick, dirty glass, with no physical contact. It was bad. No home leave, nothing.

If any of the Firm were ever unavoidably detained in prison, we'd still cut them in their whack whenever we had a touch. We looked after wives and children when their men were away and out of circulation. It was our rule, although not a lot of firms did as we did.

Around this time, we were offered some work in Ireland by an Irish connection who had worked in London and done some time in British jails. We were in a quiet period, but holding a good amount of money. The Irish firm said they had access to a bank and keys in Drogheda, Co. Louth, just 30 miles north of Dublin on the east coast of Ireland. Did we fancy going over? We liked the sound of it. In case we were stopped and questioned over there, we had the plausible excuse that we had come to look at betting shops. This was just before the British government had decided to cash in on SP betting itself. Betting shops were given a trial run in Ireland for a year or so before they were allowed in England.

The four of us went out in pairs – me and Patsy O'Mara on one flight, Micky Regan and Big George on another. Big George had already been there earlier to look at the safe and said it would only take half an hour to cut through it. The Irish firm had been given a shopping list of equipment necessary to burn open the vault and they already had access keys to let us inside the bank. All of us used pseudonyms when we booked into Dublin hotels on arrival. I stayed with Patsy at the Gresham Hotel under the name of Roberts and the other two booked in under false names at the Moria Hotel.

We were met by the Irish firm and did a little more negotiating on how to go to work. The bank was in an industrial area and all our equipment was stored in a tomb of a church graveyard adjoining our target. One of the priests had enthusiastically entered the plot and had agreed to bring the loot to England for us wearing his dog collar. That would ensure he wouldn't get a pull by police or special branch. The scheme was looking better and better. We asked the Irish firm to hire a car and gave them some money to organise it. We then drove down to look over the bank. Everything went according to plan and we were pleased with the arrangements. On returning to Dublin, we passed through a small village. Four large men driving through a quiet country village was not too clever, but we had nothing on us to worry about. The keys to the bank had been lodged with someone local and everything was above board. Or so we thought.

A lone Garda Síochána (guardians of the peace is their fancy name, but in reality they're just the local cossers) waved us down. Next thing, 20 armed Gardai were all over us. They appeared from behind walls and hedges and arrested us and took us to the local nick. We gave our false names.

It turned out that Zebedia, the geezer whom we paid to get the car, had tried to earn himself some pocket money and, instead of hiring it, had borrowed the car from his girlfriend. The problem was that she was two-timing Zebedia, and lent him a car belonging to her other boyfriend – who turned out to be an Irish policeman! That explained why they flagged us down. They had recognised their colleague's car and were convinced the four heavies inside had stolen it. Can you believe it? This could only happen in Ireland!

Thank God, they had not been on our tail when we went to visit the bank. That said, now they wanted to know what we were up to. They didn't buy our story about visiting betting shops and didn't believe we had given our proper names. They had got in touch with the girl who had lent out the car and she said that she had not laid eyes on us before, nor had she allowed us to use her car. So, now we were nicked, fingerprinted and asked for our proper names. We tried to fanny our way out, but they told us, 'We're just as clever as Scotland Yard, you know.' We couldn't get in touch with Zebedia, so they banged us up.

As our prints were on their way to London, there was no point in maintaining our false identities any longer so we told them who we were, but that caused further complications. I was OK with a name like Foreman and a cockney accent, but Patsy, Mick and George all had Irish surnames as well as cockney accents, so once again the Gardai thought we were trying to have them over.

'Do you take us for idiots?' They hit the roof when we insisted Patsy O'Mara, George Cahill and Michael Regan were Englishmen. The CRO (Criminal Record Office) files confirmed our names but, even so, it was off on remand to Mountjoy Prison charged with stealing a car.

It was a terrible prison, 50 years behind the times. Filthy wooden floors in the cells, knives and forks made from old tin hammered into shape, corroded with age and encrusted with food. You couldn't use them without risking death from food poisoning. The diet was potato soup, potato soup and potato soup. The winter was freezing cold and there was no heating in the cells. You could hear the mice scrambling under the bed. After 5.30pm, when the lights went out in winter, it was pitch black. The cons had no vests or underpants. They were lucky to have buttons on their shirts and they had no woollies or jumpers apart from old blue-dyed army battle dress as the warmest piece of clothing.

We were in nice cashmere overcoats, suits and ties – in spite of which, we still froze. Rather than being locked up in these conditions for 23 hours a day, we asked to be put to work in the woodshed, a Nissen-style building but without sides, in which we sawed sleepers and logs wearing our overcoats for extra warmth. A bell rang every quarter of an hour or so and warders and cons who observed the faith would kneel and cross themselves.

The screw supervising us was a fat little Hitler, complete with moustache. Patsy, after being constipated for a week, asked the screw for some toilet paper and, accompanied by him, went in search of a khazi, but they had all frozen over. We watched the pair of them inspect each toilet in turn, pour cold water, then hot water down the pan, and even try and break up the ice with a four-by-two timber. It was hilarious seeing them shake their heads, and discuss frozen crap. 'Cold water won't shift that,' the screw remarked. This went on for half an hour and frustration grew between the two men. They then returned, with a bucket of boiling hot water – which promptly split the basin in two. Patsy had had enough and said he'd gone off having a crap. The screw nosed up to his face and said, 'You shit when I tell you!'

Patsy responded, 'I'm not getting frostbite in my bollocks for you or anyone else.' The pair then stood nose to nose swearing at each other – until the bell rang again, upon which the screw dropped to one knee and crossed himself.

My old friend from London, Jim Murray, came to our rescue. He had an interest in a small hotel in Dublin. Jimmy was a good friend for whom I had done a favour in Soho a year before, as I'll explain. I'd visited his club with the Twins for a late-night drink. Tony Mellar tried to take over Jimmy's club and sent in some heavies on the night we visited. It was a clip joint with nice-looking girls and run properly by members of Jimmy's family. All of a sudden, several guys tipped over chairs and tables and started a rumpus. Reg got one of them just in time before he smashed a huge ashtray on my head. We laid out all five of them and dragged them downstairs to Wardour Street, where we left them on the pavement, neatly laid out side by side. Jimmy was grateful for that.

He was a real character. He once hired the Festival Hall for St Patrick's Day celebrations and laid on a red carpet with Irish pipers and the Ted Heath band. Jimmy had a lovely house in Clapham overlooking the common. I would go there for parties and he invited a mixture of showbiz people, villains and titled gentry. Lord Moynihan, despite his title, was lower than a sewer rat, and he was a frequent visitor to these parties. However, I never liked him and as events were to show, he revealed himself as a treacherous, deceitful informant. I also saw people such as Peter Rachman, the notorious landlord, Raymond Nash and famous actors and musicians at Jimmy's parties.

Anyway, Jimmy arrived at Mountjoy with style. As remand prisoners our food could be brought in, and Jimmy delivered it to us using silver service from the kitchens of the hotel. The screws had never seen anything like it. A lawyer, aptly named Mr Blood, was engaged to represent our firm. My London solicitor, Tony Block, had earlier telephoned Maureen to ask if she knew where I was. She responded as she'd always been briefed to when authority rang: 'He's just gone out to buy a newspaper.' Tony said I must have gone a long way, then, because Fred was in Mountjoy, Ireland. So Maureen came over, with Ding Dong (Dell Rudell), a close friend who handled a lot of my business. Patsy's people came with a little Jewish guy called Solly Lautman from the East End. He was in the schmutter game (rag trade), manufacturing clothes, and brought us some bail money over. We needed a lot of it.

The court appearance in Drogheda was like something out of a farce. The place looked nothing like a courtroom. At one end there was a table and chair and, at the other, a big roaring fire. The room was full of people all talking excitedly. The magistrate, a one-armed chap, wanted £10,000 bail in cash for each of us. They couldn't believe it when we piled this king's ransom on the table. I think it was probably the highest bail ever demanded for charges of being in possession of a car without the owner's consent. Let's face it, you could buy a beautiful house for £5,000 those days.

We made front-page news, with headlines referring to us as the 'London Gangsters in Dublin' and were treated like celebrities. Crowds had turned up for the court appearance. We were each sentenced to nine months, suspended, and were ordered not to return to Ireland for five years (which would have been much too soon for me, anyway).

There was a footnote to this story. Zebedia tried to leave Ireland from Shannon airport when he heard that it came on top for us. Imagining the worst-case scenario, he got himself kitted up in the priest's outfit, hat, glasses, dog collar and Bible under his arm, the whole bollocks. But he had form as long as your arm, so the Gardai recognised him straight away, kicked his arse into a patrol car and arrested him. That idiot could have got us all 14 years if we had been nicked a day later doing the bank! Another lucky escape!

After the Irish fiasco, we all went into the betting-shop business. I was not able to acquire a licence myself, so I put my brother-in-law Johnny Fitz up for it, as he knew the game and had worked for different bookmakers at the races as a clerk. Another relation of mine, Jack Darling, also had a bucket and sponge job at the dog tracks, which was a job handed down to family members over the years. It was like a pension. You were paid tips for washing down the blackboards and keeping an eye on the bookie, giving protection.

While I was setting up my betting shops, I was asked to help resolve a conflict that could have led to wars between some of the biggest London firms. It involved the Nash brothers, one of whom had been charged with the murder of Selwyn Gooney, who was shot dead in the Pen Club in Duval Street, Stepney. (Jerry and Bill both had a good touch robbing a pen company and that's how the club got its name.) The club was owned by two pals of mine, Billy Ambrose and Jerry Callaghan, who were recruited from time to time to join in some pavement work with our firm. On this weekend – 6–7 February 1960 – Billy Ambrose had been paroled while serving a 10-year sentence for robbery with violence. There was a fight in the club involving the Nash firm, which included Joey Pyle, Johnny Reed and Jimmy Nash on the one hand, and Jerry Callaghan and Billy Ambrose on the other.

Unfortunately, the barman, Selwyn Gooney, got shot in the head and Billy Ambrose got a bullet in the stomach. A few of the others had bottles smashed over their heads too. Billy, in spite of his wounds, took Gooney's body out of the club and put it on the pavement before driving himself to hospital.

Later, Jimmy Nash and Joe Pyle were arrested for the shooting and looked like being hanged if they were found guilty so we had a 'sit-down'. Both sides needed someone to negotiate, so I was called in for Billy Ambrose and the Twins for the Nash brothers. To make sure no villainy was done, I had to guarantee that Billy and Jerry weren't setting them up for an ambush. The Twins, in turn, made sure the Nashes didn't come tooled up to blast Billy and Jerry. We held the meeting at Vallance Road and pledged our help. It was a case of us against the authorities.

No one ever really knew until years later that it was me who saved their necks. It was a tough old sit-down because there was a lot of animosity in the room: these were the brothers of Jimmy Nash, who'd shot Billy Ambrose and killed their barman, so it wasn't an ideal situation. But the ethics of the criminal underworld was to save them from being hung, and we had to go about changing the minds of all the witnesses – who, of course, were all from Ambrose and Callaghan's side.

So the Nash brothers, Johnnie and Ronnie, came round. And they had their heads in their hands with despair. We had a carload of my lot as back-up round the corner too, in case it all went off. You see, the Twins didn't know what day of the week it was back then – it was the early sixties, and they were far from the established criminals they were to become.

We decided to go about getting witnesses to change their statements. Suddenly they all started to remember how dimly lit it was in there. We even went as far as to pay for one of the female witnesses to have an abortion, and flew her out to Ireland for the operation she so desperately wanted – to keep her right out of the way.

By the time the verdict was given in court, the jury was convinced, and Jimmy was acquitted of the murder and got five years for GBH – which was a good result. Joe Pyle escaped the noose too.

So effective was our work that when all concerned were acquitted, one newspaper said of the man shot dead that night that, 'As far as the law is concerned, all that happened is that he leaned on a bullet which happened to be passing.'

It's a pity that politicians and heads of state can't settle their differences as effectively as we did. That was the end of the rows between Callaghan, Ambrose and the Nash brothers.

CHAPTER 8
BATTLE OF BOW

I learned early on to keep a low profile. The last thing a successful firm wants is for the Old Bill to come moseying around or to lay itself open to an informant fingering you after a big job. You can get away with an awful lot in life if you don't shout about it. That said, our work nearly always attracted widespread publicity, not least for the huge rewards offered for information leading to our arrest and conviction. If there had been a competition for front-page splashes in national newspapers, we'd have won hands down. Not like some flash villains who couldn't resist flooding the bar with free booze and mouthing off about their latest victory. We knew when to stay shtum!

As with other trends in society, crime has a distinctive pattern of evolution and we did our bit in shaping the criminal landscape. To this day, the public has never been told the full story of what happened in the Battle of Bow, when a bank clerk shot and killed a member of our firm. His death was never recorded. Police and newspaper reports only revealed that a robber had been wounded and might need 'urgent medical attention'. They didn't explain that an unarmed man had been shot in the back of the head. Had they done so, there would have been a public uproar. It was a crazy situation. On the one hand, police were not issued with guns, while on the other, two ordinary bank clerks were allowed to discharge their lethal weapons in a busy London road during rush-hour traffic!

Neither the Home Office nor Scotland Yard were prepared to reveal the full facts of this major incident because of the potential political scandal. Nevertheless, it became the turning point in determining Home Office policy on the use of weapons and security, particularly as related to guarding bullion.

The legacy of our actions, and the actions of other firms like ours, has been the growth of a billion-pound security industry giving employment to thousands and inevitably making our task more difficult in the process. (I wish I had bought shares in the security industry!)

Members of our firm had planned the Bow theft over a period of months. As a rule of thumb, most big raids usually involved detailed planning based on inside information. Experience taught us to assess such information and to weigh up the likelihood of success.

Thursday, 14 December 1961: a cold, drizzly day. Wisps of early morning mist rose like steam from the wet, cobbled roads. The mist had almost cleared by the time the wages van came into view in Carter's Road, at the junction with Bow Common Lane near the east London gasworks.

The Firm had been in position for some time. They'd rehearsed their roles for weeks. Now, flushed with excitement and the thrill of the chase, they were counting on an early Christmas present. At today's values, the snatch, if it came off, would be worth more than £2 million.

The target bullion van had been hired by the City bank of Glyn Mills to deliver large sums of money from their head office in Lombard Street to the East End. This was a regular trip. The van set off about 8.45am with the driver, Edward Banks, two guards, Fred Dighton and Ron Harman, a bank official called Bill Shelton, City of London police constable Ted Buckle and Flash, his German Shepherd guard dog.

Their first drop was in Wapping High Street, then on to Bow, to the gasworks. The Firm, already familiar with the route, delivery times and the number of people in the van, were in place for the ambush.

One vital piece of information was missing, however. The robbers had not been told that the two bank clerks guarding the payroll were *armed*! Dighton and Harman were each carrying a loaded .22 Beretta pistol with five rounds of ammunition. And they were both crack shots.

The proposed ambush was relatively straightforward. It would take place in Turner's Road at the aforementioned junction of Bow Common Lane. The target van would be rammed by the first vehicle, another van would park across the road cutting off access from behind, and a third vehicle would come up alongside to create a diversion while the second vehicle wrenched off the bank van's rear doors.

Three members of the Firm lay in the back of the diversionary vehicle. It was a very long lorry with the side cut out and a tarpaulin sheet hanging down one side. The driver kept watch for the target van through his side mirror and had no verbal contact with the others. The target vehicle was a solid old van. Brown in colour, it had two very small windows along the side and another two on the back door.

The Firm's second vehicle was an Evening Standard Ford V8 delivery van with a reinforced iron rail welded into the back to strengthen the chassis where a hook and chain were secured. The ram vehicle, manned by two of the robbers, was positioned in front of the target van, ready to jam on its brakes and reverse into the bank van at the predetermined spot near the junction. All the gang wore heavy coats with hats and scarves and industrial face masks ready for the smother-up (disguise). Pickaxe handles with rope and taped ends to provide grip were at the ready.

Everything had been planned with military precision. Five vehicles, cars, lorries and vans had all been stolen, false numberplates fitted and modifications made. Each member of the team had been carefully chosen. Now, as the time for action drew nearer, the tension mounted. The gang's excitement was measured by short puffs of breath visibly hitting the cold morning air.

At 9.45am, the big brown van turned a corner at the bottom of Turner's Road and came up behind the open lorry, which sped forward to keep abreast. Had they tumbled that something was amiss? The Firm's other lorry, some way in front of the target van, braked suddenly and then hit reverse gear. The bullion driver must have shitted himself to see the lorry reverse at speed, making a head-on collision unavoidable. Crash! Lorry and van shuddered to a stop as they collided. The gang's open lorry then hit the side of the bank van, making a sickening scraping sound exaggerated by the ripping of metal. On impact, the three raiders in the back were thrown about like rag dolls. Scrambling to their feet, they made their way to the side of the van and ripped away the sheet of tarpaulin to expose the windows of the bank van.

Tooled up with small iron crowbars, they smashed the glass windows to create confusion inside. At the same time, the robbers in the print van reversed against the two rear doors, smashed the back windows and passed an iron hook and chain through them. On securing the chain, the signal to drive forward was given. The print van revved up and lurched forward, wrenching off the two back doors of the target van. They went flying into the air before crashing down on to the road.

Meanwhile, the three men at the side of the van had created total confusion among the bank clerks and bank official, who were screaming and shouting, running back and forth in panic. But there was to be a turnabout. One of the robbers came face to face with the clerk and was struck by a premonition of danger. His hair stood on end and his blood ran cold. Without a second thought, he ducked. A millisecond later, a bullet shattered the glass. His premonition saved his life.

At this point, the plan was going drastically wrong. The Firm should have been filling the van with a noxious substance. They were only 18 inches away from the most daring and cunning part of the entire raid: smashing a hole in the window and blasting in a mixture of pepper and talcum powder to temporarily blind the cashier, security guard and policeman.

Their apparatus was ready: a huge funnel, which was fed by a length of copper tubing attached to a 3ft oxyacetylene cylinder to force pounds of the powder and pepper through the broken window. But the driver had misjudged his crash: they were out of line with the nearest window and couldn't work the apparatus.

Instead, they concentrated on the rear of the bank van. Once the doors had been wrenched off, they armed themselves with pickaxe handles and stormed inside. Tantalisingly, halfway down the van they could see brown cricket bags bulging with cash – £122,000 in wage packets: a fortune waiting to be grabbed.

But the scene had become ugly. They were confronted by a snarling Alsatian, and out jumped a six-foot four City copper, who turned out to be an ex-boxing champ and was as determined and courageous as his dog. He was struck across the head by the driver of the print van who had come alongside. Another robber went for the dog and cracked him on the head. There was a sound of gunshots, which nobody heard at first because of the commotion going on.

Still unaware of the danger from the armed guards, one of the robbers, waving a sledgehammer, tried to climb into the bank van with a helping shove from his colleagues. The attempt was short-lived. He came face to face with two guns pointing at him and the guards standing in firing position, legs astride, shouting, 'Come any closer and I'll shoot.'

Risking the warning, he tried to grasp the end of the cricket bags, hesitantly snatching at them. The other raiders egged him on, but then the penny dropped. They could see that one of their number had been shot in the side of the head. The badly injured robber, blood pouring from the back of his head, crawled round to the rear of the van.

Meanwhile, the bank clerks inside were still shouting, 'I'll shoot, I'll shoot!' Two of the robbers threw themselves under the van to help their wounded mate. Another, half in anger and frustration, hurled a pickaxe handle into the bank van sending it crashing against the cabin wall and forcing the bank employees to duck as it clattered to the floor.

Two of the robbers then lifted and dragged the wounded man into the print van and clambered aboard themselves. Another robber had also been shot through the arm. At this stage they decided to call it a day. They'd had enough and were ready to pull away.

But it was not over yet. Two of the Firm were missing. Where were they? Down the road, some 50 yards away, a strange ritual seemed to be underway. From a distance, it looked like a dance in slow motion choreographed by an odd troupe wearing face masks and police uniforms. The policeman was twisting and turning, a pickaxe handle in his left hand and, with his right, struggling to hold a robber's neck in an armlock. Next to him, obstinately gripping the second robber's arse with his bloodied fangs, and swinging from side to side as the robber tried to shake him off, was the dog, Flash.

Two of the robbers jumped from the print van to the rescue, one grabbing a pickaxe handle, the other a sledgehammer. Running back past the rear of the open bank van, more shots were fired. Did they really think the raiders were coming back? One of the robbers shouted out, 'I think they're out of bullets.'

The rescue team warned PC Buckle, 'Let him fucking go.' Terrier-like, the copper hung on and was rewarded with a more forceful gesture. A pickaxe handle came crashing down on his head. He looked up: 'You bastard,' he yelled. A second later a sledgehammer went whizzing by and the copper got hit in the back between his shoulder blades. The hammer bounced off and went sliding 20 feet down the road. But still the PC persisted. His dog, like its master, continued to grip the other bandit.

There was only one thing for it. The copper would have to be beaten unconscious. The team laid into him. Five or six good hard whacks on his nut until eventually his knees buckled. Then someone kicked the dog in the bollocks and another robber gave him one on the nose for good measure. The robbers were finally free to stagger back to the waiting print van.

As they did so, the policeman tried to walk away, but he just crumbled. He appeared to be walking down a slope, disappearing into the ground as his legs gave way. He finally fell flat on his face and was out cold. But what a strong bastard copper. Well, they used to come big and still do in the City of London. He had to be given credit for his courage. Afterwards he and his dog received a medal. As for the Firm, they were all very upset with the morning's work and had to go away and lick their wounds.

Later that day, police issued a statement warning every hospital in greater London to be on the lookout for a wounded man. What happened to the victim was very sad. His death could not be acknowledged and it was the first time a man had been shot dead by the authorities during a robbery. To reveal his name today would only open old wounds for his widow and family. His disappearance was covered up with a story that he had run off with a mistress to Australia.

The problem now confronting all the big firms was that this episode showed the authorities were prepared to use guns while we only had sticks. We needed an equaliser. That became a turning point for criminals as well as the establishment. The whole of the underworld decided: 'Next time, we'll be armed as well.'

Police said that they found a toy plastic Luger gun in the gutter near the van and that the firm had also been armed. Which was complete bollocks, as if we had had a shotgun, we would have got the cash, believe me! For some time afterwards, there were a lot of cartoons in the newspapers with pictures of bank vans with cannons, rockets and machine-gun turrets carrying cash through the streets of London. The press also wanted to know how many armed bank vans there were. Under the headline GUN LAW PERIL IN BRITAIN, the Liberal MP for

Bolton West, Mr Arthur Holt, warned the government that the shooting of a bullion bandit by a bank guard could lead to Chicago-style gun battles imperilling passers-by. He wanted the Home Secretary to disclose how many private persons were permitted to carry arms for the protection of property.

The bank guards, it transpired, went twice a week for target practice. Dighton, who fired the shots, thought he had discharged five bullets in all but in fact only four shots were fired. The first two, he explained, had been warning shots at either side of the doors. The second volley hit home. This was more bullshit: our man was hit in the head with the second shot, and our next casualty, who was shot in the arm, was hit about five shots later.

When asked about the incident, director of the Glyn Mills bank, Mr Faulkner, made an astonishing admission. Asked by one national newspaper what would have happened if a robber had been killed, he replied, 'About 20 men at the bank employed as messengers are licensed to use guns. They collect their pistols from the bank before going on payroll and other duties. Each man licensed to carry a gun has regular marksmanship training at a police shooting range. These men are good shots. I think Mr Dighton did a damn fine job and next time I hope we hit two of the bandits.'

Dighton admitted to hitting one of the robbers. He said later, 'I know I hit one man. He yelled and grabbed his left arm. The gang seemed to panic. The whole thing was over in a couple of minutes.' The only clue left by the bandits as they made their getaway in a Jaguar car parked nearby, was a blood-soaked piece of gauze torn from a protective face mask.

Since then there have been many cases in which a robber has been killed, particularly at ambushes where police have been lying in wait for robbers to show up. Judging by what we have witnessed in recent years, it appears that police are more keen to have a shoot-out than stop the robbery. Why not nick the robbers earlier? The answer must be that they have been given carte blanche to do whatever is necessary to stop armed robbery.

So in hindsight, it really did work in the end: there are very few organised gangs prepared to do what they did in the early years of crime in London. Now, with Big Brother watching every step we take, you can't take a piss in a side alley without getting nicked!

CHAPTER 9

'GOT ANY GOLD BARS DOWN THERE, FRED?'

We'd learned a lot of lessons from Bow, and by the early 1960s the Firm were a finely tuned machine. In those days, wages were moved around on backs of lorries to factories, power stations and office blocks. Some six or seven members of staff would be chosen to guard the wages. They got a few extra pounds in their pockets for this and were armed with coshes and police truncheons. They thought it was a big giggle until a lorry or car smashed into their vehicle, sending them sprawling in a heap in some quiet street through which they had to pass. Then they would be confronted by five or six masked men standing over them with pickaxe handles. Fortunately for them, no one was in it for the violence, only the money.

As far as our firm was concerned, the less violence the better. We'd never batter people till they were on life-support machines; we just got the money and went. The element of surprise and the method of attack were the best possible way to ensure this. Usually, they were so surprised they had their mouths wide open and we'd be gone before they knew it.

Of course, there was always the Mackeson man. (Remember the stout advert? A chap dressed in a boiler suit, muscles bulging, an iron girder on his shoulder with the Mackeson balanced on it.) Macho employees who imagined we were stealing their personal money would sometimes have a go and would receive a tap here and there or a clump on the shoulder or legs – never on the head. They were only workers trying to get a bit extra to take home. Besides, our information for the bit of work usually came from inside, so we didn't want to hurt one of our own.

It was all very businesslike. We had nicked fast, reliable cars to get away with and were cool drivers. There was never any panic. Such was our success that the Post Office would be forced to reorganise security and bring in a host of procedural changes as a result of our enterprise. We were known as pavement artists because of the speed and efficiency with which we relieved Post Office and security vans of their valuable cargoes. Basically, it meant hanging about on a pavement until the target stopped off for a pick-up or a delivery. We'd strike then and it would be all over in minutes. It was a highly lucrative business.

Thursdays were the busiest day of the week. That's when pensions were paid. I would dress up as a postman in trousers with red stripes, badges, the whole gear. Through inside information, we already knew which PO van would leave a particular sorting office with bags of cash. The van drivers were never told what they would be carrying and security was surprisingly lax considering that they could be carrying up to £20,000 in cash, a lot of money in those days.

I'd be lurking on the pavement, waiting for the van to arrive. The driver was usually alone and I'd cop for him as soon as he opened the sliding door. In most cases, I'd drag him into the back of the van and wrap him up with some rope. Alf would jump up with me and go through the sacks of mail and find the four or five registered bags that had to come out. These were normally identifiable by a perforated edge on the label.

Ron would drive us away with another van or car tailing us. It was all over in minutes. We would drive the van to a predetermined spot – usually a dead turning or somewhere you would be least noticed – dump the van, and be off in the getaway car. We always prepared thoroughly in advance and noted stopping times, delivery times, routes and escape routes. The operation went like clockwork and we used to average one a fortnight.

The hauls were mostly cash, but we also got insurance and postage stamps. You could sell the insurance stamps to business firms for one-third of their face value. Mike Harris and his partner Reggie Isaacs had people lined up all over London who'd buy them. He even sold them back to post office workers, who'd flog them across the counter and get back the face value. Our 'sales force' had been established over many years and everyone was on an earner. They were all part of an established organisation and you knew they could be trusted.

Eventually, the authorities must have sussed what was going on because they started perforating stamps and putting codes on them for certain areas. But that didn't stop us. We cracked the codes quickly and made sure the post office in Southwark wasn't selling stamps destined for, say, Carshalton. Once when we raided a sorting office, we had nearly half a million pounds' worth of stamps, all coded; with our organisation it was no problem.

When things began to hot up too much, we switched to banks and sorting offices. The PO had begun countermeasures by putting two men into the vans. When that failed to stop us, they installed bullet-proof glass and panic buttons that immobilised the vehicle – but even that couldn't stop us.

The getaway vehicle we used for bank and post-office raids was a Vanden Plas limousine. The boot held all our readies – pickaxe handles, coshes and spare clothing – and we had false plates fitted for the occasion. The cap-wearing 'chauffeur' sat alone in the front, while the rest of us hid on the floor. We used that car for a long time. It was reliable, and we considered it 'lucky'.

One night, we did a factory while staff were on duty. Dressed in boiler suits, we made our way along a river towpath, clambered over an outside wall, and got into the office block containing the vault. We were told that there was no night security because the whole place was alive. But the vault door was on view to all the working staff milling about in the yard outside. To block off the view, we came prepared with a large tent, which we built in front of the vault door and set to work with the cutters. While we were waiting for the vault doors to cool down after being torched, there was time for a flask of tea and sandwiches. Big Ron and me were facing some porthole swing doors and saw a face skip away from one of the windows. Ron rushed after him. There was night security after all! He rugby-tackled the guard, who smashed his torch into Ron's face. I sat on the man's chest and told him to behave himself or he'd get hurt. He managed to say, 'You'll never get away with this,' then fainted. We dragged him back to the vault room and roped him up. We then got the money and left him protesting wildly: 'You'll all hang,' he screamed. 'I'm going to die.' He passed out again. But it was all a sham. There was quite a large air vent in the vault door after we'd been at it, so he had nothing to worry about.

Nevertheless, we packed our suitcases in a hurry, as we didn't know if the night security guard had to check in and, if so, how often. If you could possibly avoid it, you never left gear behind because of the expense, the risk of prints and the bother of replacing it. Because of our need to get away quickly, we just threw everything into our suitcases leaving us short on space. So we stuffed all the money that was stolen into the legs and body of Alf's boiler suit, making it look like a bonfire Guy Fawkes with no head, tied and knotted at the neck and ankles. We left in two Ford Zephyrs for our safe house in north London, where we would cut up the money.

I found a spot to park the Zephyr in between two other cars. It was a bit tight, but I managed to squeeze in and was just about to get out of the car when two plainclothes policemen came out of the darkness and began asking questions about the numberplate and ownership of the car. I gave the details and told them to leave us alone. I locked the car door and started to walk away when one of the clever bastards shone his torch into the back and saw Alf's boilersuit torso. 'Hello, hello,' he said. 'What's this, then?' Well, all hell broke loose. One copper was laid out and I drove down the road with the other silly bastard lying across my front windscreen, right across the bonnet, flashing his torch into my eyes:

I said to Alf, 'I'll have to stop and you get out and bash this silly bastard.' At which point, I braked hard. Alf got out, but with the rapid stop the copper had disappeared over the back, ripping off the windscreen wiper as he went. That got rid of him. We drove to a friend's flat where we could walk through different blocks of the estate out of sight with our headless dummy, which Alf and I were holding up like a drunk, and phoned the rest of the Firm to tell them of the change of venue. We'd had a narrow escape, but it all ended well and we cut up the money while Alf tucked into a rabbit stew.

For another job, we'd had the layout of a north London sorting office accurately sketched for us. Our information was that on a certain weekend there would be a load of cash coming in that would be stored in a strongroom and would amount, by today's values, to several million pounds. Our plan was to enter the building before the weekend and stay overnight in one of the recreation rooms, for which we had a spare key. Planning this operation took several weeks. By the time we were ready for the robbery, most of our gear had been smuggled inside the sorting office and hidden in lockers and cupboards.

Instead of bringing in conspicuously large oxyacetylene bottles, we converted some much smaller oxygen bottles, which we stole from St Thomas's Hospital in south London. We entered the building via the loading bay dressed in authentic post-office attire and made our way along passageways we'd memorised from the sketch to an upstairs recreation room. We brought with us our bags and sandwiches and walked about purposefully and confidently, as though we were part of the staff. Once inside the recreation room, nobody would disturb us because it was locked up over weekends.

At about 9pm on the Saturday, when only a skeleton staff were in the building, we covered our faces with scarves and made for the strongroom. On the way, we met a security man, who put up a bit of a struggle. He was a copper type, and got whacked a bit and then tied up. Another two security men gave no trouble at all, though, and we tied them up and left them in the strongroom. The cutting gear was not needed because we managed to get a key. It was an Aladdin's Cave full of cash. We sorted out all the registered bags and filled up two trolley-loads of high-value parcels filled with money and valuables. On the way out, we bumped into two more nightworkers. We copped for them too, wrapped them up with a bit more string and left them on the loading bay. Now, all that lay between us and riches were the exit gates.

They were bolted with chains secured with padlocks and we sent Paddy O'Nione (Paddy Onions) and Big George to open up so we could toss everything into our van, which was already standing by, engine running, ready to drive into the loading bay. Alas, this was where things started to go wrong.

We had used somebody in the country to provide a lot of our equipment. He was a penny-pinching bastard and had brought cheap cutters even though he'd been given plenty of money to buy the best heavy-duty gear. As a result, Paddy and George had difficulty cutting the chains and were a bit slow. Midway through this little operation, a cosser walked by the gates on the footpath outside. Instead of fannying it out, Paddy fucked up. He panicked and brought attention to himself by overreacting to the copper's presence. As far as the cosser had been concerned, the sorting office was lit up and everything looked normal. Meanwhile, we were making our way there with the trolleys full of cash. But the copper, alerted by Paddy's behaviour, ran from the gate and blew his whistle.

Me and Alf were not willing to go empty-handed. Our van was outside, revving its engine like fury. The gate was still shut, but there was a gap at the top just large enough for us to squeeze through. We tried throwing bags of money through this opening, but they were too fat. We then pushed a couple through, but things were getting too hot and, reluctantly, we left the skips and narrowly squeezed through the gap ourselves.

We went to our lock-up in Kennington. We had a nice stow for the cars off Clapham Road, left them there, and went back to my place in Vauxhall. Paddy said he'd had enough. He wasn't going to do this any more. After what happened, though, we didn't want him anyway. Our haul was only a few thousand and a bit of tom (Tom Foolery, the cockney rhyming slang for jewellery.) But it should have been millions. C'est la vie!

Some months later, four of us did the place again. I was masked on this occasion and scared two of the security men shitless when I walked in on them. With the light behind me, I must have looked a menacing sight. I had them both on the floor in an instant, and Alf joined me. We put a bit of rope around them. I asked one how many more were in the building. 'Two more,' he said. We went stalking for them and Alf copped one, head under his arm, a tap on the head, and frogmarched him to another room.

'Where's your friend?' He didn't know and we couldn't go to work until we found him. All of a sudden, we heard a toilet flush. He was in the khazi, so we got him when he came out.

He told us where the keys to the strongroom were and we got in without a problem. This time, we made our exit from the building through a side-door, sweet as a nut. It was a good bit of work. We got a lot of cash from payrolls sent through the post, and some tom – rings, watches and other jewellery in transit for Hatton Garden. Although it had been a good bit of work, it was a little disappointing as they hadn't stored as much cash and stamps as we'd hoped. That was all down to the last episode, which must have scared the shit out of them.

As well as cash, stamps and a bit of tom, one night we escaped with something completely different in the back of the motor: a top Flying Squad officer! Alf and I had been out all night looking at some business and were driving along the Embankment by Chelsea Bridge. He'd been asleep in the back and I noticed a car had copped us. Our motor had Irish plates, but it was straight. I told Alf to wake up, as I knew we'd get a tug. I reached over and locked the front passenger door and my own door and just as we stopped at traffic lights, three coppers ran from their car trying to get into ours. Only one managed it – and he was the governor! I took off and drove down a side street while the other cossers ran back to their car. Now the officer was in the back seat with Alf – and getting in the back with Alf is like getting in the back with a Rottweiler.

'I'm Chief Inspector Vibart of the Yard!' he kept protesting. Vibart was a well-known Flying Squad copper back in those days. Alf was giving him a terrible time in the back and had pinned him against the door with his feet. It was like a scene from a comedy, this top copper in a car full of crooks.

The police were going crazy, and squad cars were flying around all over the place, trying to find their man. Suddenly, they located us, and three handed, they gave us the tug.

'What's all this about?' they asked sheepishly.

'We never asked him to jump in the back of the fucking car!' we replied. They desperately wanted to pull us, but didn't want the embarrassment of nicking us for kidnapping their boss! So instead, they asked if it was a crooked car.

'No it's not a fucking crooked car!' we told them.

They phoned back to the Yard, going through the usual checks of insurance and ownership, and even lifting the bonnet up looking at serial numbers. But reluctantly they had to let us go, figuring out that reporting this sorry tale back at the yard would cause much embarrassment in the policeman's canteen.

It was the beginning of a bad run, with one disaster following another, but that's how things went sometimes. After one aborted job in which we lost quite a few tools, we went up to Manchester, where a bit of work had come our way in one of the Big Four banks. To get at the back of the bank, we had to go through a locked car park and then into another yard belonging to a funeral parlour. (This is where Alf pointed out the accident casualties in their coffins, which I mentioned earlier.) After we'd got inside the premises, a security man arrived with two Alsatians and let the dogs loose in the yard. They made a hell of a fuss by an open window through which we'd entered with all our oxyacetylene equipment. With all the commotion we couldn't go on, so we quickly collected up all our gear and got out of there.

The police put a cordon around Manchester, thinking we'd head south, and this caused us to go a long way round. We tried to fox them by doing a detour around country lanes. But hours later we ran out of petrol and had to wake up a lorry driver sleeping in his cabin. We gave him a tenner and got him to drive us to the nearest garage for a can of petrol and we were then able to return safely to London.

Christmas was coming up, though, and we hadn't earned any money for quite some time, so we raided a postie van in south London. Most of our tools were lost on aborted raids and we had to make up new pickaxe handles to go to work. All you needed was some rope, which you put on each side of the handle and then wound black adhesive tape so you could carry it easily on your wrists. The hitting end was also taped up to soften the blow. It was a good tool.

With these as weapons, we got into the back of the van. The security men put up quite a fight, but the situation got worse with the arrival of reinforcements. These were made up of local builders and scaffolders who joined in the melee. The bastards got a bit brave and put up quite a fight. The security guards were not the ordinary run-of-the-mill guards either, so we had a terrible row with them. Afterwards, my bollocks were black and blue. As we made our getaway, a big petrol tanker came up and blocked the road. We had to go up the pavement to get around it. Big Ron was a good coach, though, and we just scraped through a narrow gap.

As we did so, they threw everything at us, from bricks to scaffolding poles, but we escaped and were back in the money again. Me and Alf finished up going to Harrods and spending £600 on toys for the kids.

Some villains panic when their liberty is at stake, but we always prided ourselves on our professionalism, which included never doing any real damage to innocent parties. We had targeted another sorting office on the outskirts of London. We knew that there'd been a delivery of quite a lot of cash and we struck late at night when we expected only about six to eight staff on duty. We waited by the vans in the yard when one guy came out to do the perimeter security and let the last van in. We copped for him and got his keys, but he struggled violently and made a lot of noise. A housing estate was next to the perimeter fence and the commotion threatened our safety.

Big George, Mick and Patsy had already gone inside to wrap up the others so I told Ron to take his hand away from this noisy geezer's mouth so I could knock him out. In fact, his false teeth had slipped halfway down his throat and the reason he was being so noisy was that he was choking and fighting for his life. He was as good as gold after Ron delicately fished out the small plate with his banana fingers! After that, things ran smoothly and we had a good payday.

At one stage, we were competing with the banks in a race against time to get at their vaults. They had commissioned a leading safe manufacturer to provide new safes before we had an opportunity to crack their old ones. After seeing their vaults busted open with square holes through great thick doors and cages, and their deposit boxes plundered, all the major banks realised they would have to renew their antiquated hardware and fit the most up-to-date security systems.

With all the heavy work we had been doing, we were strong as bullocks. Our 'equipment' included about six suitcases and several oxyacetylene gas bottles weighing two hundredweight each. We used to lift these up and throw them over our shoulders, then climb fire escapes and ladders and scamper across roofs.

We used walkie talkies and we had become so professional we even had smoke extractor fans to get rid of the burning smell. It was only natural that, following all this success, we would soon begin looking for bigger and better targets...

I've had a love affair with gold ever since I first handled it at 14. It's a soft, beautiful metal with aphrodisiac qualities- you could make an impression in it with your finger, and it's so precious you don't want to part with it, but keep and cherish it. So nothing could be more tempting or alluring than the promise of 40 solid gold bars, each the size of a house brick and with a combined weight of nearly half a ton. The Firm were offered the job in April or May 1963. Bullion that, by today's values, would be worth about £5 million was the prize. Before embarking on it, there was planning to be done and alibis to be arranged.

It was a nice piece of work from friends in the East End. There were some complications, however. The timing had to be spot-on and it meant that the Firm would have to be ready and prepared to strike in a matter of minutes. For week after week, they waited for the van to show up at the right time for its delivery of gold bars.

The ideal time for it to arrive, it had been decided, was late in the morning, preferably when most of the staff had left for lunch and only a few would remain in an upstairs office and at the back of the warehouse. Importantly, there would only be one man on duty to shut the gate after the van arrived.

In order to be there at the crucial moment, the Firm would have to sit around for possibly weeks on end in a hired van. That was never going to be easy in the City of London, which was a hot area for any villainy and heavily patrolled. But after weeks of no go, the van eventually arrived late and the staff had started to leave the premises for their favourite café or restaurant.

And so, on 24 May 1963, Sharps Pixley and Co., bullion brokers in Paul Street, near Finsbury Square in the City of London, became victim to the biggest gold bullion snatch in London. The *Daily Express* devoted its front page to the theft and called it the 'hottest load of loot since Colonel Blood snatched the Crown Jewels'. Someone, they said the next day, 'is sitting on half a ton of gold bars'. The newspaper continued:

Certainly they went about the grab in deadly professional style. There were four of them in blue overalls. They were waiting in busy Paul Street, Finsbury, when a van carrying the gold from Rothschild's Bank drove up to the warehouse of Sharps Pixley and Co., bullion brokers.

Two warehouse men had just gone to lunch and Charles Houghton, the 55-year-old porter, was alone there. He opened the big double doors and guided the van into the yard. The four men in blue slipped in behind and vanished into the shadows. From the van the crew and Mr Houghton unloaded 40 gold bars weighing 27lbs a piece and the size of a house brick. Twenty minutes later the van left empty.

When the men in blue overalls came into the open they had stockings on their faces and coshes in their hands. Mr Houghton was tied to a chair. The attackers opened the gates again and backed in a waiting blue Bedford van.

Swiftly the gold bars, stamped with serial numbers, were reloaded. When this van nosed into Paul Street, noisy with traffic and drills, no one took any notice. But then the bandits made their first mistake. They turned left and Paul Street is one-way in the opposite direction. People shouted. Cars hooted. But the Bedford roared on regardless and vanished into Finsbury's warren of side streets.

Curiously, police had been literally round the corner while Britain's biggest gold swipe was taking place. They were investigating a £10 safe robbery!

During the raid, the security man, a big old boy, had picked up a gold bar and tried to hit members of the Firm with it. He was given a right-hander to slow him down and take the fight out of him. The raid was over in minutes and the Firm took the gold to a north London yard, reloaded the bullion on to a tipper truck full of rubble and took it down to the country. A back-up car followed in case of trouble.

When police called the betting shop, I was busy chalking up the runners for the last race. The Firm had done a brilliant job, left no clues, no one saw a thing. The security man turned out to be a serious suspect but he was only doing his job and risked getting hurt trying to protect his employer's money. Interpol and Customs throughout Europe had been alerted to the bullion. Everyone was convinced that it was destined to be sold abroad.

Contrary to the press reports, the robbers did *not* go the wrong way up a one-way street. Another van – one that had nothing to do with the robbery – did, though. As a result, the police were searching for the wrong vehicle. When the Firm realised this, Ding Dong took back the van he had hired and asked for his deposit, safe in the knowledge that nobody was looking for the van. It tidied up the whole business.

About a month later, in June, police searched a Dutch motorship in Amsterdam following a tip-off by an underworld source that it was carrying 40 gold bars. But the 496-ton *Zaanstroom* was innocent of smuggling. The bullion was safely buried in Britain.

People were buzzing about the robbery. I was even approached about it by a friendly villain called Mikey Harris. He was well known, because Billy Hill, the notorious gangster, had taken liberties with him and tramlined his face years before. Mikey said he could get his hands on the gold. He wanted me in on it to give him credibility so that he could have it on approval for a few days and let the people know they wouldn't get conned out of their money. Knowing it was safely hidden away for the next six months to a year, I told him, 'Of course I'd be interested.' It certainly took the heat off me with the criminal fraternity.

Soon afterwards, a policeman who visited my pub, the Prince of Wales, pointed down the stairs to my basement and joked, 'Got any gold bars down there, Fred?' I laughed along with the rest of the punters. If only they knew!

A few weeks after the raid, I was having a drink at the Spanish Patriot pub in The Cut, Waterloo, with Tommy Sullivan and Patsy O'Mara, when in walked Buster Edwards, Gordon Goody, Bruce Reynolds and Tommy Wisbey. We all had a nice drink and during our conversation I was asked if I would like to go on some work. I thanked them for the invitation but said the Firm was having a little rest for a few months.

Once I had refused their offer they didn't elaborate on what they had in mind. It was none of my business, but I wished them luck in their enterprise. Three months later, on 8 August 1963, they pulled off the Great Train Robbery.

CHAPTER 10
PANAMA GOLD

In 1963, I was approached by some very serious people to rob Panama's main bank of its gold. My contact was a retired Foreign Office mandarin who was a friend of Churchill and the Royal Family. Whether he was acting in an official or freelance capacity, I will never know, but as unlikely as it sounds, you have to understand the politics of the era to realise the 'tricks' governments got up to then. In the early 1960s, Britain was still trying to be an influential player in world politics. After the Suez retreat, its main concern was over Aden and the growing crisis in the Middle East. Julian Amery, a government minister, wanted to knock the stuffing out of the Egyptian leader, Nasser, who was set on taking the British base there.

Prime Minister Macmillan was persuaded by Julian Amery and Billy McLean, Conservative MP for Stirling, to give unofficial backing and finance to royalists opposing Nasser's troops. To this end, Amery and McLean – both former Special Operations Executive officers in the war – set up an operation run by David Stirling, founder of the SAS, to help the royalists by recruiting ex-SAS mercenaries. Because Sir Alec Douglas-Home, the Foreign Secretary, preferred appeasement to conflict, the war against Nasser became a secret war involving SIS (the Secret Intelligence Service, which later became MI6).

Further afield, in South America, the Foreign Office turned its attention to Russian influence in Cuba, and central South American politics. How could a professional robber play a part in these Machiavellian plots? The answer is that 'anything goes in international politics'. The bizarre plot in which I almost became a player, involved Britain's most famous ballet dancer, Dame Margot Fonteyn, and her Panamanian ambassador husband, Dr Roberto 'Tito' Arias. It was hinted that I would be doing a service for Queen and Country.

In April 1963, a well-connected friend of mine, who had organised the sale of bullion in Switzerland for our firm, asked me if I'd be interested in some overseas work. He said an acquaintance who had been in the government wanted to hire a team of top professional safecrackers and bank robbers for a job for which they would be handsomely paid.

At the time, Dame Margot Fonteyn was consistently in the headlines. In February, she received international accolades after performing at Covent Garden in *Swan Lake* with Rudolf Nureyev, and then more in March with Ashton's new ballet *Marguerite And Armand* at a Royal Ballet Benevolent Fund gala. She and Arias had married in Paris in 1955, having met each other years earlier when he was a student in Cambridge. In 1956, she had been made a Dame of the British Empire and he'd become Panamanian ambassador to the Court of St James, resigning two years later when he fell out with the Panama government. The Panama Canal joins the Pacific and Atlantic oceans and had been a virtual protectorate of the USA, jealously guarded for its strategic position. But the country was always having revolutions and counter-revolutions. The Arias family had been very influential. Tito's father had twice been the country's president and Tito had harboured ambitions to follow in his father's footsteps. His uncle Arnulfe had been elected president four times and overthrown three times. Dame Margot Fonteyn's husband had a wide circle of influential friends on the international scene, including President Kennedy. Dame Margot had been a guest on the Onassis yacht with Winston Churchill and had dined with the Kennedys.

I was given some of this background detail in a preliminary 'briefing' when I was taken to see the former diplomat at his Wimpole Street flat in London's West End. A lift took us directly into his private lobby adjoining a large study-cum-drawing room complete with antique furniture and a grand piano. He greeted me cordially and told me I had come well recommended. He was very much an establishment figure and his appearance reminded me of Sir C. Aubrey Smith, the famous actor who starred in films like *Rebecca*, *Waterloo Bridge*, *Clive of India* and *The Four Feathers*. He had white hair, an aristocratic bearing and was in excellent shape; I'd have said he was in his late sixties or early seventies. As a young diplomat in the British Embassy in Moscow in 1917 and 1918, he'd helped smuggle the royal family's gold out of Russia shortly before Tsar Nicholas II, a close relative of our King George V, was murdered. I made three visits to Wimpole Street to discuss the plot to steal Panama's gold. This mysterious Aubrey Smith character had impeccable contacts. Photographs displayed on shelves and on the piano included shots of him with Prince Philip, other members of the Royal Family and with Winston Churchill. My own credentials had been verified by people like Tom Driberg MP and Lord Manny Shinwell.

The FO mandarin (retired) wanted me to bring a team of five men to Panama City. He was looking for the best mercenary robbers in Britain. We would get none of the gold, but would be paid a total of half a million pounds – £100,000 each which in 1963 would make you a millionaire by today's standards. It was an attractive proposition, made even more so by the adventurous aspects of the enterprise.

The plan, which would be more fully outlined once we had accepted the work, involved us entering Panama City separately from different parts of Europe some two weeks before the robbery. We would also book into different hotels. The operation would take effect during a fiesta. All the equipment we needed for the raid would be supplied and we would each be issued with weaponry – small arms.

An armed sentry at the target bank would have to be taken care of, and we would have to familiarise ourselves with the route from the city to the port. A truck – he called it a 'camion' (a lorry) – would also be provided, together with escort vehicles, and I would have to do a dummy run from Panama City to the harbour, some 40 miles away. Our FO man would supervise operations at the bank, after which we would be on our own.

The bullion would be loaded on to a Greek vessel. Apart from the captain and first mate, none of the crew would be aware of the cargo and there was little doubt about what we had to do if there were difficulties: sling the troublemakers overboard.

The night after the robbery, we would lay off the coast at a certain point, pick up three passengers in a small motorboat and escort them to Mexico City. One would be a treasurer of the bank, another would be Roberto Arias; the third passenger remained a mystery. We were also expected to provide a 24-hour guard on the cargo until the ship reached Mexico. An armoured van would meet us in Mexico City and the bullion would be transferred to the branch of a bank that also had a base in London. We would then return to England and the money we had been promised would be sent to the account numbers we had nominated in whatever part of the world we chose. I wanted to know a lot more and did some homework in local libraries. I knew the area was a hot-bed of activity and that the Americans would be very suspicious of vessels in the area. I didn't want us to end up cannon fodder in an ill-conceived plot. It was a very sensitive area and we were not sure who was behind these plans. As bank robbers, we were easily dispensable and nobody, apart from our families, would care what happened to us. Each of us was told to take out life insurance for our families prior to departure.

I discussed the work with Patsy O'Mara, and we came to the decision that we would concentrate on a job in London, which proved to be equally lucrative. Why travel to a distant country where we ran a great risk of never coming back? The others were wary of going into unknown territory. Here in London we knew all the back streets where we could duck and dive, and we had friends with whom we could stay if we had to go on our toes. True, the money was attractive. For a working-class cockney lad, the thought of instant riches was very enticing. But the downside was the very real danger that we were being used as pawns and would be dispensed with once the work had been done. Apart from that, our new bit of work in London was looking rosier and rosier. As a result, I declined the offer.

In June 1964, Dr Arias was shot in Panama by a 'political' assassin. The official version was that he had stood as candidate for the National Assembly as a Deputy for the Province of Panama. A political colleague, Alfredo Jimenez – known as 'the expressionless one' – had asked Arias to register him as his deputy. His refusal resulted in Jimenez shooting Arias five times at point-blank range at a busy road junction. Dr Arias survived but was permanently paralysed. Knowing what I did, I wondered if Arias *had* attempted to get the gold, which would have been his springboard to power in Panama.

That year, then, proved a lucky escape for me. I refused Panama and I had also knocked back the chance of becoming one of the Great Train robbers – and the likelihood of a 30-year prison sentence. In fact, later on, the Firm arranged for Buster, and later Ronald Biggs, to escape from Britain and get plastic surgery abroad. It was done through my contact, who used a former top-ranking Nazi officer to organise plastic surgeons and safe passage through Europe. Austrian-born Otto Skorzeny fulfilled the popular concept of a Waffen SS officer in every way. His face was lean, mean and authoritative. And in common with others of his kind, he proudly bore the status symbol scar inflicted on his face while fencing at university. But the man's enterprise was not in question.

In September 1943, he had led a detachment of men in gliders and landed on a short, inclined slope in front of the hotel on the Gran Sasso Range, Italy, where Benito Mussolini was held prisoner. After a brief battle, he liberated the fascist Italian leader and brought him to Hitler's headquarters in East Prussia. For his bravery and enterprise, Hitler awarded him with the Nazis' highest honour: the Iron Cross. In September 1944, he infiltrated the Citadel of Budapest and forcibly prevented the Hungarian puppet leader, Miklós Horthy, from making a separate peace agreement with Stalin. Then, during the Ardennes counteroffensive in north-east France in 1944, he caused widespread sabotage behind Allied lines. His activities included dressing up as an American army officer with his men as Allied military police and changing road signs over a vast area, leading to utter military confusion among Allied convoys. After the war, he stood trial as a war criminal but was acquitted. Now he and his wife Else ran a profitable business as 'fixers' for people all over Europe. Buster invested £20,000 with Otto's wife Else for a share in a holiday complex under construction in Algeciras, southern Spain. Although he got some returns, however, the whole thing was a rip-off.

Ronnie Biggs escaped from Wandsworth Prison with a friend of mine, Eric Flower, on 8 July 1965. They were sprung by Paul Seabourn, who drove a furniture van alongside the prison wall and threw over rope ladders, which got them out while other prisoners held down two screws. Although they no longer sew mailbags for the GPO, screws at the prison held an unfinished mailbag 'for the day Biggs returns'. Of course, today he is imprisoned in Belmarsh, after returning voluntarily from Rio – against my advice, I might add.

Eric Flower rang me from the 'safe place' he and Biggs were deposited in Dulwich by Paul Seabourn. He said he didn't think security was as good as it might be. We said we'd be over straight away. I had never met Biggs before, although I knew most of the main men in the train robbery. As I've said, Buster, Tommy Wisbey, Gordon Goody, Johnny Daly, Jimmy Hussey and Bruce Reynolds were all pals of mine. They were all from south London and our paths had crossed many times. I felt outraged that they had been given 30 years for the robbery. That was a fucking liberty. Nothing short of barbaric. I still believe to this day that someone probably sweet-grassed them.

Eric Flower was doing a 12 for robbery at the time of the escape. When Alf and I went to the Dulwich flat to see him and Biggs, Paul Seabourn was not too happy. He recognised Alf Gerrard immediately and took Biggs to another room and told him (as Biggs confirmed in his autobiography *Odd Man Out*), 'I know Alfie and I can tell you he's bad news. They're not here to do you any favours and they know you've got lots of dough tucked away. Take this [he offered a pistol, which was refused] to look after yourself. You're out, now make sure you stay out. Use this if you have to.'

He was right about one thing. We were there to help Eric rather than Biggs, but we had no designs on Biggs's money. We were only doing this as a favour for a friend. We didn't need the money and all 'fees' for services went directly to the parties involved and not us.

We moved Biggs and Flower to a safer address in Bermondsey, knowing that Seabourn would be in the frame, as Biggs and Seabourn had been close in prison. I didn't know Seabourn either and therefore had no reason to trust him. We moved Biggs and Flower from Bermondsey after we'd been tipped off that Seabourn had again been interviewed by police. The following night, police raided the block of flats where Biggs and Flower had been staying, but smashed into the flat directly below! They'd made an error, though the fugitives had gone the day before anyway.

Safely ensconced in one of the Firm's safe flats in Camberwell, where my sister-in-law Nellie looked after them, Eric and Biggs spent most of their time watching television. My Nellie looked after them for weeks without asking for a penny, or receiving any money. She did their cooking and washing and risked her own liberty without demanding anything. And she knew they were loaded because there was a suitcase stuffed with money behind her sofa. They did not venture out while we arranged passports and travel to Belgium and France for their plastic surgery.

But then Biggs got restless and wanted to move down to Bognor Regis for a couple of months to get rid of his prison pallor and link up with his wife Charmian and his kids. We only agreed reluctantly to this, because of the obvious risks. Later, we brought him back to Camberwell and arranged for a boat moored on the Thames at London Bridge to take him and Eric to Antwerp. We provided 'seamen's' clothes for them and drove them to the docks. They were to walk through the dock gates, where the ship's mate would meet them and hide them both on board. They were given seasickness pills and told that no matter what happened they had to stay in hiding on the boat until told to go ashore. A yellow DAF car would pick them up once they had walked out of Antwerp docks. The passports the Firm provided were in the names of Terence Furminger and Ronald King. We did not profit from the transactions and that was the end of the Firm's involvement with Biggs. All we knew was that he might possibly be in Australia.

Life is full of ironies and coincidences. In 1969, when Biggs fled Australia, Alfie Gerrard, Ronnie Everett and Jerry Callaghan were also there. They'd been on their toes, having fled Britain after a fight with police. While in south Australia, they had started a road haulage business and a store and were doing really well driving lorries across Australia. Alfie loved it. But their freedom was short-lived because of the introduction of a satellite TV link between Britain and Australia. Scotland Yard organised pictures of Biggs and members of my firm to be beamed across the Pacific and they were arrested hours after the transmission. Eric Flower was also arrested and they were all extradited to Britain. Eric was sent back to Wandsworth to finish his 12 years and the other three stood trial for assault on police and vehicle theft charges. I was away doing my 10 for Jack McVitie. Meantime, lucky Biggs had successfully evaded arrest and was on his way to Brazil and a new life.

Many years later, when I was on my toes in Spain in the mid-1980s, I met a Polish film director called Lech Majewski at the Red Pepper restaurant in Puerto Banus. He wanted to make a film on Biggs. I got the pair together and Biggs went ahead with the movie: *Prisoner of Rio*. I don't think it was very good, but Biggs made a few bob from it.

Majewski and his girlfriend Julia Frankel wrote the script. Paul Freeman played Biggs, and Steven Berkoff and Peter Firth had starring roles. It was released at about the same time as the film *Buster*, starring Phil Collins and Julie Walters.

Buster had escaped the police net in exactly the same way as Biggs and together with June and Nicky, had gone to Mexico and met up with Bruce Reynolds and his family. But life in Mexico was not for Buster. The family missed London and Buster returned to Europe in September 1966 to give himself up. On his way back, he asked me to meet him in Cologne, Germany, to help him with a plan of action.

Just before that, I had been a go-between for several others involved in the Great Train Robbery who were being hassled by Tommy Butler, the Flying Squad chief in charge of the case. By then, Detective Superintendent Frank Williams, whom I trusted and who had helped me in the past, was his deputy.

Butler was obsessed with catching all the men involved. To stop him pestering the men, I was asked to offer him £50,000. Frank Williams put it to him and Butler seemingly agreed. I made a meet with Frank to take the £50,000 cash stuffed in two holdall bags to Nunhead Station in south London, close to my betting shop in Nunhead Lane. When I walked into the station with the money, however, Frank Williams, looking a bit flustered, told me, 'Fred, I can't take it. Tommy's backed out.'

I told him it was no big deal and I'd take it back. He offered to act as my minder while I returned the money. 'No thanks, I can manage,' I said and got the fuck out of there.

I returned the money, only to go through this business all over again. This time, arrangements were made for me to leave the money in a telephone box in Great Dover Street, where I could mind it from my brother-in-law's flat. A separate bundle of £10,000 had been left on top to be dropped off at Albert Connell's betting shop. But Tommy Butler didn't want to stop at Albert's. He insisted on going straight to Scotland Yard, where he declared the lot. Oddly enough, the ones who got away weren't bothered by him any more.

I took Maureen with me when I went to Cologne as she had wanted to see her old friend June and we spent a few nice days together eating at restaurants and enjoying nightclubs. June had been very unhappy in Mexico and wanted to be back home with her family. Buster asked me to make a deal with Butler. I said I didn't trust him and that I thought he would double on him. But I promised to speak to Frank Williams.

I treated Frank and Tommy Butler to a lunch at Simpson's-in-the-Strand, one of my favourite restaurants. We sat in one of the box seats upstairs and I gave them the full treatment: plenty of fine wine, roast beef, cheeses and vintage port. By the time we'd finished eating, they were both relaxed and feeling mellow. All Butler wanted to talk about was cowboy films. He knew all there was to know about Westerns. Frank kept looking at me as if to say, 'Don't upset him, Fred.' Anyway, eventually we got to an arrangement where if – and only *if*, I emphasised – we could put Buster down as a minor participant in the robbery, such as cleaning up at the farm and being paid only a small amount of money, would Butler agree to do whatever he could to get him a lighter sentence. We all shook hands on this, then I explained it to Buster and got him back into a safe flat in Russell Court, Holborn. He and June shared a few days together and I kept in touch with Frank Williams.

Although everything had been agreed, I still did not trust Butler and asked Frank his opinion. Frank told me, 'Let's wait until Butler takes his leave. He goes to loads of European countries with field glasses, looking on the beaches for train robbers. That's his holiday. While he's away, bring Buster in to me, then I'll be the arresting officer and will be able to give my evidence *after* Butler has given his.' Frank Williams was a good man, considering he was a copper. In his Welsh accent, he said he thought 30 years was much too much time for a man to do.

So that's what we did. I arranged for Buster to come to the Prince of Wales pub on 19 September 1966 while Maureen kept June company. We sat in my lounge above the pub and got stuck into vintage brandy – Camus, I think it was. Frank, me and Buster spent hours chatting and got plenty of drink down us. I felt really worried in case it went wrong, though. I didn't like the idea of seeing a man throw himself in, knowing he faced the possibility of a 30-year sentence.

Buster got up and went to the loo at one time and Frank said, 'He can go if he likes, Fred. If he has changed his mind, I don't really care.'

So I got Buster in the bedroom and said, 'Look mate, if you want to go, I'll take you back to June.' But he wanted to get it over with and said, 'Let's go through with it, Fred.' It was a sad night as he walked out of my pub, got in Frank Williams's car and drove off to the

Borough High Street nick, where Frank sat Buster right under one of his wanted pictures. Not one copper, not even the Flying Squad team, recognised Buster. Mind you he did look different. He had lost lots of weight and the plastic surgeon had done a good job. I visited Buster in Bedford Prison with Maureen and the press were waiting outside thinking she was June. They drove us nuts following us around Bedford taking hundreds of photographs. June was known to the press as the 'Black Rose' and looked very much like Maureen.

I engaged George Stanley, a solicitor from Stratford Broadway, and we had the trial moved to Nottingham Crown Court. We got the best QC available, a leader of the circuit and a very nice man to talk to – Bernard Caulfield. He was shortly to be made a judge and many years later went down in history in the Jeffrey Archer libel case for his chivalrous commentary on Lady Archer.

Buster and I put together a story that Buster had been at another address at the time of the train robbery. We contrived to say he only went to Leatherslade farm where the money was counted, *after* the event, and that his job had been to burn it down and destroy the evidence. One of the prosecution team was Tom Williams QC, another Welshman, who had impressed me and so I made a mental note of his name for the future. Halfway through the trial, I considered Buster's case was not going very well and had a word with George Stanley: 'I don't like it George, I'm going to pull one of the jurors and try and get Buster a new trial.'

He was shocked: 'You can't do that! That would be illegal – and not only that, you'd go to prison.' I told him I didn't care; I was worried sick that Buster would go down for 30 years. He told me not to worry: Bernard Caulfield wouldn't let us down.

When it came to Tommy Butler, true to form he never helped one bit and he even tried to get Frank Williams to double on us. During the trial, when Frank Williams was about to enter the witness box to give his evidence, Butler grabbed hold of his arm and whispered in his ear, 'We can't let him slip, Frank.'

But Frank was a man of his word and went along with our defence. When Bernard asked him what scale or position Buster would be on the train-gang ladder, Frank replied, 'On the bottom rung.' Buster got 15 years, which was half of what the others got, so it didn't turn out too bad – at least, not if you say it quick and you aren't the one who has to do it. Buster did eight, and the others between 12 and 14 out of the 30.

Some time after his trial, Bernard Caulfield came to my pub the Prince of Wales with some friends, and we had a drink. He was a very nice man. I followed his progress and found him to be a very fair judge. He could dish it out with the rest of them, but he did show compassion and humanity when he had to sentence someone, not like Melford Stevenson and Sir Frederick Lawton. They were dogs, as I was to find out at a later date.

June had no money left over after all the expense of the trial and what they had spent to live on the run in Mexico and Germany. Buster had also been ripped off by a guy who had an office in the City. He was a right smooth operator; we nicknamed him Hunchie because he was short and had the start of a hump on his back, which would have got worse as he aged. He conned Buster for £20,000 in 1964 – and that was a lot of cash back then. To help June, Alf and I paid Hunchie a little visit: He was full of the usual shit, but I was not prepared to listen and told him so. We gave him a week to come up with the money and left him alone for a few days. Then we picked him up on another day in Hyde Park and kidnapped him for few hours before dropping him off at his Chelsea home. It was just to let him know that we knew where he lived and to give him a reminder about paying the money he owed Buster.

It turned out that Hunchie was a right rascal and owed a string of debts. People were queuing up to be paid. Before I was due to visit Hunchie again, I got an excited phone call telling me he was dead. I asked my informant how it happened and he said that he was found in his bath having suffered a heart attack, or something like that. There was no chance of money from him now, so I got in touch with Peter Wickman from the German magazine *Stern*. We organised a feature article, which was sold to the Sunday newspapers here and in Germany and made June £25,000. It helped her out until Buster got home.

I have to say this about coppers in those days: they never took it out on your wife like they do today. Tommy Butler, for all his faults, behaved like a gentleman around a lady and wouldn't dream of nicking them like today's police. If she loves him, a wife will stay with and support her husband, no matter what he has done. Most wives I have known are strong and loyal to their men, suffer with them every inch of the way and are still there waiting for them when they come home from a long sentence.

I take my hat off to you, ladies. You are by far the stronger of the sexes. I love you all.

CHAPTER 11
'GIVE ME A NAME'

My brother George was lying close to death in the surgical ward of St Thomas's Hospital in London. He had taken the full blast of a double-barrelled shotgun aimed at his groin at point-blank range. Although heavily doped up, he was still in agony after four operations. His upper thigh had been so badly wounded that there was talk of amputation. George and I had always been close and now I shared my brother's pain. His eyes were like deep, black holes in his pallid face. He looked like death. I felt anger, sorrow and the urge for revenge as I watched his suffering.

A policeman was at his bedside and I asked for a moment alone with my brother. After he left, I bent down and whispered in George's ear, 'Give me a name'. George's eyes turned to where the copper had been. Satisfied he was out of earshot, he uttered the words, 'Ginger Marks'.

George was shot on 17 December 1964, in a reckless, foolhardy attack. The assault was over in minutes, but the repercussions continued for years, jeopardising the liberty of innocent people, dividing friends and destroying families. His assailant was George 'Jimmy' Evans, who is only alive today because of the cowardly way he used his accomplice and friend Tommy 'Ginger' Marks as a shield, avoiding being shot himself. My brother George, who is one of the chaps, stuck to the time-honoured code of the underworld: he told police nothing. The comeback was our business.

Evans was a safe-blower who worked with his own little firm, which included David Norman, a man called Sams (who knew George) and Tommy 'Ginger' Marks, who was a good friend of Evans. He was also involved with Joe Wilkins, who ran escort agencies in the West End. To give you a small insight into his character, Evans had a monkey that he dressed as a policeman and, to the amusement of his friends, he'd whack this poor animal with a rubber truncheon: 'Hit the copper. Hit the copper.' Evans was not only violent but also an insanely jealous man. Pat, his wife – a lovely lady – was terrified of him.

He was gun mad. Firearms were an obsession that he continually indulged in. He'd talk about every gun that was ever built, giving all their technical details.

My George and Pat Evans fell in love shortly before the shooting. Their feelings for each other were genuine and deep and they are still together now, more than 30 years later. When they first met, both were married with children and homes of their own, so they used to meet at George's flat in Cable Street, Stepney. But Evans got suspicious and started spying on her. Shortly before 17 December 1964, he saw Pat driving George's car and challenged her. She told him the car was a repossession and that she had borrowed it, but Evans searched the glove compartment and found an electricity or phone bill belonging to George showing his home address: 12 Bland House, Lambeth Walk. Evans knocked at the door, but George wasn't there. He was told to try the betting shop in Nunhead Lane, again without success.

A couple of days later, George went to look at a car showroom in Rotherhithe, just by the tunnel. Sams and Evans happened to be there and Sams pointed George out to him. (There had been some confusion over tracking my George down, because there was another George Foreman living in Essex at the time.) On Thursday, 17 December 1964, Evans hid in the boot of Pat's 'repossessed' car when she drove to George's flat. He jumped out just as she was about to enter the flat and pushed her inside. Slamming shut the door he pulled a knife on her and demanded to know whose flat it was. Pat said it belonged to her girlfriend, but Evans didn't believe her. In a rage, he kidnapped Pat and drove her to the house of David Norman, who was a loyal friend, and asked to borrow a tool. He was given a 4.10 single-barrelled shotgun.

Norman was told to keep Pat away from the telephone and to stop her if she tried leaving the house while Evans drove back to Cable Street to confront George. My George was standing outside the flat talking to several other people, one of whom had called the police after hearing the fracas involving Evans and Pat. By this time, however, the police had gone. But with so many witnesses about, Evans was not prepared to use the gun.

Instead, he returned the firearm to Norman and went off to borrow a 12 bore double-barrelled shotgun. He cut down the barrels with a hacksaw and then drove around to Marks's flat in Stepney. The three of them then went to George's marital home in Lambeth Walk. Norman was the getaway driver while Evans and Marks went to do the business. Evans hid the sawn-off shotgun under his coat. By this time it was dark and he removed the bulb from the landing outside George's front door.

Marks, wearing his usual hat and glasses, knocked at George's door. Fortunately, his wife and kids were not in. George opened the door to him and Marks gave him a moody name, pretending he was looking for someone else. A few minutes later, there was a second knock on the door. George opened it and this time Evans came out of the shadows. 'Hullo, George,' he said, and blasted him with the shotgun at point-blank range. The impact sent George the full length of the hallway.

Fortunately, hearing the shot, a Polish neighbour investigated. Finding George in a pool of blood, he quickly rang for an ambulance. Evans returned to his home and told Pat he'd killed George. She was kept a virtual prisoner for the next 10 months.

Evans and Marks hadn't anticipated the strength of the Foreman brothers, though. After a while, and having made a few enquiries, Evans began to worry about the comeback. Marks, on the other hand, was gung-ho about the affair. He was seen at an East End party, sitting in the middle of a room with a shotgun across his lap saying, 'Send the fucking Foremans across here, I'll deal with them.'

Soon after the shooting, I was tipped off that Evans's firm were going to rob Attenborough's, a jeweller's in Bethnal Green Road, on 2 January 1965. My information was that they were coming five-handed: Evans, Marks, David Norman and two others whom I didn't know. David Norman and the fourth man would break in while the fifth man and Marks would keep watch. Evans would blow the safe. Their point of entry would be through St Matthew's churchyard, which joined the rear of the jewellers' shop.

By now, I knew that Marks lived in Redman's Road, Stepney. I waited for him with Alfie and another man who was a solid chap, and identified each member of Marks's firm. He then left us to our work. Alfie and I followed Marks, first to Attenborough's, then to Norman's flat, where they collected more tools, and finally back to Marks's flat in Stepney. After half an hour or so, Marks and Evans drove to the jeweller's in one car, and Norman and the fourth man followed them in another. The fifth man had been left at the bus stop opposite the shop.

Alfie was at the wheel. He reckoned we were sussed and to avoid further suspicion he turned off just before we got there. We later learned that the men were concerned about our car and had talked about it. Marks said it was a police car. He claimed he knew that because he had the registration number at home. We drove around the block and past the bus stop, where the five of them were talking and then turned into St Matthew's Row and parked in Goldman Close, where we could watch the road. We waited a few moments in the car. Neither Alf nor I spoke. We just watched.

Suddenly, our luck was in. Marks and Evans began walking towards us down St Matthew's Row. Alf's hands gripped the steering wheel. They strolled past us without looking and turned left into Cheshire Street by the Carpenter's Arms public house on the corner. Alf started the motor and slowly drew out. My right hand closed on the .38 revolver and I wound down the passenger window with my left. Alf gently eased the car forward and drew alongside the pair as they walked past a school playground adjoining the pub. I leaned out, my gun at the ready: 'Ginger!' Marks stopped in his tracks. Unsure of who we were, and startled by the recognition, he stepped towards us. I let fly a hail of bullets.

There was no sound from Marks, but Evans reacted instantly. He crouched behind Ginger and gripped his shoulders, using him as a shield. The pair of them danced like puppets on a string, jumping and twisting about in the street trying to avoid the volley of bullets. Ginger took most of the bullets, although one entered Evans's coat, missing him by a hair's breadth. Evans could no longer support his shield. He let go of Marks's shoulders. The man dropped to the pavement as Evans ran away. I dived out of the car and stood over Marks with my gun pointing to his head. He didn't move.

Alf tore after Evans in the car. Panic-stricken, Evans banged on the door of the Carpenter's Arms pub, which still had its lights on. Nobody answered. He ran back up the road and dived under a lorry in Wood Close as Alf chased round again. He pulled himself up off the ground and hugged his body to the underneath of the lorry so he couldn't be seen from the road.

Marks was still lying on the ground. We picked him up, slung him into the back of the car and tore off in the direction of Vallance Road. It was pitch black and without street lighting so we knew we would not be identified. The Carpenter's Arms pub customers had come out when they heard shots but quickly went back inside. This was the East End and people didn't want to see anything that was not their business.

When he thought the coast was clear, Evans came back to look for Marks. All he found on the otherwise empty road was a pair of spectacles and crumpled hat at the spot where Marks had fallen. He collected Ginger's things, ran to the churchyard and told his firm that Ginger had been shot by: 'Someone in a car.' The four of them drove back to Cheshire Street to have a last look. Evans, who was now in a state of frenzy, drove round the corner to Vallance Road and knocked up the Kray Twins to tell them what had happened. Reg and Ronnie told him, 'If you've any trouble with the Foremans, you get on with it yourself, don't come to us for help.' Until then I had no idea he had been friendly with the Twins. But it wouldn't have made any difference. They knew the sort of person I was and no one could have stopped me from making a comeback to avenge my brother.

Evans and his firm then drove to Ginger's wife Annie to break the news. It was now the early hours of Friday. Annie broke down uncontrollably when given the glasses and hat, the last memento of her husband she would ever receive. Pulling herself together, she phoned Ginger's brother Walter (Terry), who immediately came round and together with Evans, went out looking for his brother. Again this proved fruitless. Checking with hospitals in the area they were told nobody had been admitted with gunshot wounds.

They returned to Annie's just before dawn and rang the police to tell them that Annie had received an anonymous phone call informing her that Ginger had been shot in Cheshire Street. When the police came to interview her, Annie gave them Ginger's glasses, but as they were leaving her home, one of them picked up Ginger's hat and put it on his head as if it belonged to him. He was politely told by Ginger's daughter to leave her dad's hat alone.

During the daylight hours, police searched the area around Cheshire Street and found blood spots, spent bullets and a cartridge. A bullet had entered the brick wall bordering the playground next to the pub and from its height, they reckoned Ginger had been shot in the stomach. Detective Chief Superintendent Townsend was put in charge of the case.

Losing Ginger did little to damage Evans's appetite for the bit of work his firm had set out to do. Two nights later, they were back at the same spot trying to break in to the jeweller's again. It wouldn't have needed the brains of Lloyd George to work out that he would now be under round-the-clock surveillance as the star witness in a potential murder inquiry. To expose his firm to the risk of capture by attempting a robbery at the scene of the murder just two days later was sheer madness. No wonder they all got nicked.

In fact, Evans himself was interviewed as a possible suspect in Ginger's disappearance. His home was searched and a shotgun found. When asked to describe the 'murder' car, he replied that it was red with the first three letters of the numberplate reading: 'BLA'. In doing so, he was purposefully misleading police, because those three letters were the same as on Ronnie Everett's red Simca. The car I used was nicked and rung specially for the job; Alf and I destroyed it immediately after.

Police continued their efforts to solve the mystery over Marks's disappearance. More than 40 owners of cars were interviewed and in the absence of a more mundane motive, there was speculation that gang warfare had been behind it all. Police were told by one witness that Ginger had cheated someone out of their share in a cigarette robbery and was expecting trouble from that source. He was also wrongly linked with the Great Train Robbery.

A publican claimed Marks had asked him to look after a gun and on 18 January, Ronnie Everett's car – registration number BLA 876B – was stolen in Romilly Street, Soho. He reported the theft at Tottenham Court Road police station. Although this had no bearing on what happened, it was to figure prominently in the future, when Evans tried to implicate members of my firm who were innocent of involvement.

All the Firm and my personal friends and known acquaintances were questioned by police during their routine enquiries. But unknown to us at the time, Evans had already put several of us in the frame: me, Alfi, Jerry Callaghan and Ronnie. A south London informer who had served in borstal with Evans had given him a list of names of my close friends and associates in case of reprisals and it was in Evans's interests to convict as many of us as possible.

Evans seemed to live a charmed life. He and two of his accomplices were charged with breaking and entering Attenborough's the jeweller's. His accomplices were each jailed for six months at the Old Bailey, while strangely the case against Evans only got as far as the magistrates' court, upon which he was acquitted. I wonder why?

In February 1965, Evans was charged with shooting my George, who still refused to identify him. It was only his own mouth that got him nicked. He was bragging to people about what he'd done and word got back to the police. While on remand in Brixton, he told an old friend of mine from the East End and a good pal of the Twins, Colin 'The Duke' Osbourne, that George Cornell – who'd been rowing with Ginger shortly before his disappearance – had killed Marks. Cornell was shot dead in the Blind Beggar pub in Stepney a year later.

Evans was again acquitted on 9 April 1965 – both of shooting George and of possessing a shotgun that was found in his home. He claimed he was continually being hassled by police for not cooperating over Marks's disappearance (which was hard to believe). In the meantime, police enquiries about Ginger widened. French police were asked to interview two drug smugglers who were convinced that Marks grassed them on a drugs deal in return for police favours and assistance to get a US visa. In an exclusive *News of the World* article on 11 April that year, Evans claimed he had not shot George and that Marks's disappearance had no connection with the shooting. The newspaper offered a £5,000 reward for anyone who could provide them with Marks's whereabouts.

There was also continued speculation, which has lasted to this day, over what happened to Marks's body. It has been suggested he was disposed of by a bent undertaker, buried in a motorway, or set in concrete and dumped in the Thames. All wrong…

I owned the Prince of Wales pub at the time and police were slipping in and out keeping watch on me. Their operation was dual: undercover and open. One PC and WPC pretended to be a courting couple and began using my pub every day. You could spot them a mile off. They watched me round the clock and waited for me to make a move. Cossers would come in to the pub and say, 'Aren't you worried, Fred, with your back to the door?' When I said there was no reason for me to worry, they intimated that there was going to be a gang war.

After Evans was acquitted, and as time went by, I used to go over and plot up on him. I wanted to do him badly. At the same time, I didn't think it was worth going to jail for a mongrel dog like him. But I kept watch nevertheless. He had about nine lives and I kept thinking he was going to run out of luck. I once missed him coming out of a club belonging to Joe Wilkins at the back of the Strand. I got a phone call tipping me off that he was there with Joe, and I drove over from south London as fast as I could, with a tool. I hoped I'd catch him outside the club, but missed him by seconds. The street was dark and I had parked well away, in Villier Street. I was walking very fast, on a mission, only focused on getting to the nightclub before he left. My informant was standing outside the club and informed me that Evans had left moments earlier. 'Fuck it!' I said, and then I remembered a strange guy giving me a funny look as he got into his car on the opposite side of the road. I'd just missed him!

I then tracked him to a block of flats in Hackney and sat there night after night, waiting for him to come home. He never stuck to a routine, arriving instead from different directions, even climbing over walls. Above the entrance to his block was a flat roof with a railing. A perfect spot to conceal yourself. I slipped on an old boiler suit over my clothes, a balaclava to hide my face, and got up there and waited with a rifle and silencer. Early one morning, as dawn broke and people began moving about, I packed up, took my gun to pieces and got into my car. As I drove towards Bethnal Green Road, a car came up in front of me. It was him. And he got me in an instant. His eyes were everywhere. He was like a hunted animal. He knew he had escaped death by inches and it was only a matter of time before his luck ran out.

A while later, I was arrested together with the Krays as an accessory to the murder of Jack 'The Hat' McVitie and sent for trial at the Old Bailey on 28 February 1969. I was sentenced to 10 years, during which I faced a second murder rap, for Frank 'The Mad Axeman' Mitchell.

All the time I was serving my sentence over McVitie, I had no idea police were still investigating me over Ginger Marks's disappearance. The crucial turning point came in 1972, when Evans was charged with the murder of a young Scottish carpenter. Apparently, on 28 July 1972 he killed an innocent young man who was larking about with a group of friends. They had surrounded Anick Webb's car (Evans's French common-law wife) after she stalled at the exit of a car park. Evans, who was driving his own car in front, jumped out and chased after two of the men, stabbing William Fernie, a 21-year-old Scottish carpenter, who died instantly, cradled in his girlfriend Pamela Lawrence's arms. Evans was charged with murder and Anick Webb was arrested the following day in Plymouth but released without charge. Evans was acquitted of murder but found guilty of manslaughter at the Old Bailey in February 1973, and jailed for seven years. While he was on remand awaiting trial, he was again seen by several officers of the law and asked to help in the Marks affair. This, in my view, was the time when a deal was struck with between Evans and the police. They must have promised him he would only serve three years if he gave evidence – and in the end, that's what happened.

Other problems were also getting on top of him now. Anick Webb wrote to say she was fed up with him being in prison – he had been on remand for six months – and that she wanted to end their relationship. Evans wrote back to her and said he had sold his soul to these people to be with her, and that he would soon be out.

After he was sentenced to seven years for the stabbing, he discovered he was to be sent to Albany Prison on the Isle of Wight and immediately protested, demanding another prison. Why? Because Alfie Gerrard was serving four-and-a-half years there and Evans said he knew he was a friend of mine. The request was refused. At Albany, Evans got a friend to point out what Alfie looked like and then confronted him. Suspecting Evans might be bugged, or looking for witnesses to make up false verbal statements, Alf walked away, saying he didn't know him. I knew what was going on in Albany Prison at the time because no one can have police visits without the rest of the prison population finding out. I had many other good friends doing time there during the same period, among them Mick Regan and Roy Hilder.

From my Category A cell at Wormwood Scrubs, I organised someone to screw Anick Webb's flat and find those letters in which Evans said he had sold his soul to the devil. I got the originals and made a number of copies.

In 1974, Evans finally cracked and told police he wanted to see them. Evans named four of our firm as being involved in Ginger Marks's murder: me, Alf Gerrard, Jerry Callaghan and Ronnie Everett. He'd already talked to the prison deputy governor and chief officer to ask how he could help police enquiries. His statement now was vastly different to what he had told them 10 years earlier. In the fresh statement, he confessed to shooting my George and said that David Norman was with him at the time. Marks, he claimed, was shot for boasting that he had supplied the gun and driven him over there.

It seemed that despite all the intervening years, Evans was still miraculously able to recall, and recognise, four people from that dark night in January 1965. He said Jerry was driving and Ronnie had stepped out of the car to stretch himself at one point before the shooting, and that he saw Alfie filling up at a petrol station at 2.30 in the morning after the killing. This proved to be untrue. Checks were later made and it was found that the garage in question always closed at 11pm or earlier. Soon after this false statement was made, Evans got his transfer to Pentonville Prison. Marks's brother Terry was interviewed, but he refused to cooperate. He was old school and good stuff.

In November 1974, another prisoner, called Baker, with a string of burglary convictions, who had absconded while on home leave, made a statement to the effect that Alfie had said to him, 'I will make you a lump of bacon, like I did that cunt Marks.'

David Norman was arrested on 3 January 1975 over an offence on which he had jumped bail four years earlier. He was charged with armed robbery and possession of weapons. Now questioned by the police about Marks for the third time over 10 years, he suddenly remembered that a red car – an 1100 type – had followed them from Redman's Road, Stepney, to Bethnal Green Road. He also admitted accompanying Evans to my George's when he was shot, and to breaking into the jewellery shop in Bethnal Green Road. He said he had heard a shot and that Evans told him they had got Marks.

Ronnie Everett was arrested on 6 January 1975 in connection with the murder of Thomas 'Ginger' Marks. Jerry Callaghan and Alfie Gerrard were arrested the following day and taken to Leman Street and Arbour Square police stations. All three were interviewed on 8 January in a question-answer session.

I'd nearly served my time for McVitie when they finally came for me. I had nine months left to serve out of my 10 years, only to face another murder charge that could have put me away for life! Superintendent Chalk and Detective Sergeant Troon visited me in Wormwood Scrubs after the others were arrested. I was taken from the laundry block to the admin block and ushered into an empty room; the door closed behind me. Chalk and Troon suddenly entered from a side door. The moment I realised it was those two, I headed for the door, banging on it with my fists and demanding to be taken out of there. I yelled, 'Open this fucking door, you've set me up!'

Ignoring my protest, Troon and Chalk, announced, 'We want to ask you questions about the disappearance of Thomas Marks.'

My response was as before: 'I've got nothing to say to you. Open this fucking door or I'll smash it down.' The screws finally got the message. The door opened.

'What's up, Fred?' the screw asked.

'Take me back to the laundry, you bastards. You set me up!'

I was taken from the Scrubs to Arbour Square police station, where a questionnaire was given to me. I answered 'no comment' all the way through and signed every answer, initialled every page.

Next, I was formally charged with murder, taken back to the Scrubs and put in the hospital observation wing (the rule is 28 days in the hospital wing for all prisoners charged with murder). One day, to my amusement, my door was opened for breakfast and I saw a screw standing there in his white overalls with a food trolley. Next to him was a con with hair slicked back and a little Hitler moustache. He wearing a prison shirt and tie, looking very dapper. I pointed my finger at him and said, 'I know you,' to which the little guy nodded his head like a toy dog. 'You're Graham, Graham Young,' and he carried on nodding his head vigorously and shaking with glee. Young, had poisoned his own mother when he was 11 years of age and then poisoned his work colleagues when he was released, 10 years later. 'Don't you get up to any of your tricks with my breakfast, Graham!' I warned him.

'No, not you Fred,' he replied. I didn't know whether to keep him as a friend or enemy and tell him to fuck off because all the people he befriended were now poisoned. He would have made a brilliant chemist if he hadn't been such a nut. In fact, eventually the Home Office began to consult him about poisons because he had become such an authority in that field.

After surviving Graham Young's cooking, and 28 days' round-the-clock observation, I was sent to Wandsworth as a Category A prisoner again. Maureen visited me and two screws sat beside us, writing down everything we spoke about. I told her, 'Say no more, love. Just wait eight months until I finish my sentence and go to Brixton [on remand]. At least there we will have decent visits.'

When I arrived at Brixton, Ron, Alf and Jerry were all there to greet me. I hadn't seen them since they'd left for Australia around 1967, so it was quite a reunion. Also in the Cat A wing were all the men arrested for the £8 million Bank of America robbery in Mayfair, one of the biggest at the time. Among them was Johnny 'the Bosch' – the best key-fitter in the business, whose real name was Leonard Wilde – Peter Colson, John Mason (who was cleared of the robbery), Henry Jeffery, Micky Gervaise (who later became a grass), Jimmy O'Loughlin, Billy Gear and Stuart Buckley (who was the insider). Philip Trusty, who shot a constable at the wheel of his car during a raid, was also there and later got a 20.

I appeared at Old Street Magistrate's Court handcuffed to two screws. My three associates stood behind me in the dock and, to my left in the public gallery, were my brother Wally as well as Harry Smith. Harry was a good, solid man, one of the chaps, for whom I had done a big favour some years before. He caught my eye as he was as white as a sheet and he seemed to be winking at me. Harry's brother, Patsy, was downstairs in the Old Street cells, waiting to give evidence against the four of us. Harry had asked if he could visit his brother in his cell. The police, thinking they were simply doing Patsy a favour, allowed Harry in to speak to him. The so-called favour may have backfired. Harry told me that he told his brother that if he did get in the witness box, he would personally drag him out of there and jump all over him. The prosecution called their witness but he refused to come out of his cell. Who's to know whether it was Harry's visit that influenced Patsy or whether he just didn't want to give evidence anyway?

At the hearing, our defence lawyers were Louis Hawser for Jerry Callaghan, Hutchinson for Big Ronnie, Barry Hudson for Alf and William Denny for me. Chalk and Troon were questioned about the visit they paid me when I was in Wormwood Scrubs. They claimed that when I'd been interviewed about the disappearance of Tommy Marks I'd said, 'That Evans has grassed me up. One of these days I'm gonna shut him up for good.' Their evidence was the same and was struck out by the magistrates.

Now, the interviews are recorded and more than one police officer is always present. Our case must have stood out because it had generated so much publicity; on top of that, it showed that something had to be done to ensure that police interviews were conducted in a more open manner.

In the end, all applications for bail were refused and we were committed for a trial at the Old Bailey.

We were in Court Number Two in front of Judge Wein. The prosecution went through the whole case, but a technicality arose when one of the jury stood up and said he couldn't continue because he had knowledge of the case and the people charged with the offence. That made the whole affair a nice little rehearsal to tighten up and polish the prosecution's evidence for a second trial.

You see, the Guildford Four who were on trial at the time, were in Court Number One. They came up before Judge Donaldson, who weighed them off for 30 years apiece. Of course, with this case now over, Court Number One was now available, so we were swiftly transferred there to stand before Judge Donaldson. Brilliant.

We came before Judge Donaldson at the Old Bailey in November 1975. Evans, the first prosecution witness, admitted he had lied under oath at his own trial, and at a divorce court hearing. He also admitted that he had lied for money when he wrote his story in the *News of the World*.

When shown the original letter he had written to Anick Webb, which stated, 'I have sold my soul to these people to be with you,' he became extremely angry and refused to answer counsel's question.

Louis Hawser, QC for the defence: 'Did you write that?'

Evans: 'I don't know where you got this, it is personal and nothing to do with you.' Unable to control his rage, Evans then tore up the letter in a frenzy.

Mr Hawser watched on with amusement. 'Tear them up all you want,' he said, 'I have the originals here.'

David Norman's evidence did us no harm. He also denied hearing any comments made by Marks or Evans that night about the description of the car or the people in it – in other words, 'That's a police car, I have its number written down at home.'

Above left: Me aged two.

Above right: My father, Albert.

Below: Family group – my parents visit Brighton, to where we were evacuated. (*Left to right*) My father, me, my mother Louise, and my brother Bert.

Above left: The five brothers – Wally (*top left*), Herbie (*top second right*), George (*middle right*), Bert (*below left*) and me (*below right*).

Above right: Me boxing at Jack Solomon's gym.

Below: The family outside Croxeth House during the war: (*left to right*) Herbie, Wally, George, Father and Bert.

Top: *(left to right)* – Charlie Kray, Reggie Kray, Terry Allen, Ronnie Kray, Barnie Beal, me, Johnny Fitzgerald and Buster Edwards, 1962.

Middle: Me and Maureen's wedding – *(left to right)* Nelly Puttman, Maureen, me George, mother and father.

Below: *(Left to right)* My sons Gregory (top and Jamie, my daughte Danielle, Maureen anc me.

How the Curtain Road crooks pulled off the most sensational banknote robbery of all time

THE £7M CUPPA!

Tea-up guard gave gang their big break

THE GREAT BANKNOTE ROBBERY

Blaze torture

IT'S PURE MAGIC, SAYS BUSTER

TREASURE IN CHESTLOADS

Evening Standard

Crash-helmeted, gas-masked thieves with pepper spray-gun ambush wages van

BANK GUARD SHOOTS £100,000 BANDITS

Five bullets then the gang cry 'Beat it!'

AND HIS DOG COSHED IN BATTLE IN A BOW ROAD

THIS WAS THE PLAN

LORRY USED TO BLOCK ROAD

THE Sun

Britain bags Foreman

Nat West allowed innocent Eileen to face a theft charge

COSTA CROOK SLUNG OUT SNARLING

£70,000 LOTTO £31,000 BINGO

Above and below left: Making headlines.

Below right: The Sun reporting my deportation from Spain.

Above: This picture was taken four days before Charlie Kray died. (*Left to right*) Wilf Pine, Diane Buffini, Charlie Kray and me.

Left: Newspaper clipping reporting the opening of the Borough Boxing Club gymnasium at the Marshalsea. I am in the middle.

London's latest gymnasium is opened and it's congratulations for the proprietor. Left to right, Terry Spinks, Teddy Waltham, Tim Riley, Fred Foreman, Reg Gutteridge, Dave Charnley, Mark Rowe.

Left: Helping Ronnie Biggs over the wall in Rio!

Right: Me with my brother George, Terry Murphy and Jamie. Terry is the only boxer in history to have knocked out the referee during a match.

Below and inset: Enjoying Ronnie Biggs's famous 'Post Office Port'.

Left: Me, Telboy and world lightweight champion, Roberto Duran.

Right: Me and my son Gregory.

Below: With film director Roman Polanski. We met when Jamie played Bill Sykes in the 2005 film *Oliver Twist*.

Top left: Me in Full Sutton Prison, AA category prisoner.

Top right: Me in Maidstone Prison with a few of the chaps.

Centre right: My security prison book, from HMP Maidstone.

Below: With the chaps. (*Left to right*) Roy Shaw, Joey Pyle, Tony Lambrianou, tilks, Charlie Richardson and me.

Evans had said in his evidence that his response to that had been: 'Don't be silly. I've just seen Callaghan driving it and Ronnie Everett in it.' Neither of the two other burglars who had been convicted of breaking into the jeweller's were called to give evidence about the mystery red car.

Louis Hawser then asked Evans about guns. Evans became so engrossed in talking about his pet obsession that he went on and on, detailing all the different kinds of shooters without realising the effect this was having on the jury.

On the second day of the trial, Mr Justice Donaldson told the jury to discharge Ronald Everett, on the flimsy evidence relating to his car.

After hearing evidence from other witnesses, the prosecution then called the two police officers Chalk and Troon to the box one at a time, to give their evidence. First up was Chalk. He was cross-examined by Lewis Hawser, who dropped something of a bombshell during Chalk's time on the stand. To allow you to experience the full effect of the drama, I present the following excerpt, which details the moment at which the case started to unravel:

This is the outline of one man's story of the events that led to four men being charged with the murder of one Thomas 'Ginger' Marks.
    DCS Chalk gave evidence of arrest and the taking of questionnaires producing the originals as exhibits.
He was followed by Sgt Troon, the officer who had been actually writing the questionnaires.

Mr Lewis Hawser for Callaghan:
Q. Did you write these questionnaires?
Sgt Troon: Yes Sir.
Q. Let's go through from the beginning. You and Chalk take Callaghan to an interview room. You have a blank sheet of paper, you write on there Callaghan's name, the date, the time, 10am. Then as DCS Chalk asks the questions you write that down, and against the question you write the answer Callaghan gives. Is that correct?
Sgt Troon: Yes Sir.
Q. Then some four hours later at another police station, Arbour Square, you interview Gerrard. Same procedure, fresh paper, Gerrard's name, date and time. Questions and answers?

Sgt Troon: Yes Sir.

Q. All these interviews took place on the same day, the 8th January 1975?

Sgt Troon: Yes Sir.

Q. Have you your police diary with you?

Sgt Troon: Yes Sir.

Q. May I see it please?

Sgt Troon: Yes Sir. [Hands over diary]

Q. How long after each interview for the questionnaires did you make a note of it in your diary?

Sgt Troon: About half an hour after each interview.

Q. So three times you wrote down the date on these questionnaires then some half an hour later after each one, three times you wrote the date and time in your diary. Is that correct?

Sgt Troon: Yes Sir.

Q. Can you tell me how on three separate times you wrote the date on the questionnaires the 6th January 1975, when in fact the date of the interview was the 8th January 1975?

Sgt Troon: [No Answer] [Long Silence]

Q. Then again, can you tell me on how three separate times, half an hour after each interview, you made a note of it in your diary and wrote the date the 8th January. Which was the correct date?

Sgt Troon: [No Answer]

The silly fools not only made up the entire questionnaire, they did it two days before they'd even interviewed any of the suspects! After the cross-examination of Chalk and Troon, the judge and jury said that they had heard enough and did not want to continue. The foreman told the judge they'd heard enough too, and the trial was stopped. We were all discharged and no defence witnesses needed to be called. The remaining three of us walked free, much to our relief.

That afternoon, we celebrated our freedom at the A and R Club in Charing Cross Road, which was owned by Micky Regan and Ronnie Knight. The place was packed out with friends and relatives. Mick Regan has shown himself to be a true and loyal friend for over 30 years now. He is a man who commands immense respect. Mick and I shared many great times and many anxious moments when things looked bad. This is the true sign of friendship, something no amount of money can buy. I would have done anything for Mick and still would, make no mistake about that. God bless you and yours, mate.

Chief Inspector Chalk retired a year after the trial and Troon was later promoted to the rank of Detective Inspector. I heard of Troon many years later, when he was called on to investigate some political deaths in Nigeria. Apparently, there was a power struggle between two political parties who were killing each other off. While he was out there somebody tried to poison him, but failed, and I thought at the time that the Devil looks after his own.

I make no apologies for my own role in this affair. Alfie and I were not innocent. We followed an underworld code, which in its own way is as strict – if not stricter – than the statutory laws governing the general public.

This episode, more than most others, showed who the true chaps were. My George might have died from Evans's attack, but even in the face of death he honourably stuck to our code of not grassing who shot him. As a result, Evans was acquitted. But what about Evans? He broke every code in the criminal world we lived in. He gave statements and evidence when he wasn't man enough to do his bird.

This is a person who wants and asks for respect with his own kind? No way. He will have to live with what he has done for the rest of his life. He's even going to try to grass me from the grave. He has left statements with his solicitor, Fellowes, in the event of his death, stating that I would be responsible for it. He didn't mind going around shooting people, but when things got a bit rough, he just couldn't be a man and face the consequences – or stand and take the comeback. He did everything he possibly could to get rid of his enemies by sweet-grassing to start with and then, after his arrest for the killing of that Scottish carpenter, went all the way and committed the *ultimate sin*: he became a police prosecution witness. The police were true to their word. Evans was arrested in July 1972 for murder and released in 1975 right after he gave evidence. He served just three years in total for taking that young, innocent civilian's life. As that court document noted elsewhere, 'So much for doing deals with the police.'

The question has been asked: do I have any regrets about Ginger Marks and Evans? The answer is: yes. I regret that I did not shoot the two of them that night.

CHAPTER 12
BUILDING THE EMPIRE

Harold Macmillan, Britain's then Prime Minister, was right when he told the nation in the early 1960s: 'You've never had it so good.' Those years were some of the most lucrative in our career. Continuing success from pavement work and robbing banks and post offices meant I could now begin to invest money into straight businesses like the betting shops, and clubs and pubs. Ironically though, Scotland Yard kept putting obstacles in the way of me 'going straight'.

When my brother-in-law Johnny Fitz (Fitzgerald) applied for our first betting shop licence in Lower Road, Bermondsey, we were heavily opposed. At the hearing in Walworth Road Town Hall, half a dozen coppers crashed in like storm troopers and accused Johnny of being 'a front man for Frederick Foreman, a known criminal'. Well, as it happened, I knew the mayor, Bill Gates, who was chairman of the Licensing Board. I had raised money for his favourite charities and Bill, wearing his mayoral chain, was photographed in the local newspaper arriving at my pub, the Prince of Wales, in his Rolls-Royce. In response to objections from the police, he pointed out, quite rightly, 'It is Mr Fitzgerald who is applying for the licence, not Mr Foreman,' and he granted the application.

My mini empire was expanding rapidly. My pub, the Prince of Wales in Lant Street, Borough, was proving very popular; Maureen and I lived there in an upstairs flat. The area was famous. One of Lant Street's noted previous residents was Charles Dickens, who had lodged there when his father was in Marshalsea Debtors' Prison, which used to be around the corner. The house Dickens stayed in had been demolished, but one of my locals, Terry Fermature, brought me Dickens's old lock and key, which I proudly displayed in a glass case in the Prince of Wales.

I had another flat on the 14th floor of the Brandon Estate, which was a prestige block when built and included members of parliament among its tenants. We used it as a quiet little bolt hole that only close friends knew about. I had also invested in a house converted into five flats facing Clapham Common, and we still had the house in Milton Road where Ronnie King lived.

Over a short period of time, we built up a chain of betting shops. In addition to Bermondsey, I owned another with Tommy Wisbey and Billy Gorbell in Borough Market, one in Brixton run by Reggie Isaacs, another in Rotherhithe New Road, and two in Croydon. The most successful was the shop at Nunhead Lane, Peckham, where one of our punters was Ronnie Corbett, the TV comedian, who lived around the corner. It was managed by Ding Dong with my George and a young chap Kenny behind the counter. I would occasionally chalk runners up on the board and pay out the winnings on days when it suited me. It was a very good front after I'd done a bit of pavement work, as it provided me with the perfect alibi. I'd get back there as fast as possible and be chalking up more winners for everyone to see. They'd be so absorbed with betting they never missed me while I was out and would later swear blind that I had been there all the time.

Whenever there was a big robbery, police would telephone around and ask to speak to whoever appeared on their list of suspects. If I wasn't there, Maureen or one of my staff would tell them I was 'just around the corner buying a newspaper' or 'busy chalking up winners'. I also bought a 20-year lease on a large building around the corner from my pub in Marshalsea. I turned one floor into a gym with a boxing ring, punch bags and the usual boxing apparatus; it was christened 'The Chaps' Gym' by boxing commentator Reg Gutteridge. There was a disco in the basement, a photo agency at the top and an SP office on the other floor. At the beginning, it was a rehearsal studio for rock bands, including The Small Faces, Cat Stephens, Spencer Davis and a whole host of others. Mick and Big George had also gone into the betting-shop business with large premises in Poland Street (which they eventually sold to Ladbroke's for a small fortune), so they were semi-retired and with Alf doing nine months and Ron away for three years in prison, it left just Patsy and myself to make up a firm. We pulled in another two men who were good workers and had been with us on several big jobs whenever we needed extra help. Big Tommy Sullivan was one of them – he was another big lump who was capable of any work that had to be done.

One little job that came up at the time involved a guy called Charlie, who put up the work and insisted on making one with us 'just for the crack'. The money came down Silvertown Way in a taxi and we waited on the corner. Our smash-car overtook the cab and forced it into our street, where we were waiting on the pavement. We smashed the cab windows to cause confusion and ripped open the doors for Patsy to grab the money bags with no trouble. It was done right outside an electrical firm. Our escape van was in place and we dived headfirst into it, lying flat while the wheel man put his foot down and tore off at high speed. But Charlie came unstuck. Unused to this kind of adrenaline-pumping exercise, he became very excited as we took the cash bags and the silly bastard stood upright in the back of the getaway van, shaking his fist and laughing at the workers who, hearing the commotion and all the shouting and windows smashing, had come out of the electrical firm to see what was happening. Within seconds, the street had come alive with people.

As we'd clambered on board, the wheel man was urged, 'Go, go, go!' But Charlie, in his excitement, failed to hold on as the van took off and went flying through the back doors, falling flat on his face in the middle of the road. Our driver was already in second gear when we shouted for him to stop. 'Hold on! Hold on for Charlie!' as the van roared on down the road. Now that we'd gone, all the bank clerks, security men, the taxi driver had got brave and ran towards Charlie. We screeched to a stop. Charlie was a long way back down the road and limping badly as the mob got closer and closer. Our driver reversed backwards at speed and just managed to get back there before the mob grabbed him. We dragged Charlie into the back of the van and told the silly bastard to lie down as we sped off once again. After that he became known as 'Hold On Charlie', and over time the nickname was abbreviated further. So if anyone asked after Charlie in the future, they'd just say, 'Have you seen Hold On?'

It was a nice payday. We also cut in two of our other men, who were otherwise indisposed at the time.

Another venture we considered getting into around this time was the bookshops in Soho. People like Jimmy Humphries, Bernie Silver and the Greeks and Turks were making a fortune from them. But you had to clear this sort of enterprise with the Old Bill so they wouldn't come and nick you all the time. Our introduction here was through Mick. Regan had saved a couple of coppers by getting them out of trouble after they were nicked for something and now they owed him a favour. We were told to see one particular cosser and we met up with him at a Soho pub. This man was puffing away at his pipe saying, 'Yes, we might be able to work this out. All I need is a body now and again. You scratch my back and I'll scratch yours.' This was silly talk to someone like ourselves.

It was Patsy who said to him, 'How would you like that pipe stuck right up your fucking arse?' Needless to say, that was the end of our little venture into the West End. It just shows you: nobody could work in that business without giving up bodies. It makes you wonder about people who have businesses there and are allowed to reign.

In my next attempt at building up a 'legal empire', we got together and formed the Bookmakers' Guardian Association, an insurance company catering to the interests of betting-shop owners. I rented a lovely suite of offices in Regent Street, close to Piccadilly and the Stork Club, and had them professionally furnished and decorated. Ding Dong fronted the organisation and Major Collins, a very well-known bookmaker, Jimmy Lane and Johnny Parry were made directors, as was my brother-in-law Jimmy Puttnam, who bet under the name of Jack Ray. Jimmy was credited with being the first bookmaker to take bets on away meetings. He had a moody phone on his pitch in Tattersall's and he rigged up a bell that he could press with his foot and then answer, pretending to get the odds from the other race courses. Punters would then place bets with him, accepting his moody odds.

So, our proposed insurance company would take care of bookmakers in court, lend them money for new premises and insure their businesses. They would be represented by our retainer, the (one-armed) barrister

William Rees-Davies QC and MP, who was known as Dracula in the House of Commons for his habit of sweeping through the House wearing a black cloak. Rees-Davies, who at the time represented Thanet in Kent, was instrumental in drawing up the gaming law for street bookmaking. His father, Sir William Rees-Davies, was formerly Chief Justice of Hong Kong. Dennis Wheater and Brian Field, well-known criminal lawyers, were our solicitors and also board directors. Both were later arrested in connection with the Great Train Robbery.

We paid for a full-page advertisement in the *Sporting Life* to publicise the company and sought £5 insurance for the first shop and a lesser figure for every subsequent one. To give the enterprise a kick-start, we had to create a little tension and of course, the only thing to do was to go around and set light to a few of those bookmakers who tried to win unfair advantage over little shops by paying out on the fourth horse. By doing that, they used to crucify the other smaller businesses, so we considered them fair game, though we always made sure the shops were empty and there were no livers above before giving them the old fireworks.

About six bookmakers went up in this way. I remember one shop where we poured a mixture of fuel through the letterbox. Our lookout warned us that a cosser was coming down the street, so we went away for a little while. We had been experimenting with a mixture of petrol and oil to give us enough time to get away before the fire took hold. On this occasion, the mixture had been too rich and by the time we returned, all the fumes had built up, so when we threw in a lighted rag, the whole shop blew up and windows shattered. Fortunately, we were behind a solid old door, otherwise we would have been blown across the street. One of our target shops was let off the hook because when we checked it out in the dead of night, we found the manager having a right old rump across the office desk with a female member of staff.

The response to our advertisement was unbelievable. Bags of letters flowed in with requests to join the association. Word had spread almost as quickly as the fires. Although I had not been linked to the arson attacks, rumours had started about my involvement by the fact that Ding Dong was managing the organisation. Major Collins then pulled out and the lawyers were having trouble getting a board of directors together because after a couple of fires, their bottle went and their arseholes fell out. They didn't want to be associated with it. They should have stood their ground and said those fires were nothing to do with us. Instead, they lost their nerve: Gus Dalrymple from the *Sporting Life* then started making himself busy writing articles about the Bookmakers' Guardian Association and his reports were taken up by national newspapers who wanted to know who was behind this venture.

I don't know why they were so worried. The original BPA (Bookmakers' Protection Association), which we were effectively copying, had been started by three local businessmen, a butcher, publican and builder – so why not have one like ours? Police also began taking an interest when mailbags full of cash from prospective customers began arriving at my Regent Street offices. Our new company would have been a goldmine. After the initial villainy it would have been a straight business, but it was not to be.

The loss of that enterprise was disappointing, but the shops and pubs were doing really well. Considering that I had only paid £5,000 for it, the Prince of Wales was probably the best investment I ever made. The whole place was buzzing and jam-packed with people. I would buy the latest hit singles of the day from the A1 store in Walworth Road – songs like '(Sittin' on) the Dock of the Bay', Chris Montez's 'The More I See You' and 'River Deep – Mountain High'. As the top singles came out, I was the first to play them. At times, I had to bolt doors to stop people coming in. There were many marriages made from that pub because so many young people found a kindred spirit there. Many of those relationships grew and have survived to this day.

The cellars would be stacked full to the brim with booze, and crates would spill over into the yard. I earned more money out of that little pub than any other straight business I had ever invested in. As my reputation grew, so the business got better. Everyone loves a face.

The Peckham betting shop became the head office and from there we interacted with all the other shops. George also opened up a minicab office in Peckham, a small café next door, and a 'Shush' club – a speakeasy, or drinking club – down the street. Our customers would gamble their money in our shops, use George's minicab firm, eat at his café and then go to his Shush club. It acquired its name from people asking George for its address – he'd put his finger to his lips and say, 'Shush'. Those little clubs were unbelievable. You could drink around the clock and people said they had the best time of their lives in them.

We had a piano and dancing and we could move the club within a day if it was discovered by the licensing authorities. George was in his element in the Shush clubs. Always the party man, he loved entertaining people and enjoying himself, whereas – although I liked socialising – I probably appeared more sullen and menacing to those who didn't know me. People warmed a lot more easily to George, while I kept a distance. I was always in the background, a bit heavy, but people knew they couldn't fuck with George because I was there. I'd find people who misbehaved and bar them. Bertie Summers, a long-time friend, and Ronnie King were on the door. Johnny Borsch was another one who minded for us.

I was also very friendly with Ronnie Oliffe, from Bermondsey. His family were dockers, a good little family. There were five or six brothers, and they were a force to be reckoned with. Ronnie was good at running spiels and we had several in partnership in the Marshalsea building and the Old Kent Road.

Bernie Colman, who owned a chain of south London pubs left to him by his father, asked me to be his partner in the 211 Club in Balham. Bernie was involved with the MCC and went all over the world with the England cricket team. Now he needed someone strong behind him. A good friend of mine, a district surveyor called Ronnie Stafford, introduced us. Local villains, including someone involved with the Nash brothers, were trying to muscle in on Bertie, but once he told them I was his partner, they left him alone. We agreed that I would run the casino upstairs and he would run the bar and restaurant on the ground floor. The 211 Club in Balham High Road was a lovely property. Known as Hamilton House, it had at one time belonged to Lady Hamilton, Lord Nelson's fancy bit, and was later turned into an embassy. Inside was a magnificent ballroom and gardens. The venue attracted people from all over London.

We laid out a small fortune doing the place up. We had French roulette tables, a crap table, three blackjack tables, a *chemin de fer* table and the décor – arranged by Maureen, who was good at interior design – was Regency style. Fred and Joe Scala, two friends who started their career in this country making ice cream in Fulham, took care of the casino.

The 211 was a posh place. Staff were dressed in dinner suits and we had glamorous croupier girls who wore low-cut dresses. Clubs were the rage at the time, and I was involved in several clubs with the Kray Twins, including a share in the Starlight Club off Oxford Street. The Krays, the Nashes and I each carved a share from the Colony Club in Berkeley Square, Mayfair, too. It was run by George Raft, the American actor who starred in early gangster movies and who was swooned over by most women who met him. The Colony's patrons included Frank Sinatra and Robert Ryan. Dino and Eddy Celini ran the casino and the real owner was the MD of American crime, Meyer Lansky. The Colony went on for a couple of years and was a good earner. George Raft, who had Mafia connections, wanted us to keep a low profile, though. He didn't want faces to frighten away guests. In those areas it was not the done thing.

I asked George Raft to officially open the 211 Club, and he first came to my pub in a chauffeur-driven Rolls in the company of Ronnie Kray. While we were drinking at the bar, I asked George who, in his opinion, was the main man in the prohibition era and he replied without hesitation that – oddly enough – the main man was an Englishman by the name of Owney Madden from Leeds, who was raised in Wigan and became known as the Duke of the West Side. He owned the Cotton Club and was well involved with bootlegging. George Raft rode shotgun on his expeditions.

Anyway, back to the story. We were then chauffeured in a convoy of stretch limousines to the 211 Club, where we were joined by actors, bookmakers and fighting personalities. George Raft was very impressed with the layout and did his celebrity bit in style while photographers snapped pictures of him playing dice and meeting local celebrities such as Barbara Windsor and the Carry On team, whom I had invited for the opening. Mick Regan, Ronnie Knight, Ronnie Oliffe and the rest of the chaps who were on hand every weekend to help sort out any aggravation were also invited.

While I owned a number of gambling premises, I was never a gambler myself and discouraged my friends from this habit, knowing it was always the house that would win.

When punters left the 211, they'd inevitably move on to my George's late-night drinking club in Clapham South called the Red Sail. Coppers caused panic once by coming around after hours one Sunday afternoon. George quickly ushered everyone out the back and then let the coppers in by the front door. As it turned out, all they wanted was to give him his late-night licence for a hospital charity do. The police were not aware that the 50 drunken revellers standing at the bus stop had just emerged from George's back door.

George's lease for the Red Sail was in the names of Mr Green and Mr Brown. Our Polish landlord, who had been a secret agent during the war and was always worried about us, had a heart attack while on a holiday beach. His dying words to his wife were: 'Don't forget Mr Green and Mr Brown, they're behind with their rent!'

'Saturday Night Cowboys' were our biggest problem at the 211. They were workers who were in straight jobs during the week and who let loose on Friday and Saturday nights when they came in mob-handed and thought they could get away with doing as they pleased. They had to be taught a lesson to stop them picking fights, smashing glasses and upsetting other customers. My own team included Johnny Cook, Lenny White, Ding Dong, Ronnie King, Ronnie Oliffe and his brothers Joey and Danny, and quiet Jimmy Turner, which was enough to keep most people in line. But all the same, we had to teach these mugs a lesson.

One of the people who gave us problems was a fellow called Johnny Hanlon, from west London. On one occasion, he and a few of his mates – who were publicans – and their wives and girlfriends – who should have known better – were making a nuisance of themselves. So I took his drink out of his hand and told him to leave. As I put it down he made a move on me, but didn't take into account Ronnie Oliffe who was leaning against the wall, minding me. Ronnie poleaxed him with a right to the jaw and he was out before he hit the ground. I grabbed a shillelagh hanging behind an office door and put it about a bit lively. Billy and Mary Gorbell were also there and had some German *swaschenbachers*. These consisted of metal springs with a steel knob on the end that came out of a metal rod and wrapped around the victim's head. An old pal, Tommy Flannagan, who was playing the roulette, saw the fracas and quickly joined in – it was promptly sorted.

Years later, I met Hanlon at the doctor's when I was doing my 10 for McVitie in Wormwood Scrubs prison. He looked at me and asked, 'Are you Fred? Freddie Foreman? I'm Johnny Hanlon.'

I said, 'Oh yeah, do you want to step into the recess?'

'No, no, no,' he replied, and asked me if he was out of order that night. I told him he was, he apologised and we shook hands there and then.

Some years later, when I was living in Spain, a consortium of publicans came over to see me. Their spokesman told me they wanted rid of Hanlon, for a price. I told them I was not a paid hitman: 'I don't do those things for money.' Hanlon would wreck pubs and was such a nuisance that publicans gave him money just to go away. He's still around, all 20 stone of him.

One night, I had a terrible cold and was home in bed trying to get over it with a bottle of Scotch, which I don't normally drink. The club rang to say they had trouble and would I please come over. I tried to get them to sort it out themselves, but they insisted I come as they couldn't handle it. I instructed them to get the main troublemaker, a tall geezer, bigger than the others, and the rest of them downstairs to the bar. 'Give them a drink and say Fred's on his way and he wants to talk to you.' I then put a suit over my pyjamas and, although it was late, Ronnie Oliffe was still running the spiel at the Marshalsea so I asked him to pick me up and run me to the 211.

The manager had been told to hang about near the troublemaker and nod in his direction when I walked in. As soon as I arrived, I went up to the geezer and asked, 'Now, what's this all about?' Without waiting for a reply I knocked him spark out and asked the rest of his gang if they wanted some. I told them never to come there again and then dragged the big fellow across the floor into the toilets. I got my shillelagh and lifted his legs up to his chin while he was still out cold and battered his legs. 'That's for getting me out of fucking bed, you cunt!' And I'm belting him with the stick. I gave his legs a good hammering. He would feel the effects the next day when he woke up. Ron told me I was getting a bit carried away, so I stopped and we got his pals to take him home. I was really pissed off dealing with these mugs, though. Week after week, the same thing. When would they learn to behave in my club and places of business?

Throughout my life, I've always felt revolted by liberty-takers and bullies. In the eyes of the law and society I am seen as a villain, but I have always strived to be quiet, polite and well mannered. My father's belief in civility was ingrained in me. Whatever club, pub or betting shop I owned, I treated people decently and with the same respect that I expected from them. When that respect was not returned, I would get very angry and the response could be severe.

On one busy weekend evening, there was a disturbance in the bar downstairs. Our staff had become anxious because a gang of about a dozen guys – some of them very ugly, with punched-in faces, led by a bloke I called Flat Nose – were causing mayhem.

My mate Micky Regan and I were upstairs. I grabbed a tool from the office and Mick and I raced downstairs, to find them leaving. Mick suggested we wait until they were all outside and then deal with it. At that stage, we didn't know what had happened, but our blood ran hot when we saw a young girl who'd been knocked spark out, her jaw broken. She was only about 17 and Flat Nose, obviously an ex-fighter, had punched her lights out.

Angrily, Mick and I ran out of the club to follow the gang, who were getting into several cars with their women. Flat Nose was shouting directions to his friends so they could meet up at another venue. They were on the other side of the road and I waved my arms, signalling to him that I wanted a word. Flat Nose and his partner both stood on the far kerb, beckoning for us to come over. But as we got closer, the sight of big Mick and myself clearly appeared a bit formidable to them, so they made a run back to their car, parked in a side street. We followed, swiftly crossing the road as the two guys pulled out pickaxe handles from the boot of their car. 'Come on, then,' they sneered, smacking the handles into the palms of their hands.

It was the wrong move for them. I pulled out the equalizer – a .38 pistol that I had grabbed from a hidey hole upstairs in the casino. They froze. 'Just drop the sticks,' I commanded. The pickaxe handles clattered to the road.

'There's no need for that,' they said.

'No need for that?' I retorted angrily. 'After what you just did to that little girl!' Crash! I gave Flat Nose a right to the jaw. Mick went for the other one who, with fists raised, was dancing around the street doing a Cassius Clay. I laid into Flat Nose and pistol-whipped him five or six times around the head and then put the gun into his shoulder and pulled the trigger. Unknown to me at the time, the bullet didn't go clean through him as I would have expected but ricocheted off his shoulder blade and travelled around his body, missing several major arteries and his heart, before emerging from his side. Apparently, that often happens when someone is shot at close quarters.

While I was sorting out Flat Nose, Mick had chased and caught 'Cassius Clay'. They sparred for a little bit and when he'd had enough of that, Mick battered the granny out of Cassius and tossed him over a hedge on to someone's front garden.

After I'd shot him, Flat Nose had dropped to the ground like a sack of potatoes. I then went over to where Mick had tossed Cassius and got to him just as he was picking his face off the ground. I put my knee into the middle of his back, grabbed his hair and pulled his head back, whispering in his ear, 'If I ever see you out here again, this is what you're going to get.'

With that, I put the barrel of the gun behind his ear and let one go. Blood splattered everywhere as the bullet took his ear right off and the blast from the explosion burned him all over the face. Covered in blood, we returned to the club and cleaned up in our private bathroom. Then I sent Ding Dong Dell to check out the two guys. Apparently, the one whose ear had been blown off managed to stagger to the car and drive Flat Nose and himself to the local hospital. We then sent another member of the Firm to check out their ward and report on how badly damaged they were. In the meantime, the young girl with the fractured jaw was taken to the same hospital.

Police were called, but no statements were made. Both Flat Nose and his companion had been spoken to on my behalf. They understood that all they had received was a 'taster' and it would not be a good idea to take it any further. We never heard from them again.

On another occasion at the 211, Jack 'The Hat' McVitie, who was losing money that night, pulled a knife on my croupier. Then, when he realised I was on my way upstairs to speak to him, he threw it under the table. It landed near where a friend of mine, Bobby Neil (an ex-lightweight boxing champion) and his wife were dining. I knew Jack: he was on the Kray firm, but they told me he was unreliable. He had taken money to kill Leslie Payne but never went through with it and still spent the money. Anyhow, he was a loudmouth. He went around saying he was going to kill the Twins and boasted that he had tried to run Ronnie over. He'd also gone to the Starlight Club, where Micky Regan and I had some roulette and blackjack tables, held up the place and made all the guys drop their strides. All told, McVitie was a bit of a nut. He lived in a shithole with no furniture. When he was high on drink and drugs, he would fire his big .45 gun into the chimneybreast.

That night at the 211, I came up behind McVitie and asked him what the problem was: 'Misbehaving again, Jack? Come with me, I just want to talk to you.'

He looked at me and replied, 'What, and get a fucking bullet in the head?' I told him I'd go downstairs and that when I got back in 10 minutes I didn't want to see him there. When I returned to the casino, he'd left. Later I mentioned the incident to Ronnie Kray, who bollocked him for causing trouble in my club.

When the gaming laws changed in the mid-Sixties, restricting gambling to the West End, we lost our licence, so I took all the units out of the 211 and opened an illegal casino in Strood, near Rochester, Kent.

The Colony Club also closed down and George Raft was stopped from entering Britain. Nevertheless, we did further business importing one-armed bandits from the Americans. I had a van-load of machines given to me by this nice American guy called Dave Dick, and another called Gabe Foreman, my namesake. I took loads of machines off him, although a boat-load of them were smashed up by police and Customs. Lots of little cafés and clubs on both sides of the water had one-armed bandits working day and night, bringing in plenty of cash for the Firm. But there was no denying it: another era was coming to a close.

While he was working on the counter of my betting shop, Kenny Martin was beaten up in the Stork Club toilet. The culprits turned up at my brother George's club, The Red Sail, and George rang me to mark my card. I put a .38 pistol in my pocket and headed off for the club, picking up my pal Ronnie King on the way. When we arrived, most of the Richardson gang were there, with the exception of Charlie and Frankie Fraser. Charlie tended not to go around much with his brother and in fact it was Eddie and Fraser who really wanted to be the gangsters.

'When you kick the dog, you also kick the master,' I snarled at the group of six or seven men. As soon as I had their attention, I pulled out the pistol and stuck it up Eddie Richardson's nose. 'This applies to that little c**t Fraser as well. If any of your firm interfere with any of my staff, friends or family again, I'll bury the lot of you.'

Around this time, there was another incident involving Fraser and Eddie Richardson's firm which goes to show the madness of those years. If I had acted as I had intended it would have changed the face of British crime history. A close friend asked me to avenge another liberty taken by Fraser and Co. The nephew of a friend of mine had been hit with a hammer by 'you know who'. A friend informed us that a meeting would be taking place at a Mayfair office one Sunday morning at about 11 o'clock.

I sat in the back seat of a black Rover car outside the Mayfair office, with my pal at the wheel, waiting patiently for the culprits to come out. I'd acquired quite an arsenal of weapons, one of which was a Belgian FM automatic rifle with a 30-bullet magazine, so we could have been looking at another Valentine's Day massacre. We got into a position across the street with a clear view of their office door. We had been waiting for quite a long time when suddenly, the office door opened and seven or eight men strolled out talking, arms around shoulders, shaking hands, laughing. I got ready to squeeze the trigger when who should walk out of the door but Kenny Hampton. He was the very person who had told us about the meeting. He was our buyer of jewellery from Hatton Garden. Also talking to him was Paddy O'Nione, who was a really close friend of mine at that time. They all stood there chatting away and what else could we do but slowly pull away?

It just goes to show how things were during those years. I must have been a crazy bastard to overreact like that about people who took liberties with innocent friends of mine. Looking back, it would have been total madness, but that was the climate at the time. I was a suitable case for treatment.

I was just getting over my birthday celebrations (5 March), playing the part of mine host in the bar of the Prince of Wales. I was feeling just a bit tired and jaded – well, in fact, completely knackered. It had been a really hectic week, the pub was busy every night and this particular night, 7 March 1966, was no exception. The place was already packed, when in walked Peter Hennessey, Billy Hayward, Billy Gardner, Dicky Hart, Johnny Perry, Duggie Horn and several others. They were all nice guys who, as well as being regular customers that spent well, behaved well and gave me no trouble, were all good friends of mine. The drinks were flowing and Billy Gardner – a larger-than-life character and brilliant raconteur who'd once won the first prize on Michael Miles's TV show *Double Your Money* on the subject of boxing – was on good form.

The conversation turned to the new club that had just opened in Catford, called – rather strangely – 'Mr Smiths and the Witch Doctor'. Billy Hayward and his brother Flash Harry had pubs and clubs in that area and felt it was their manor. If anyone opened a similar business they thought – and rightly so – they should be consulted and given a share in the new enterprise. Especially as the club owners had come all the way down from Manchester to take bread out of their mouths. Paddy McGrath and Owen Ratcliffe, the new owners of 'Mr Smiths', had a number of clubs up north and felt there were rich pickings to be had down south, but Catford should not have been one of them. I had my own place, the 211 Club in Balham, to worry about. You see, the West End had all the licences, so when punters stepped outside, they could walk straight in to another club, casino or restaurant. Everywhere was still open, the West End was buzzing. But step outside in Balham High Street or Catford at 2am in the morning, and it was deadsville, not a soul in sight. That's why all other clubs and casinos in the sticks were doomed to failure.

Unfortunately, Paddy and Owen's other big mistake was to go to old-time villains Billy Hill and Albert Dimes, who were not the right people to get advice from. They didn't know fuck-all about what was really going on in London, or who was who. There were a lot of very dangerous firms around, armed robbers, who didn't give two fucks about names or reputations – especially when, as far as they were concerned, those old-time villains had not done anything on the scale of villainy as the men who were active at that time. If Paddy and Owen had come to me, I would have told them forget about Catford, keep their money in their pockets and go back home to Manchester.

Getting back to my story. Come closing time, we had all enjoyed the night's drinking, and then Peter and Billy asked me to go with them to Mr Smiths. There was no talk of any trouble, or that Eddie Richardson and Frankie Fraser were going to be there that night. The invitation was to carry on drinking and take a look at their new watering hole. I declined their offer, telling them 'another time, chaps'. I had hardly slept since my birthday and I still had to attend to business at the 211 before trying to grab some well-needed shut-eye. At 11 o'clock we went our separate ways. I drove to Balham, and Peter, Billy and the others all piled into several motors and headed for Catford. After spending a few hours at the 211 Club, I returned home and crashed out.

I was awoken by a quiet tapping outside and a few gentle rings on the pub door. I threw on my dressing gown and opened the upstairs window. Through the darkness, I could just make out a crowd of men. At first I thought it was the Old Bill, but it wasn't the rat-a-tat or continuous banging of the police, it was more polite and gentle. I called down, 'Who is it?' and heard Peter Hennessey's voice. 'It's me, Fred.

Can we come in, we need to speak to you for a minute?' I knew that something was seriously wrong. They told me the full SP, how the Richardsons had come down to take over the club, which they considered was their domain. Frank and Eddie had arrived firm-handed, so when Jimmy Moody arrived with even more reinforcements, it was time for Billy and Peter to send out for some tools. When you have two firms facing each other, tooled-up ready to settle old scores and grievances, it's gonna escalate into a full-scale war. With 15 hard men involved, there had to be a few casualties...

My visitors told me that they thought Frankie Fraser, Dicky Hart and Harry Rawlings were dead, and that Eddie Richardson and Ronnie Jeffreys were wounded. A .45 revolver and two shotguns had been used, leaving blood and bodies everywhere. They needed advice and a safe house. I got dressed, told Maureen not to worry and to go back to sleep, and took Peter, Billy Gardner, Duggie Horn and John Perry on to a safe house, telling them to stay put until we could find out what real damage had been done. Then we took Billy Haywood, whose head was gaping from a bayonet wound, to one of my doctor friends. After a few weeks, I managed to get Peter Hennessey, Duggie Horn and John Perry to go into Catford police station, and admit that they were there on the night, but that they had left before any trouble started – that would explain why their names were in the members' visitors book and why the bar staff and hat-check girl could identify them. This having been done, no charges could be brought against them. They all walked. Only Billy Hayward went down for eight years, for affray.

It took a bit longer to get Billy Gardner off the hook, as he had been identified as one of those brandishing a shotgun. The police still wanted him bad. I had to keep him holed up in my brother-in-law's flat for about four months, then move him down to a campsite in Battle, just outside Hastings, where I owned a caravan. In those days, many houses still had outside toilets and a tin bath hanging up on the scullery wall, but this had all mod cons (toilet, bath and TV) so he didn't have to show his face too much on the campsite, just venture out occasionally at night. This he did. Only one night, he ventured into the village pub. After a couple of hours plying the locals with drinks and regaling them with his jokes and stories, 20 gin-and-tonics later he returned, paralytic drunk and staggering around the campsite firing his shotgun into the air, shouting, 'I'm the man who shot up the Richardson gang!'

This did *not* please me. I had to send three 'chaps' to drive all the way down there to rope him up till he was sober. Bill apologised for his bad behaviour and I forgave him. After all, he was a good, loyal and solid man, who after spending months on the mattress had simply got drunk and let off a little steam. Eventually, through good friends of mine, Bill was given a job working in a Portsmouth casino. As time went on, Mr Smiths ceased to be a problem for Billy Gardner. Not so for Frankie Fraser, who was arrested and charged with affray as he lay almost bleeding to death, his leg shattered by a .45 bullet.

Five people were shot that night, but apart from the tragic death of Dicky Hart, they all miraculously survived. Billy Hayward received eight years, and Henry Bottom a five. Frank Fraser was tried separately for the Dicky Hart shooting, and found not guilty – and rightly so. He didn't shoot Dicky, but we all know who did. And that man wasn't even arrested that night. Fraser received five years for affray, though. Ronnie Jeffrey, Harry Rawlings, Jimmy Moody and Billy Stayton were all found not guilty. Eddie Richardson, who was attacked and also shot on that fateful night, had to endure a retrial, only to be found guilty and receive a five-year sentence. Personally, I thought that on all the evidence he should have walked. If a man is challenged to a fight, he's entitled to defend himself. To be blasted with a shotgun, arrested while lying in hospital and then sent to prison for five years – where's the justice in that? Eddie has had some raw deals in life. Later, he got another 10 years for a torture trial, which brought it up to 15. As if that wasn't enough, due to a drug-related offence, Eddie was sentenced to a further 25 years. Isn't it about time someone gave him a break?

I knew both camps and was sorry that the night at Mr Smiths had ended in such carnage. If I had gone with Peter and Billy, perhaps – only perhaps, mind – I may have prevented the events that took place. On the other hand, knowing myself, I would have been right up at the front, and the body count may have been higher.

CHAPTER 13
THE MAD AXEMAN

Until I was arrested with the Krays as an accessory to the McVitie murder, I lived the life of Riley. All my legitimate businesses turned over vast sums of money and the Firm continued with lucrative pavement work and bank and wages robberies. The Twins were in a different business to me, so when they were offered work that was not in their line, they'd pass it my way. I would do the same for them and we'd each get our cut.

The Prince of Wales pub had become a centre for socialising and business. Even my doctor enjoyed his visits there. But then Dr Fred Coffey, a lovely man, was very sociable. He was a tall, introspective fella with a touch of the actor Alastair Sim about him. Generally, he was unflappable. I saw him get excited only once, and that was when Maureen was about to give birth to Danielle. We had to race against the clock to get her to hospital in case the baby was strangled by the umbilical cord. We got stuck in a lift coming down from our 14th-floor flat and he really lost his rag.

Fred was no alcoholic, but like many Irishmen he loved his drink. The cellar at my pub was supplied by a friend who worked for ICI. He was a multi-talented chap and was involved in one of their hotels used by top executives as a weekend retreat. They had the best cigars, champagne and liqueurs. Stephan La Fay would come over every month with cases of vintage port and Margaux wine, which I bought off him at a knock-down price. He was a regular presenter on the TV series *Café Continental* and appeared on this programme with Helene Cordet, a very close friend of Prince Philip. I wasn't aware of how wonderful wine could be until I met him. He taught me a lot about the different vintages, and Fred Coffey, a connoisseur of fine drink, loved my cellar – the brandies in particular. I always gave him a 25-year-old Camus brandy, which he loved.

Through him, I met a succession of other Irish doctors. Dr Steven Erner was a rugby international. He had a surgery on Gipsy Hill and helped deliver my Jamie into the world. Then there was Dr Leo Barrie, who had a surgery in Peckham, another lovely man like the previous two. He gave evidence for me in the Mitchell trial. Leo was due to come to our home remove Maureen's stitches from an earlier operation. For some reason, he was unable to come, but made a note in his diary that I had called from the Harley Street clinic that Maureen was being discharged from. When he gave evidence for me, confirming I had been at the clinic when the shooting took place, Judge Lawton went red and exploded. He told ushers in the court, 'Take that man back to his surgery and bring me his diary.'

Leo couldn't believe it. They fetched his diary and scrutinised the details in case he'd written it in a different pen. But everything was in order and the jury were obliged to accept the evidence.

Fred was a very trustworthy man and – again, being an Irishman – the authorities didn't matter to him. He didn't feel the need to report every incident that occurred. Whenever any of us got cut or hurt, Fred and the other doctors would attend to our wounds. Joe Carter, my old ram-raiding mate, once got a big stripe down his face when a guy on the Twins' firm cut him up at a party. That geezer was thrown off the Twins' firm for misbehaving with my friend. Dr Fred always did a neat job! One night, years later, Joe was driving home from a West End spieler very early in the morning, very tired. He crashed into a milk lorry and was killed instantly.

One afternoon, on a robbery in south-west London, we had a bit of a run-in with security guards delivering money. All were well-padded, wore visors and crash helmets and were armed with clubs and liquid dye-guns. We were also tooled up. I had a .38 and a club around my wrist and Alfie had a shotgun. They sprayed dye at us as I ran towards them. I slipped and as I went down, a big guy in front of me whacked me on the nut with this big club, which was like a long baseball bat. I had on a trilby hat, which softened the blow a little bit, and I retaliated by battering him across the jaw with my .38 revolver.

As he came forward to have another go at me, Alf let him have it in the shoulder with his shotgun. It spun him around like a top. He was not badly hurt, because we'd taken out most of the shot from the cartridge and replaced it with rice. It was used mainly to make a noise and frighten, rather than to injure people.

We managed to get away with a few bags and it turned out to be a nice touch. On returning to the Prince of Wales pub, I ran upstairs to the toilet. One minute I was having a piss and he next thing I'd passed out, hitting my nose on the cistern. Maureen was behind the bar and heard the thud, so she and Ronnie Oliffe rushed upstairs to find me unceremoniously draped across the pan – not a pretty sight! Dr Barrie was called and their description of me led him to believe I'd had a heart attack. Later it all became clear. The bang over the head had given me delayed concussion.

That evening, we were due to go to the Dorchester to a dinner and dance to which I had been invited by Ronnie Knight and Barbara Windsor. Maureen was looking forward to it and I couldn't let her down.

But by then word had got around that a robber had been cracked on the nose during a raid (they got it wrong again, it was *my* head) – and here I was, at a top dinner attended by some of Scotland Yard's finest, answering the description of a man with an injured nose wanted for armed robbery! Worse still, I hadn't been able to scrub off all the dye, which would have shown up under ultra-violet lighting. During the dinner I got one or two long-and-hard looks but nothing was said.

I was always in the bath after that trying to get rid of the last traces of dye, and the joke went around: 'Where's Brown Bread? In the shower again?'

Throughout my long career, I was only set up once. And that was at a jeweller's in Holborn. We were told about this jeweller whose shop was on the first floor in a building, next to a Lloyds bank. He'd collect money each day and exchange it for a bag of uncut diamonds. It was suggested we take the parcel of diamonds and sell them to another jeweller. This sounded quite tasty, so we said we'd have a look.

On the stairs leading up to the shop was a landing with a cupboard and we fitted it up so we could go in there all tooled up and wait for the parcel.

The day we were due to carry out the hold-up, Mick called me and Alf over to see him. He had a betting shop in Red Lion Square, right next to a big old pub where we met to finalise our plans. Sitting at the bar as we walked in was Alec Eist from Scotland Yard's Flying Squad. Mick greeted him and asked what was happening. Alec replied, 'I've just been to a meeting at the Yard this morning. We've all been handed guns to foil a robbery, but fuck that, I don't want no shoot-outs. The Guvnor told us, "This is a right heavy firm involved, so take no chances. You've all got to be tooled up."' He said they had been told it would happen outside the bank and that they'd been sitting here all week waiting for the robbers. What a lucky break! Prevention is always better than cure. We slipped him a monkey (£500) and stayed out on the piss with Alec all day to show our appreciation.

Alec Eist was a rebel cop. He'd stand on tables and sing and make a right pest of himself when he was drunk. But he was as much a crook as any of us and quite capable of doing anything. It was much easier to hold your hand out for a few bob than to have a shoot-out, and he was a pragmatist. He had his ear to the ground and knew who was who on the London scene. Often he worked undercover and posed as a crook. He was a right rascal, but you could live with him. At the same time, he also nicked a lot of people. He'd nick you as quick as look at you if it was safe to do so. But he was very good with us. If anyone was in trouble he'd work a bit of bail and try and help us in court. It was very easy for a copper to fluff his lines or make a pig's ear of the evidence without arousing suspicion.

In December 1966, the Twins were having terrible problems with Frank Mitchell who, for a very good reason, was known as 'The Mad Axeman'. They had organised his escape from Dartmoor on 12 December, but came to regret their action almost immediately. To unleash him on the public was as irresponsible as taking the muzzle off a crazed Rottweiler and letting it loose in a playschool. He was a backward, disturbed child living in a man's body possessed of almost superhuman strength. It had taken 13 coppers to hold him down on one occasion in Marylebone Court and everyone was terrified of him. He had a fearsome reputation for slashing screws and inflicting violence on anyone who crossed his path.

When Frank Mitchell was nine years old, he stole another boy's bicycle. His father, rather than dealing with the matter himself by returning the bike to its owner and taking his son in hand, decided to turn Frank over to the police. The cossers took a dim view of the offence and the young lad was brought before a juvenile court. From there on in, it was that slippery slope, down which many kids from working-class families went: probation, approved school, borstal, prison – the usual pattern, year after year, getting deeper and deeper into the quagmire. He grew into a big strong lad at six foot 2in tall with a 54-inch chest and arms the size of most men's legs.

Frank began to earn respect from other prisoners for attacking screws and some other inmates but eventually, around 1950, was sent to Rampton, a secure mental hospital. He and another prisoner escaped from Rampton and, while on the run, they got hold of an axe and threatened people with it ... which earned Frank his nickname.

After that, it was Broadmoor for Frank and, when he escaped once more, he broke into the house of an old couple, stealing clothing, ten shillings and the old boy's watch. In spite of what he'd done, the old girl offered to bathe his sore and bleeding feet. He thanked her for her kindness and took off in their Ford Prefect, only to be caught again and sentenced to life. The press claimed that Frank had threatened the couple with an axe which he balanced on his knee while drinking tea.

Mitchell had been sentenced to life imprisonment and had done nine years of his sentence. He now wanted a release date that the prison governor, though a sympathetic man, was unable to deliver. The Twins told him that once he had escaped, they would help him appeal to the Home Secretary, and the plan was for him to stay on the run for six months, petitioning the authorities for a release date, then supposedly returning to prison to finish off his sentence. (How ridiculous does that sound?) The Home Secretary, however, was Roy Jenkins, who famously made a statement in the House of Commons regarding lifers, that 'life should be life'. It sent shock waves all through prison system, especially as he was supposed to be a 'Liberal'. Could you imagine being inside and hearing that? It was a statement that caused the loss of people's lives – Frank Mitchell, for one, because there was no way he wanted to stick around inside prison until he died. Politicians should think before they open their mouths.

Anyway, the scheme was doomed to failure with someone like

Mitchell. You couldn't trust him, and the Twins aged five years while he was out. He threatened to kill a dozen policemen rather than go back to prison. They were losing sleep and he was becoming a real threat. He wanted to go out at nights with a mask on his face, saying he wouldn't be recognised. He would demonstrate his strength by heaving up his minders by their belts and doing 100 press-ups after having it off with his bird all day and all night. From the time he stabbed Bruce Reynolds in a bath house in Wandsworth, I knew his reputation. He would pick up screws and crack their ribs in a bear hug, pretending to be friendly. Word got out that search parties looking for him after his escape would have shot him on sight.

Mitchell was holed up in a place near Canning Town, where he originally came from. He'd wanted to see his parents, who were nearby, but the Krays dared not let him out of their sight and kept minders with him 24 hours a day. Reg arranged for a girl to keep him quiet and brought in Lisa, a good-looking hostess. She tamed him for about a week, but then he got up to his old tricks again and became aggressive, pulling a knife on one of his minders and later arming himself with one of their shooters. The situation became even more harassing when he began to feel he was being snubbed by Ronnie, who wouldn't visit him.

The final straw came when Mitchell said of the Twins, 'I'll hold their mother responsible if anything happens to me.'

I mean, that's childish, threatening to go round and tell your mum. So Ronnie asked me over for a meet in Hackney and we had a private talk. There was no solution to this problem other than the decision a veterinary surgeon has to make when confronted with a mad dog that is a danger to everything and everyone else. Ron and I decided he would have to go. I didn't know Mitchell personally, but Ron asked me if I could do him a personal favour. I agreed to help him, just as he had helped me and others on my firm many times before.

Our meeting was on 23 December, the last day anyone was to see Mitchell again. Albert Donoghue, whom I knew and liked, was in the next room. He'd taken part in Mitchell's escape and helped mind him. While he was working for the Krays, he came to see me on a regular basis, bringing my share of money from occasional joint ventures in which we were involved.

Donoghue would play a key role in Frank Mitchell's disappearance, while the Twins would stay out of the way (although in a recent book he wrote, *The Krays' Lieutenant*, he denied knowing Mitchell was going to be killed).

The operation to get rid of Mitchell went smoothly. It was a shame that more than two years later, Donoghue decided to grass on us. There was no need to do that, he did not have to name names, although I have some sympathy for him in as much as the Twins wanted him to take the sole blame for Mitchell's death. It was a dark winter's night, almost pitch black, when Donoghue coaxed Mitchell from the house to the back of the waiting van, with the engine running. There was no way he could have seen anybody else in the van. All he had to say at a subsequent trial was that it was too dark to identify anybody and that he returned alone to the house. Donoghue told a number of lies about the incident although his description of the killing itself was fairly accurate. The worst thing was that he said I had done it for money.

As I've emphasised before, this was never the case. I had no need to kill anybody for financial reward. Mitchell was a problem, a threat to all of us. I took part in his killing as a favour to the Twins. There was no financial incentive whatsoever. Donoghue and others on the Firm used to bring me money all the time from the Colony Club and other West End interests. And, when Charlie Kray and some associates got nicked in Nigeria, I helped them out with £5,000 to secure their release. So to claim he handed over £1,000 after Mitchell's disappearance is an insult.

Judge Lawton, who tried me on the Mitchell case more than two years after the event, asked about 'grassing'. Detective Superintendent Leonard 'Nipper' Read told him that the criminal world had its own rules of conduct:

Read: 'There is an association of criminals in the same echelons.'

Lawton asked him, 'For criminals in the First Division, what would you say was the sin of sins against the world in which they live?'

Read replied, 'The sin of sins is, in the parlance of criminals, to grass.'

Lawton: 'Would you put Donoghue in the First Division?'

Read: 'I would put him in the bottom half of the First Division.'

Lawton: 'He will have to keep his eye on the relegation.'

Ha, ha, ha. Lawton's joke may have brought a laugh in the courtroom, but outside it was serious business. Until the Krays and I had been arrested, nobody wanted to give evidence against us. It was only when they were convinced we would be safely locked away for many years that some people agreed to talk to police.

Read told the court that Donoghue would know about grassing being the sin of sins and said his life in prison would be most uncomfortable. He added, 'For this reason I have taken certain steps...'

Donoghue was charged with conspiring with Billy Exley and 'Mad' Teddy Smith to effect Mitchell's escape from Dartmoor Prison. He was further charged with harbouring Mitchell between 12 December and 24 December 1966 and of murdering Mitchell on 24 December 1966. Kenneth Jones QC, prosecuting, said no evidence would be offered on the murder charge as it was proposed to call him to give evidence at a later stage. He stated that Donoghue took Mitchell some clothing and told him he was being taken to another place. He took Mitchell from the flat and, shortly after, shots were heard coming from the direction Donoghue and Mitchell had taken.

Alfie Gerrard was on his toes in Australia in April 1969 when the three Kray brothers and I appeared at the Central Criminal Court charged with killing Mitchell. We all pleaded not guilty to the charge and the Krays were also charged with helping Mitchell escape from Dartmoor.

Several others were charged with conspiring to help Mitchell escape and with harbouring him. The jury were told they would be kept under police surveillance – which, of course, always looks bad for the defendants in a case.

The Crown prosecutor, Kenneth Jones QC, outlined the case against me. He said money was handed over to the killer by a man named Albert Donoghue who had seen the shooting, been involved with Mitchell, the Krays and others, and had himself been accused of Mitchell's murder but who had decided to make a statement to the police.

Jones stated that Mitchell had been serving a life sentence for robbery with violence and was killed in a van outside a flat in Barking Road, in the East End of London on 24 December 1966, 12 days after being sprung from Dartmoor while on an outside working party. He was taken to a hideaway flat where a young nightclub hostess was ordered to comfort him and sleep with him and he found himself in a very nearly hopeless position. He was subject to a life sentence and had escaped from one prison on Dartmoor to a flat in Barking, which in many ways must have become like a second prison. He was entirely dependent on others and obviously this couldn't go on, Something had to happen. It was then, Jones stated, that Mitchell was murdered by Foreman and Gerrard.

On the last day of Mitchell's life, 24 December, the Crown prosecutor continued, Donoghue arrived at the flat and told the 'Mad Axeman' he was going away. Mitchell said he wanted to take the girl, of whom he had become very fond, but Donoghue said she could follow an hour or so later. Mitchell and the girl packed their bags. The girl was then paid off with an envelope containing about £100. Donoghue, who had left the flat, then returned to collect Mitchell. It was alleged that Mitchell kissed the girl before he departed, to indicate his affection, and then left with Donoghue.

The girl saw them turn the corner into Ladysmith Avenue, there was a pause and then she heard three or four muffled bangs. Perhaps they came from inside the vehicle, as they were very muffled. They certainly came from Ladysmith Avenue. She thought they were shots and asked someone to see what had happened but she was restrained from leaving the flat. What she had heard, according to the prosecutor, was an 'act of murder': the shooting of Frank Mitchell in a vehicle in Ladysmith Avenue.

About five or ten minutes later, Donoghue came back to the flat and announced that it must be cleared up. He then made a phone call and the girl heard him say, 'The dog is dead.' Jones suggested this could be an oblique reference to the fact that Mitchell was dead. He said Donoghue then took the girl by car to see Reginald Kray, who told the girl that if she ever said a word to anyone, they would get her. He said this coldly and calmly and deliberately. It was a clear threat to her.

Jones alleged that Ronnie Oliffe and Jerry Callaghan were also by the van (in fact, this was wrong: there was only me and Alf from my firm). It was alleged that Foreman and Gerrard shot Mitchell as soon as the van doors were closed and that a gun with a silencer was used. (Another mistake: Gerrard's gun had no silencer.) There were four shots, said the prosecutor. 'Foreman fired twice more into Mitchell's chest and head until he must have been dead. Donoghue was dropped off, and he made a telephone call to Reginald Kray to tell him what had happened. Mitchell's murder was planned by Ronald and Reginald Kray. When Donoghue took him from the flat on Friday evening, 24 December, he was taking him to his death. Afterwards, Donoghue had gone to Ronnie and been required to repeat details of the murder, telling him exactly what had happened. The prosecutor alleged (again, wrongly) that Donoghue then went to my pub in Lant Street and paid me £1,000 on the Twins' instructions. At the same time, he said, Donoghue had a discussion with me about the final disposal of Mitchell's body, which had now apparently disappeared off the face of the earth.

William Henry Exley told the court he was a minder at the Mitchell flat in Barking. On the night of the alleged murder, he said, he was at a party with Reggie Kray and others when Donoghue came in and said, 'The other fellow's gone.' Reggie and Donoghue went outside into the passageway and he followed. He overheard Donoghue say, 'They gave him four injections in the nut but he was still moaning.' He thought they said there was some in the body as well.

Cross-examined by Reg's QC, Paul Wrightson, who asked him whether he did as he was told by Reg, Exley said in a raised voice, 'I slept with a loaded shotgun for four months. They wanted to come and get me in the same way they got Jack 'The Hat'. They shot and wounded Nobby Clarke, Donoghue and Jimmy Field.' After being calmed down by the judge, Exley admitted he had been convicted of shooting with intent to murder. He denied that the murder vehicle belonged to him. He told the judge he was in prison and that, 'If I live long enough, I will get released in October.'

Mitchell's hostess gave evidence in court as 'Mrs C'. She said she was taken to the flat from a club where she was working by a man named Donoghue. She spent several nights with Mitchell and once she tried to leave and got a spanking from him. 'He was trying to protect me,' she said. 'If I had got out of the flat, he would not have been able to protect me.'

Another witness (referred to as 'Mr B') said Mitchell was in his flat with a man called Scotch Jack, whom he later discovered was actually called Dixon. He said Frank Mitchell stayed in his flat for 11 to 14 days and that while there Mr B was a general errand boy. Asked if anyone else visited Mitchell, Mr B said, 'Yes, Ronald, Reginald and Charlie Kray, a man called Cowley and another called Dixon and Albert Donoghue.' He said on the night of the alleged shooting, Mitchell left the flat with Donoghue and Cornelius Whitehead at about 11pm, shortly after that he heard about three or four bangs as though a motorist was in trouble and all his tyres had burst.

Donoghue's evidence, given on Tuesday, 22 April 1969, was potentially the most damaging: he described how he had collected Mitchell at the Monkey's Fist pub in Dartmoor and brought him back by car to London. Foreman was going to take him to the country, where he would spend Christmas with Ronnie Kray. After that, he was to be put on a boat and sent to the continent somewhere. 'A meeting was arranged by myself and Foreman for the evening so I could prepare Mitchell for the trip,' Donoghue stated. 'I met Foreman... I went back to Mitchell's flat. I told him we were leaving and he became agitated when the girl could not go with him. I told him we would arrange for her to follow. I went out at about 8pm and saw a dark blue van in Ladysmith Avenue with one of the men standing by the back doors. I went back and collected Mitchell who shook hands with everyone and made a fuss of the girl before walking out.'

Asked by the prosecutor when he first knew that Mitchell was to be shot in the van, Donoghue replied. 'When the guns opened up.' He said he saw two men pump about 12 bullets into Frank Mitchell. 'Frederick Foreman and a man called Gerrard were sitting on the left. Foreman told me to go to the front of the van and tell the driver the route.

'As I walked up and got in the van, both doors closed and two guns started firing as the van drove off. I spun around and saw Mitchell on his knees, clutching his chest. The guns were just blasting away at him. One was a small revolver, which Gerrard had. The other was a black automatic with a silencer. It was Foreman's.

'Mitchell fell back on his shoulders. His knees were up. Mitchell started making noises from his throat. Foreman held the gun about a foot away from Mitchell's chest and fired three shots. The material of Mitchell's coat was jumping up and down.'

Donoghue added that Mitchell made some more noise and Gerrard said, 'Give him another, Fred, I'm empty.'

Mrs C, the blonde nightclub hostess, said she had stayed four nights with Mitchell and had been given a brown envelope containing money on the evening of the last day. She also said Mitchell had been given a long scarf by Albert Donoghue. Mitchell and she had grown to like each other during their four days and nights together, she stated, and had kissed goodbye when he left. Then she heard bangs like gunshots. 'I shouted out, "Oh, God! They've killed him. They've shot him",' she declared. She heard three, four or five shots fired, the sounds coming from the side of the flat; the sounds did not echo, they were muffled. About five minutes later, Mr Donoghue came back in the flat and made a telephone call. Mrs C was taken to a party after Mitchell had left, although she had wanted to go home: 'Reggie, Connie Whitehead and Albert Donoghue would not let me go home and I stayed the night at the party with Albert.'

On 24 April, the judge directed that the Krays be found not guilty, through lack of evidence. The case against me continued, though. Terry Spinks, the Olympic gold-medallist boxer, was called to give evidence and said he had been drinking with Ronald Oliffe on the night he was alleged to have been driving the van in which Mitchell was shot. Spinks said on 24 December 1966 he arrived at the Log Cabin, a club in Soho, at about 5pm and stayed about four hours. Oliffe and his brother were there and dropped him home in his cab at about 9.30pm. Terry said he was a friend of mine and the second time he met Donoghue at the Stork Club, he came across to his table with three other men and said he recognised him as the man with Foreman who had thrown him out of the pub. 'He picked up an ashtray and hit me across the eye with it. He said the matter was not finished and he was going to burn down Foreman's pub.'

A number of witnesses were called by my QC, Tom Williams, Labour MP for Warrington (his junior was Ivor Richard, who became Labour leader in the House of Lords in 1992). I had an alibi: that I had visited my wife Maureen in a Harley Street clinic on the night Mitchell was killed. To prove this, I tried to get a statement from a nurse, who had since emigrated to Australia. I sent Maureen Down Under with a top detective agency, Pinkerton's, but Maureen was arrested the minute she set foot in Australia. They then took the nurse into protective custody and said she was in danger of being nobbled, when Maureen only wanted a statement from her. The nurse confirmed that she remembered I had asked her for a cup of tea or coffee but wouldn't say it was on that particular night – she thought it may have been the day before. When Lawton gave his summing up, he put doubt into the jurors' minds that these might have been genuine events occurring on a different day. I have never spent a more anxious time until the jury came back and announced their *not guilty* verdict on 16 May.

It would have been very unsafe to convict on the evidence of a man who was himself implicated in the crime. Even the prosecutor said that everything that happened in the van at the time Mitchell was allegedly killed rested on the evidence of Albert Donoghue. My defence brought 17 witnesses to establish bias by Donoghue and four alibis as to my whereabouts.

Prison officers at Leicester told me that if I was indeed guilty of the crime, I had performed a public service and should be awarded a medal the size of a dustbin lid. That's how much terror Mitchell had struck into everybody's heart. And in a sense, when Mitchell climbed into the back of that van, it marked the end of all his troubles too.

CHAPTER 14
MUDDY WATERS

Although his conduct of the case was disgraceful, Judge Melford Stevenson will never know how accurate some of his remarks were when summing up in the Kray trial in March 1969. Before sentencing me to 10 years for being an accessory *after* the fact in the McVitie murder case, he said, 'The needs of justice sometimes require that truth should be dredged from very muddy waters. When you start that kind of dredging, what you may bring up from these muddy waters may be very disagreeable indeed.'

Well, that worked both ways. I agree that some of the things we did then were murky, but I was not happy about the administration of criminal justice. Before Melford Stevenson sentenced me, he asked the crown prosecutor, Mr Jones QC, what the maximum was, adding that he was thinking of giving me and Charlie Kray life imprisonment. Mr Jones told the judge the maximum was 10. Until 1967 you could receive a life sentence for it, but this was 1969.

I've had a lot of time to think about the reason I got such a stiff sentence. I started to think about the trial, and in particular what happened as I stood in the dock, when Melford Stevenson began to stare at me across the courtroom. It was an evil stare, and he held eye contact for what seemed like an eternity. Everyone was wondering what I'd done to piss him off. I came to reckon it was because my old friend Bernard Cauldfield had mentioned my name to him, perhaps in the hope it might make him give me a leaner sentence. I had noticed Bernard on the bench when the trial began, but he had disappeared just after the lunch break, making me wonder whether he'd come to dine with Melford Stevenson. As my old friend Joe Pyle said in one of his poems:

It's said a good lawyer has plenty of punch,
But the clever one though,
Takes the judge out to lunch!

I can only assume that this had backfired, and the judge had been offended by the suggestion. When the sentencing came around, he tried to life me off. He read out the verdict of life imprisonment, but the prosecution, Kenneth Jones, QC, stood up, and announced, 'M'Lord, this doesn't carry a life sentence, it was accessory after the fact of murder.'

I had nothing to do with the McVitie killing. My role in this never-ending saga, which I now hope to put to rest, was a very limited one. I got rid of the body for two reasons. One: because it had been put on my doorstep and threatened my own safety. And two: as a favour to the Krays.

Dumping Jack 'The Hat''s body on my doorstep was stupid. I was one of the last people who had a public showdown with McVitie when he caused trouble in my 211 Club in Balham. It would have been very convenient for the police if he'd been found dead on my side of the water. It put me in great jeopardy. Not only was I charged over his disappearance, but I found myself in the dock of the Old Bailey with the Kray Firm, who faced *two* murder charges – for George Cornell and Jack McVitie.

The two cases were tried together. For those who were not involved in the Cornell affair, this was an affront to natural justice. You became 'guilty' by association and that same jury who watched you in the dock now had to decide about you in a second trial. If ever there was a miscarriage of justice, that was one!

Cornell was shot in the Blind Beggar pub on Mile End Road on 9 March 1966. He and a bookmaker friend, Albie Woods, had visited Jimmy Andrews, who'd been shot in the leg and was recovering in the

London Hospital, Aldgate. Cornell was connected to the Richardson firm and had called Ronnie Kray a 'big fat poof' behind his back, so he was a marked man. It was claimed that Ronnie boasted to associates about killing him – 'I put a couple of bullets in Cornell's head. I took his fucking head off' – though this was not true.

McVitie had worked for the Krays, but was eventually regarded as a liability. The Twins said of him, 'His big problem was he liked to drink a lot, but he couldn't hold his drink. He got nasty. McVitie started to let us down. He went into the 211 Club in Balham High Road, which was owned by our friend Freddie Foreman. McVitie was drunk, so Freddie told him to leave and he did.

'He upset another friend of ours, Ron Oliffe, in a club called the Log Cabin, in Wardour Street, which the boxer Billy Walker had an interest in with his brother George. Then he misbehaved himself in our club, the Regency. He took a gun out and fired a couple of shots at a fella called Tommy Flannagan. Thank Christ he missed. Then he cut a fella with a knife in the basement, walked upstairs and wiped off the blood on his knife on the dress of a woman who was having a drink at the bar.'

McVitie was killed by Reggie Kray at a party in Blonde Carol Skinner's flat in 71 Evering Road on Saturday, 28 October 1967. His cousin, Ronnie Hart, who later gave evidence against all of us, was present. As far as I can make it out, and from what the Twins told me, it was not premeditated murder but a spontaneous action that resulted from Jack's behaviour at the Regency Club, which the Twins minded for the Barrys, one of whom was in the dock with us. Jack 'The Hat' had shot the place up and the Barrys demanded to know why the Twins couldn't keep 'this cunt out of here'. The Twins called Jack to the party in Evering Road, where they were going to chastise him. The Lambrianou brothers, Chris and Tony, were despatched to the Regency to bring him over to Blonde Carol's. But the whole thing got out of hand. The Barrys had supplied a gun with a faulty mechanism. It would not shoot, but it was intended to scare him. I think they forgot there were other ways to skin a cat.

When he came to the flat, Reggie went through the motion of shooting him, but of course the gun didn't work. Instead, they were going to give him a good battering. But it went too far: someone brought Reggie a carving knife from the kitchen, which he used to stab

McVitie, plunging him in the body. I can confirm that there were no injuries to the face or neck as has been reported. The fact that there were a lot of people there – more than a dozen witnesses – is additional proof that it had not been premeditated. If Jack had played his cards right he could have walked away from that flat, but he was so high on amphetamines that he became brave. He even took his coat off and challenged them. This is when Ronnie told Reg, 'Kill the bastard.' If, however, they had intended to kill McVitie from the start, they would have done it differently. Looking back on it now, the lawyers could have emphasised this point more at the time: it was not a premeditated killing, but a fight that went wrong. Those harsh sentences of 20 and 30 years resulting from this gangland fight would never have been applied today. Ronnie Bender got 20 years for cleaning up blood stains!

The Lambrianous and Ronnie Bender dumped the body on my doorstep in Bermondsey, just down the road from the pub. Ronnie had a go at them. 'You fools,' he roared. 'You went and dumped it right there on Fred's doorstep, knowing he had a row at the 211 Club a few months earlier!'

McVitie was wrapped in Blonde Carol's bedspread, and the cleaning tabs would have traced it back to her flat immediately if the police had found the body. The corpse was slumped in the back seat of the car, which had been parked outside a church in Bermondsey. Afterwards, Charlie Kray was woken up and taken to a safe house in north London where everyone was stowed away. Like Charlie, I'd also been in bed that night and neither of us knew what had gone on. Tommy Cowley came over to my pub between two and three o'clock in the morning to knock me up and tell me that they'd dumped Jack 'The Hat' down the road, not far away. I didn't see who was with him, because whoever it was, had parked round the corner. Hart swore in court that it was Charlie, but in fact it was Tommy Cowley. It would not have been sensible to go out between 4am and 5am, before there was any traffic on the road.

At about 5am, a few hours after Cowley left, I went out to look for the body. The Lambrianous and Bender couldn't remember exactly where they'd dumped McVitie, so I drove around the streets searching for the car. I spotted this battered old Zephyr with a different coloured wing, broken lights and only one windscreen wiper working. It was all locked up, so I had to force the window open with a screwdriver. I could see McVitie lying across the back seat. Fortunately, it was a horrible winter's morning, pissing down with rain. I had a set of keys and found one that would fit the ignition but I could hardly see a thing as I drove away. Alf tailed me in a back-up car and I drove with the body in the back all the way up to Camberwell Green and garaged it in a lock-up. I took a liberty with myself doing that. It wasn't daylight and I could easily have got pulled for a number of reasons. I transferred the body to a van and disposed of McVitie's Ford Zephyr motor in a wreckers' yard. No trace of it was ever found.

On the following Monday, I drove his body down to the coast with a back-up motor minding me off. And that was the end of Jack 'The Hat' McVitie. We had a friend on the coast who wrapped him up in chicken wire attached to weights. Our contacts with certain fishermen who'd helped us with smuggling had been kept alive and they were now called in to help out again. As with Ginger Marks and Frank 'The Mad Axeman' Mitchell, Jack 'The Hat' McVitie was buried far out at sea, away from the fishing lanes, deep beneath the 'muddy waters' Justice Stevenson spoke of in his summing-up to the jury. We had been told by American contacts that bodies weighted down in this way would never find their way to the surface but would slowly be disposed of by crabs and other deep-sea dwellers. Many people prefer burial at sea...

I was protecting the Twins. The rule of thumb was, where there is no body, there is no evidence and therefore no conviction. Before McVitie, the one exception to this rule that I could remember took place on an ocean liner when a steward was convicted of the rape and murder of a young woman called Gay Gibson. After killing her, he pushed her body through a porthole into the ocean and she was never found. In spite of the lack of evidence, he was convicted.

For our part, we felt fairly safe once we had properly disposed of a body. But I felt very bitter about Hart involving my friends and it seemed very odd that Tommy Cowley walked out of the case at the early stages. He was a ginger-headed little geezer who thought he was something special because he worked for the Twins. Tommy was a collector; a nothing. If he hadn't been with them, he would have been annihilated for his flash behaviour. Tommy had also brought the Mini car used by Reggie Kray to drive away from the scene of the murder. He parked it near my pub with telltale blood stains in it. They wanted it cleaned and washed up, which it was. A few days later, they picked it up again and took it to a black cab depot near Vallance Road. Witnesses who spotted the car there were called to give evidence at the trial. Tommy Cowley was a slippery little fucker whom I never liked and one of the first to grass to Nipper Read, whom he secretly met in Wandsworth Prison library in the dead of night. He was on remand with us in Brixton, a couple of cells along from Charlie, myself and the Twins. On returning from a court appearance, Tommy was transferred to Wandsworth Prison, and we never saw him again.

I was also surprised that John Barry, whom I later met in prison when he was awaiting trial for armed robbery, had also given evidence against us. Even one of the Mills brothers from Ladbroke Grove, one of the respected families, gave evidence against us, which was very disappointing. Another was Charlie Mitchell (no relation to Frank Mitchell). He too gave evidence for the prosecution at Bow Street Magistrates' Court and was never seen for years until he turned up in Spain. He came to a sticky end – battered by a Spanish doorman, he drowned in his own blood.

On the day the Twins were arrested, I went to their flat in Bunhill Row, Clerkenwell. There had been nothing in the news, so I wasn't expecting any bother when I took the lift to their floor. As I got out of the elevator, though, the whole landing was full of policemen. The Twins' front door was off its hinges and leaning against the wall. The police were all standing about. I walked straight through them and past, as if on a mission. I didn't know where I was going and it was a long corridor. They would be watching me, so I didn't want to head for an exit. Thankfully, they were local cossers and hadn't recognised me. As I got to the end of the corridor, I rang at the door of one of the flats. It was opened by a young married woman. 'Excuse me, love,' I said. 'There's a bit of a problem up the end at Mrs Kray's, do you mind if I step in for a bit?' She invited me in for a cup of tea. I told her I was sorry to intrude and explained that I had called to see the Twins and had clearly not picked a good time.

She told me the cossers had been there and smashed the door down. 'There's hundreds of them, but you can stay as long as you like,' she said.

We chatted for a while and then she showed me the exit downstairs, which I used to get out of the building. Fortunately, I managed to slip the net and didn't return to my house or to the flat above the pub but went straight on my toes again. I didn't want to disappear in case the Twins needed my help, but I was told to fuck off by Frank Williams. He said I would be better off keeping out of it.

I kept in touch and stayed at a hotel for quite a few weeks. Apparently, Nipper Read was very keen to arrest me because Hart and one or two of the other witnesses wouldn't give evidence while I was at large. But I didn't know that at the time, otherwise I would have made sure I stayed well away, even though I would have had every copper in the world looking for me. Eventually, I was arrested in my pub after going there to see if everything was all right. I met with a few friends – Micky Regan, Patsy O'Mara and Ronnie Oliffe – and after they all went, I left the pub to walk over to my Mercedes. As I got in, they sprung me: Read, Cater and a copper called Ian St John – the murder squad. They took me to Tintagel House, where I was formally charged. Nipper Read was an unassuming type and didn't employ any bullying tactics. In fact, both Read and Cater were quite polite to me.

One of the police officers said I was a bonus to the Twins. They knew I would move heaven and earth to help anybody. At one stage there was a suggestion that I was implicated in the Cornell case. It was claimed that I had delivered the guns to the Twins at a party and that one of those guns was used to kill Cornell. Thankfully, the court accepted it was untrue. Nevertheless, I was made to sit in the dock for six weeks with people like the Lambrianous, whom I'd never seen before.

When I complained, I was told by my QC to keep quiet and not to make a fuss and upset the judge, who would carry on with the trial with or without me. The lawyers promised they would try and get a severance of the trial so that the Cornell case and the McVitie case would be tried separately. Neither me, Charlie, Tony Barry, Ronnie Bender nor the Lambrianous was involved with Cornell, yet we had to sit through the Cornell trial without our names being mentioned at all. At one stage, Judge Melford Stevenson even tried to hang numbers around our necks like Nazi war criminals. I shouted out, 'What's this, a fucking cattle market? Or are we fucking Nazi war criminals? I'm not putting that around my neck,' tore it up and threw it in the air resulting in an awful commotion in the dock. Screws were leaning over trying to quieten people down and there were a number of scuffles and chairs going over. At one stage it got quite ugly in the dock, until finally the judge relented about the numbers. I spread further chaos by changing seats with Scotch Pat so they didn't know who was who. He had been 24 stone, but had now apparently halved his weight! Scotch Pat and Fat Wally had been in bed with a barmaid and the question had been raised of whether the bed had been constructed with scaffolding, because their combined weight of about 60 stone would have been too much for any bed in the UK! The trial was a complete farce.

Even the way we were brought to the court each day from Brixton Prison was prejudicial to our case. We were bundled into a 'meat wagon' (prison van) and locked inside rabbit-hutch cells – they were like empty cupboards with nothing to hang on to and driven at high speed with motorbike escorts and a fanfare of sirens and klaxons blasting away until we reached the Old Bailey, making it look like we were all highly dangerous enemies of the state. Fumes would escape into these hutches and most prisoners were sick in them.

Each day a different route was used, although you could hear us coming for miles. One time, a police outrider went skidding along the road and we all tut-tutted, saying what a shame it was. But there was no need for the break-neck speed. The drivers were simply intent on beating their record (under 10 minutes) in getting from Brixton to the court. It was frightening and we used to give the warders a lot of verbal over the way they treated us on the journey. They'd race through red lights and police ahead would stop traffic. The only light note to this was when we drove down The Cut near Blackfriars, and past my old favourite pie and mash shop. All the staff knew me there because I'd patronised the shop with my family and had once tossed out four pests who were drunk and being silly and the staff were delighted. Now, when we drove past their place, they were all waiting to cheer and wave to me as the prison van blasted its way down the road.

In his summing-up, Judge Stevenson observed, 'No one disputes the fact that Cornell was murdered. That he died as a result of a pistol wound in the Blind Beggar. In the McVitie case there is no body. There is no clear, undisputed evidence of his death, and the prosecution say that his death is a matter you are forced to infer from the evidence they have been able to call. The witness Ronald Hart called for a closer consideration than anybody else in the case... the suggestion is made that Hart is really the murderer... we start on the fact that he is himself a self-confessed murderer. He has admitted joining in the violence as a result of which McVitie is said to have died. He has implicated a large number of people in the dock and that excites dislike in all of us. The dislike of what we used to call a sneak.'

The jury delivered its verdict on 4 March 1969 after retiring for 6 hours and 55 minutes. The trial had lasted 39 days and we were sentenced the next day – my 37th birthday. I was found guilty of being accessory after the fact of McVitie together with Charlie Kray and Connie Whitehead. Later, Charlie and I were taken separately from our cells to the solicitor's room, where further charges were made. Nipper Read, Cater and my defence counsel had heads bowed and looked very glum. Nipper Read said, 'I understand it's your birthday Fred – I have some very bad news, we are charging you with the murder of Frank Mitchell. Have you anything to say?' I looked at my lawyers (Tom Williams and Ivor Richard). They just shook their heads so I replied, 'No comment.' I was returned to the cell, where Charlie and Connie Whitehead were waiting anxiously. Charlie was next to be charged with the Mitchell murder and came back visibly distressed.

Ronnie Kray was found guilty of the murder of George Cornell and Jack McVitie. Reginald Kray, Christopher Lambrianou, Anthony Lambrianou and Ronald Albert Bender were also found guilty of McVitie. Anthony Thomas Barry was found not guilty of the murder and discharged. John Alexander Barrie, a Scotsman who was not in any way connected with the London Barry family, was found guilty in the Cornell murder. All he had done was to discharge a gun in the ceiling, and for that he received a 20-year sentence.

The Twins were sentenced to life imprisonment and Melford Stevenson recommended they be detained for a minimum of 30 years, the longest murder sentences ever passed at the Central Criminal Court. He said to Ronnie, 'I am not going to waste words on you. The sentence is that of life imprisonment. In my view society has earned a rest from your activities.' Reggie was handed out the same treatment and Charlie, like me, got 10 years. Donoghue, who admitted guilt and grassed on us, got two years for the same offence.

There was a curious sequel to this case. On 20 January 1970, three men were sent for trial at the Old Bailey from Bow Street Magistrates' Court. They were accused of conspiring together, between 2 December and 12 December 1969, to defeat the course of public justice by attempting to persuade Ronald Hart, by threats and inducements, to make a written statement that differed in material particulars from the evidence given by Hart on oath at the Central Criminal Court at our trial, which had ended on 5 March 1969.

Understandably, there had never been a case quite like it. Two of the men, Derek Higgins, a private investigator, and Alexander Thomson, my solicitor's managing clerk, were both ex-policemen working on the case for my appeal. The third man, Kenneth Prater, was a journalist. All were respectable people gathering evidence for Brendan Quirke, my solicitor. They had arranged to see Hart – at his suggestion – to question him about the evidence he had given in court. After my trial, Maureen got a call out of the blue from Ronnie Hart. He said that he had told a pack of lies at the trial and was now under a lot of pressure and needed money to get away, but wanted to put things right first. Maureen was too clever to take this at face value. She told Hart that if he wanted to talk about my case, he should ring my solicitor and gave him the number. Hart said he would ring again and this time she had Higgins there to record the conversation. Hart repeated what he said before but kept asking for help. Maureen then came to see me at Leicester Prison to discuss his offer. I told her I didn't trust him one bit. If he had been prepared to tell lies at our trial he was probably just trying to set us up for something now, I warned.

My lawyers felt they were on the verge of winning my appeal and were quite excited by the prospect of getting a statement from him. The worrying thing, though, was the way he said he wanted money to disappear. He asked, 'How much will you give me to go away?' and other leading questions like: 'Will I be all right with Fred afterwards? I know what I done to him but I will say whatever you want me to say. How much will you give me?' At the meeting, the three men were set up for a police bust. Holes had been drilled in the walls of the room from the adjoining house so police could listen in and bug the conversations. During the meeting, DCI Frank Cater arrested Higgins and Thomson. The original charge of conspiracy without details of the accusation was withdrawn at the request of the prosecution.

At their Old Bailey trial in May, the prosecutor John Leonard claimed that Hart was threatened by one of the accused and that the journalist had asked Hart to provide 'loopholes' so that the Home

Secretary could be petitioned for my release. It was alleged that Hart was told by the accused that I had access to the proceeds of the Great Train Robbery.

Quite rightly, the men pleaded not guilty. Mr Leonard said that Hart had given evidence in the trial to the effect that once McVitie had been stabbed, the Krays gave orders for the body to be taken 'over the water' for disposal by 'Freddie'. After the trial, Hart and his family were given a secret address in Essex, but Prater the journalist traced him and introduced him to Higgins and Thomson. The prosecutor said the impression was given that they were planning a French TV film on crime in London. After their first meeting, a '£5 note was left on Hart's table for his trouble'. Higgins was reputed to have said, 'Foreman is a rich man and you will not come to any harm... If Foreman has to sit for 10 years thinking about the man who put him away he is bound to get him when he comes out.' Hart was allegedly offered £500, or the cost of fares for his wife and family to emigrate or take a holiday to Australia. Another meeting was arranged, but only Higgins and Thomson arrived. The prosecutor said the journalist had got 'cold feet'. A two-hour interview at that meeting with Hart was recorded on tape by the police. But after just one-and-a-half days of the trial, the judge ordered their acquittal. Common Sergeant Judge Griffith-Jones observed, 'There was no doubt that the defendants were employed in various inquiries and to see whether anything could be properly done to submit "something" [fresh evidence] to the Home Secretary regarding Foreman.' Nevertheless, the men were not reimbursed for the money they had deposited towards their legal-aid costs. Bearing in mind the tapes and transcripts, Griffith-Jones said they had 'brought matters upon themselves'.

His view was not shared by the press. The *Sunday Times* took up the cudgel, describing the proceedings as THE CASE THEY HAD TO DROP. The newspaper said the case 'represents an amazing piece of back-tracking by the Crown in two hazy areas of British law – conspiracy and the perversion of public justice. On the charge sheet these two were linked together and resulted in what is thought to be a unique indictment... there have been many cases in which it has been alleged that people have tried to sway the evidence of prospective witnesses *before* a trial but never *after* a conviction. It is significant that the original charge had to be amended three times before the trial and that the Crown seem to have had considerable difficulty in preparing the indictment.'

Originally, the charge had simply been 'conspiring together to defeat the course of public justice'. At the committal, the prosecution added the following details: 'by attempting to persuade Ronald Hart by threats and inducements, to make a written statement that differed in material particulars from the evidence he gave at the Old Bailey Kray trial'. The 'threats and inducement' were omitted on the indictment and before the case opened the defence applied to quash it by suggesting it disclosed no offence in law. Judge Mervyn Griffith-Jones did not accept this, but agreed to an alteration in the wording of the indictment so that the final version read: 'attempting to persuade Hart to make a false statement...' The jury was told the police had set up the meeting when Hart contacted them after he had been approached by Higgins and Thomson to talk about the Foreman conviction. The police recorded the two-and-a-half-hour conversation from a vacant house next door.

On the morning of the second day of the trial, the prosecution asked for a one-hour adjournment. This was granted and at the end of it, prosecution counsel made the surprise offer of 'no evidence'. The explanation for this was quite simple, the *Sunday Times* said, 'For the case to succeed the prosecution would have to prove that Higgins and Thomson believed Hart's evidence at the trial to be true and they were therefore trying to persuade him to make a "false" statement. If they had merely tried to discover if he had lied, they were committing no offence and therefore it would not be right to leave it to the jury. For this reason, no evidence was offered.' The *Sunday Times* was surprised that in view of the cost it would have taken to bring this prosecution to trial, it was remarkable they proceeded without more careful examination of their chances of success. The newspaper said the plain facts were that the two former policemen appeared to have been acting quite lawfully in carrying out the instructions of a reputable firm of solicitors, Quicke and Co. 'Furthermore such inquiries are carried out regularly by solicitors and bodies like Justice and the National Council for Civil Liberties and from time to time by newspapers and it has always been accepted that prosecution witnesses may be interviewed in such circumstances.'

Writing to the president of the Law Society, Mr Brendan Quirke noted, 'It is a sorry day when the managing clerk of a responsible firm of solicitors who was acting properly, regularly and in consultation with counsel can be arrested and thrown into prison and detained for 14 hours.' Thomson, his clerk, was not allowed any contact with his solicitor. The *Sunday Times* commented, 'One can only ask why the police brought this prosecution. The effect of it could only be to deter perfectly legitimate inquiries. In the circumstances the judge's decision that the two defendants should pay towards their costs seems completely unjust. Bearing in mind the fact that these men will receive no compensation for their loss of business it seems a particularly harsh one.'

After the failed prosecution of Higgins and Thomson, on 13 June police went to Hart's Harwich home, apparently by chance, and found him bleeding heavily from deep cuts in his left arm. Hart had apparently tried to kill himself and had written a letter in which he revealed he had been 'under constant worry and pressure' over what was going to happen to him for telling the truth. Based on what Hart told Higgins and Thomson, a petition was sent to the Home Secretary asking for my case to be reopened.

But the authorities focused on fighting my appeal. Fresh statements against me were now made by Chris Lambrianou, who had been sentenced to life with a recommendation of 15 years and clearly thought that by telling the police everything, he would do himself a favour. He tidied the case up for the prosecution, filling in the gaps regarding all the details, taking McVitie through the Rotherhithe tunnel and leaving the body in the car near the church. Afterwards, my solicitors said it would be better if I didn't see his statement. It was very damning for me. That clinched it as far as they were concerned. My appeal was thrown out. But his statement did him little good. At the end of the day, he didn't get any remission and served his full 15 years.

Tony Lambrianou was a different class altogether. He had the bottle to drive the car with McVitie's body in the back seat and the sense to keep his mouth shut afterwards and do his bird like a man.

I felt sorry for Ronnie Bender when he was sentenced. He got 20 years, five more than the Lambrianous, for annoying Melford Stevenson and disrupting court proceedings. Melford Stevenson had annoyed all of us by putting on a great show for the jury whenever something was said in our favour that he disagreed with. He'd sit up and contort his face in a way that undoubtedly influenced the jury. Ronnie Bender got his own back by blowing his nose very loudly whenever the judge spoke. Stevenson would glare at him, but got his revenge at the end when he dished out five years to him on top of what the others got. So much for impartiality and treating people equally. But in this case, the government really felt they had nailed the sixties gangs and cleaned up London. The Richardsons were first, followed by the Krays, the Tibbs and the Dixon families. If I had got off the charges, Charlie Kray would also have to be acquitted and that was the last thing the judiciary wanted.

CHAPTER 15
BANGED UP

On the night of Saturday, 21 December 1991, six screws, a senior officer and a deputy duty governor were held hostage by masked prisoners at HMP Full Sutton, in York. I was asked by other prisoners to help resolve the situation. During the five-hour siege, the deputy came to within a hair's-breadth of having his throat cut with a pair of garden shears and the six prison officers were in danger of being battered to a pulp. The atmosphere was charged to the point where it was ready to explode into violent blood-letting. Outside the prison doors, armed police officers, wearing visors and padded jackets, wielding tear-gas, clubs, and riot gear, were impatient to rush in and put their sticks about. It was strange you could never recognise them – they must have been brought in from other prisons. (Later, I found out that the government use the SAS to do the dirty work.)

I was caught in the middle with 300 angry prisoners around me, some of them inciting fellow inmates to kill the screws. As frequently happens with these situations, the Home Office was brilliant at covering up the incident – to this day, the press and public are unaware of what happened. During the riot, thousands of pounds of public money was wasted and I put it down to the obstinacy of those in authority.

While serving time, I made many friends among chaps in prison and I owe a debt of thanks to an articulate and clever pal called Norman Parker for defining the meaning of the phrase 'one of the *chaps*' in his book *Parkhurst Tales*. I have used his definition on the first page of this book: 'Chaps, an almost mythical grouping of criminals whose ethos includes: professionalism in the pursuit of crime; loyalty to others of their kind; hatred of and non-cooperation with authority; and courage. Many aspire to membership, few qualify.'

Chaps who are sent to prison always remain the same. I have always come out of prison the same way as I went in. It has never changed me. That is what makes villains 'chaps'. They don't graft or grovel to people. They just get their heads down and get on with it. And they are better prisoners to have, because they keep a steadying influence in prison life. The people who run prisons – the governors and prison officers – usually appreciate their level-headedness, too. They stand for common sense and fairness, but in sticking to these principles, they can just as easily be sent down the block as they can be instrumental in saving lives of prison staff. In either case, they expect no thanks. All they expect is to be treated in a civil and fair manner, a basic courtesy that should be extended to everybody, regardless of their status. What the authorities have not yet woken up to is that taking a man's liberty is sufficient punishment. You don't have to take his dignity as well. A short, sharp shock is much better.

Joe Martin is probably the longest-serving prisoner in Britain. He was jailed for 18 years, but he's been inside for 32! It seems like the Home Office has been interfering with the judge's recommendations again. The killing he was accused of was accidental. He might have lost a little remission when he once tried to escape, but to keep a man locked up for so long is unacceptable. By coincidence, some of my mates – Joey Martin, Tommy Wisbey, Bobby Welch and Georgie Stevens – were all involved in that escape bid from Leicester security wing. When I arrived, Bobby had just undergone a simple cartilage operation to his knee in the prison hospital. But complications set in and he has suffered great pain ever since and can only get about with the aid of two walking sticks. He is a lovely man and a good friend and I am sorry to see him suffer all these years after that prison operation – but he may well talk about that one day in his own book.

George was a real character. His pet budgie, his only friend in life; flew away. He was in an adjoining cell to me and drove me fucking nuts calling out to his budgie; he was always asking me if I could spot it. From our cells we could only see the top of a tree across the prison walls, the highest in the country, and I told Georgie that if he was up there, other birds would eat him. He spent hours calling to his little friend. The next day Maureen visited and to shut him up I asked her to buy him a budgie. Maureen, who hates birds owing to a traumatic incident in her childhood, went to great pains to buy him a pair, which he named 'Maureen' and 'Fred'. This was a great sacrifice for my Maureen, whose phobia about birds wouldn't normally allow her anywhere near one of our feathered friends, let alone to walk into a pet shop to buy one.

The thing about being one of the chaps is that you acquire a high profile. The screws see the way other prisoners treat you and that identifies you as a high-profile prisoner, which has its good and bad points. The upside is that you get respect; the downside is that you prejudice your chance of parole.

So while I was commended at Full Sutton for defusing a powder-keg situation, it did me no favours regarding early parole. The six officers were held hostage in D wing over an incident that could have been solved within minutes. A prisoner from up north had received a visit on the Saturday afternoon and word spread that he had been beaten up afterwards. The prisoner's pals demanded to see the prison officer in charge to make sure their mate was all right. By 7.30pm the situation had become so volatile that I was called to try and straighten things out. I went to the main office on the wing to make some sense of what was going on as the prisoners refused to be banged up in their cells until they were sure nothing had happened to their pal.

The prison governor was not on duty that night. I told his duty governor that all it needed was for one prisoner to go down to the block and see if his mate – whom they thought had been beaten up – was all right. If he was, they'd all go back to their cells. But the duty governor refused. He said he wasn't going to have prisoners dictate to him. The situation became more charged.

Among the prison population were a large number of political prisoners who helped stir things up. Next thing we knew, the authorities called for one of the visiting magistrates, who sat on the prison board, to come in as a negotiator, together with the number five governor, an ex-priest. It was all a waste of time.

The prison exploded. A lot of angry and frustrated prisoners broke into the kitchens at about 11pm, grabbing kitchen knives and any other tools they could lay their hands on, including the garden shears. Some disguised themselves in home-made balaclavas and began smashing up toilets and sinks. By now, the prison authorities had a full-scale riot on their hands.

While the northern boys were foaming at the mouth, a few of us London fellows were trying to be sensible. I even tried to get authorisation for a signed note from the prisoner to say he was not injured, which would have appeased the men. But it was not allowed.

At midnight, the screws had to run the gauntlet to a back room. Some of them were as young as my sons and they were really frightened, on the verge of tears. They were pleading: 'Don't leave us, Foreman, stay here!' The corridor outside was crowded with prisoners wanting to have a go at them.

I told the cons to calm down: 'We're looking at a 10 stretch on top of our bird,' I warned.

As I say, there were a lot of Paddys trying to incite the riot and disrupt the prison system. People had their own motives and you found yourself being manipulated by a number of sectional interests. On top of that, I was being put up as the number one rioter. The prison governor and several POs were now talking on the telephone. The guv'nor came on the phone to me and said, 'Foreman, you are now in control of the wing.

'Its not my fucking wing,' I replied.

Outside, the riot troops eagerly awaited a chance to get at us and were only stopped because of the ridiculous design of the doors. They opened inwards and the prisoners had jammed them tight with furniture from cells. There was no possibility of escape, but quite a lot of damage had been done. I still had to wrestle a couple of mad Paddys to stop them cutting an officer's throat and getting us all extra bird.

Eventually, someone was allowed to go down to see if the 'injured' prisoner was fit. There wasn't a mark on him. It had all been one gigantic fuck-up. I then negotiated with the authorities for an undertaking that there would be no recriminations. I told them that providing no prisoner was arrested or charged, everyone would return peacefully to their cells. Both sides honoured the undertaking. But none of that should ever have happened. Apart from the financial loss, several men nearly lost their lives, all because the men were not given proof that a fellow prisoner had not been assaulted. Once again, the taxpayers were the losers, and the incident was hushed up to save embarrassment to the prison service and the Home Secretary.

Thank God, an old pal of mine wasn't there at the time. The notorious Charlie Bronson is a legend in British prisons up and down the country. A brief rundown of his record explains why. Charlie has spent more than 25 years in prison and has been moved over 135 times to 60 different jails. He's ripped off about six prison roofs, taken some five hostages, and assaulted about 20 screws. He arrived at Full Sutton just after the riot. I'd met him a few times over the years and we had mutual respect for each other. His real name is Peterson, but he changed his name, claiming that he was the 'real Charlie Bronson' and that prison authorities should recognise him as such. He is built like a brick shithouse with the strength to match and once did a record 2,000 sit-ups with a medicine ball.

Originally, he began a simple four-year sentence, but because of his behaviour in prison, he ended up doing 14 years inside. He is now institutionalised. At present he is in top-security Belmarsh jail after taking a prison doctor hostage at Winson Green.

I had the pleasure of his company for about two months at Full Sutton. On one night two brothers badly upset Charlie after trading verbal insults with him across the yard. Frustrated, Charlie smashed up the furniture in his cell. In the morning, at opening up time, everyone stepped out of their cells into the corridor, yawning and scratching their bollocks, when out jumped Charlie into the passageway like Rambo. He was stark bollock naked, covered from head to toe in black shoe-polish and only wearing a bandanna around his head. Wielding a table leg in one hand, and a broom handle sharpened into a spear in the other, he raged down the passageway. As he did so, all you could hear was cell doors clanging shut as other prisoners stepped back into their cells a bit lively at this awesome sight. Charlie's tantrums resulted in four assaults on screws and one fractured skull, which he'd cracked with the table leg.

Some two hours later, while he was still on the loose, I asked to see if I could deal with him together with another young lifer called Mark Edmonds who was also a pal. We found Charlie crouched in a small recess ready to do battle. Preparing for a counter-assault at each end of the wing was the mufti in full gladiatorial regalia. We coaxed Charlie into the bathroom, got him into a nice hot bath and began scrubbing the boot polish off, while I scolded him like a naughty schoolboy: 'You fucked up again, Charlie. I thought you liked it here. You are with nice people, we have a drink of hooch over weekends, you sing your songs [he did a great impersonation of Louis Armstrong singing 'What A Wonderful World'] and now you've fucked up.'

After we'd made him presentable, Charlie said to me, 'Don't let them take me down the block, Fred, you take me.'

So I spoke to the PO and they were quite willing to let me and young Mark escort him down the block without any aggravation. Obviously, Charlie is a sick man and needs help. But the prison system has brutalised him.

He was later moved to Parkhurst, where he upset some of the chaps – though I think they might have overreacted, bearing in mind Charlie's reputation. Charlie, in his crazy way, had decided to dig a fish pond near the running track. As prisoners ran past, dirt was falling back into the hole, which upset Charlie. He jumped out gesticulating and calling them 'Fucking LGs', meaning London Gangster – fighting talk used by non-Londoners. As a result, Charlie was served up severely by a number of the chaps and he got himself stabbed. He lost six pints of blood and was in intensive care, but survived and is still up to his old tricks. I'll always have fond memories of Charlie, but on that occasion he stepped out of line when he should have known better.

I have spent too many years in prison. But compared to some people, I haven't done badly. Most prisoners I knew didn't look on prison as a reforming institute. It was more a breeding ground of information, like university; a place where you learned all the tricks of the trade. That's why they don't work. They just teach you better skills and show you your real vocation in life – doing something you're good at, like thieving. They leave men bitter and twisted and break up families. Children forget their parents and the whole family unit breaks down. Long sentences have never achieved anything.

I began my sentence for McVitie at Leicester. We had been dispersed from Brixton to different prisons around the country. The Twins and Charlie Kray were sent to separate prisons. Ronnie to Durham, Reg went to Parkhurst and Charlie to Chelmsford. Whichever prison you go to, you are bound to know people. At Leicester, apart from Bobby Welch, whom I've already mentioned, I ran into Charlie Richardson, who was doing a 25 over the torture trial; Billy Gentry, serving a 17 for armed robbery; Tony Dunsford, a double-lifer; and Nobby Clark, also a double-lifer who looked like the old film actor John Carradine. While in prison, both Tony and Nobby had killed again. They found Nobby dragging a young guy down a corridor with wire flex around his neck, attempting to hide him in a cupboard. I'd known Charlie and his brother Eddie, and Billy Gentry prior to arriving, and got on OK with them. But I also met other prisoners such as Micky Kehoe, who was to become a friend for many years after.

Leicester special wing, occupying an isolated high-security corner of the prison, was to be my home for the next four years. To reach our quarters, visitors would be brought through a series of passageways and gates and then made to sit across a large table. No physical touch was allowed and two screws sat next to you with notepads, listening to every word you said. Prison life was extremely limited. The only time we left the wing was to go to the sewing-machine shop and a small, caged exercise yard. We were completely isolated and never saw other prisoners in the main wings. There were only eight prisoners at any one time, year in year out; and you got sick to death of seeing the same faces. The security was unbelievable.

One of the madmen in our section was Arthur Hosein. He and his brother Nizam kidnapped and murdered Mrs Muriel McKay, whom they mistook for Anna Murdoch, wife of media tycoon Rupert Murdoch. Hosein would walk around singing, 'I want to be a millionaire…' He was completely round the twist. We'd play football and he would snatch the ball and run away with it, giggling and laughing. He wasn't special-wing material and everyone despised him for what he'd done. He wasn't accepted as one of the chaps. It was only a matter of time before one of us knocked him out. That honour eventually went to 'Hate 'Em All Harry'.

Hosein had grown his thumbnails to an extraordinary length and filed them to a razor-sharp point. He slashed his own brother, Nizamodeen, across the cheek when he'd made statements to assist the police. The other cons in the wing were concerned about his 'lethal' weapons. An opportunity arose one day when Arthur volunteered to cook one of his curries. I booked out a pair of scissors, grabbed his arm under mine and cut off both thumbnails: 'You can't cook food for us, Arthur, with dirty fingernails,' I told him. Arthur protested loudly, 'No, no, no Mr Freddie,' but it was too late. I had cut him down to size.

Naturally enough, living in such close quarters resulted in tensions and fights; having eight prisoners crammed in a small space was bound to have this effect. You get on one another's nerves and the slightest little thing upsets you. Charlie Richardson had a proper row with Ronnie Bender, providing us with good entertainment. People fought each other for no reason at all. Every few months, a new face would appear and you'd drain every bit of information and news out of him. It was always a disappointment when an old face returned, because you wanted somebody new.

Reggie Kray arrived at one point, in exchange for another con. After a few days he had a few heated words with Peter Hurley, a strong and fit young guy. I stepped in just before the row started, to make sure Reggie didn't get hurt, and was glad I acted quickly. Hurley grabbed a knife from the kitchen sink and I managed to grab his wrist and arm before he had a chance to do any damage. Reggie than sank a few left hooks into him and that was the end of the row. Reg was grateful to me for what I did, but then again Hurley, a bank robber from Liverpool, wasn't a bad kid and I felt sorry for him. He was just out of his league.

On another occasion, Charlie Richardson was moved out to another prison. To the remaining inmates' dismay, his brother Eddie took Charlie's place. Charlie was alright, we'd got on with him, but Eddie never stopped moaning. He also thought that we presented some kind of threat to him so, for over six months, he went behind his door. It was a right pain because whenever he came out of his cell, we had to bang up and vice versa.

I'd managed to persuade the governor to let me have extra food from the kitchen so that we could cook our own meals. One Sunday, I'd got a nice bit of beef in for a roast dinner. Previously, we'd only been allowed plastic knives and forks but the screws trusted me to be responsible for a carving knife. Just as I finished preparing the meal and was ready to dish up, Eddie decided he wanted to come out of his cell to make tea and toast. As usual, the rest of us had to bang up. When we were eventually allowed back out of our cells, the knife had disappeared. There was a lockdown while they turned the whole wing upside down – they even brought in a metal detector. They finally found the knife, stuffed down the hole in the urinal. That was the end of our Sunday roast. We were all pleased when Eddie was moved out but all my hard work in getting us the additional food and extras like a punch bag and better visits had been wasted – it was back to the old days, no more little perks.

Other faces to pass through included police-killer John Duddy, who was arrested with Harry Roberts. John often spoke to me about the incident and used to shake his head, saying, 'As the police car drove away, I went down on one knee and fired a shot through the back window and it hit the copper in the back of the head. How unlucky can you be? If I'd tried it a million times, I would never have pulled it off. It was a total freak shot. Even Annie Oakley couldn't shoot as straight as that.' He said it had been a reflex action and not a premeditated act. Afterwards he lost the will to live, wasted away and died in prison. He knew he would never get out.

Conditions were medieval. You couldn't see daylight because of the extra bars they put on windows and the whole unit had a ridiculous number of bolts on every opening door. The cells had no heating. In winter, you were given a jug of water, which would turn to ice by your bedside. That's how cold it was. Prisoners named the wing the 'submarine'. When you woke in the morning, your nose would be frozen. As a Cat A prisoner, you were shifted around to different cells, sometimes up to three times a week. Just when you'd arranged everything and cleaned up the cell, they'd tell you to pack everything up again. It was soul-destroying. Then they would also knock on your door every 15 minutes during the night. A red light was left on all the time and if they couldn't see your hands above the sheet they'd flash the light on and off. I'd throw my boots at the Judas hole where faceless screws peered at us like perverts at a seedy sideshow. It was mental torture. All through the night they would kick the door. When they'd finished with your cell, you'd hear them kicking at the next cell door. It was an extreme case of sensory deprivation, the kind of torture you think only goes on in Third World dictatorships.

During this period of time, we had many important visitors to the wing. The then Home Secretary (later to be Prime Minister) James Callaghan paid us a visit and we complained to him about our conditions and treatment. Charlie Richardson was well up-front and had plenty to say. Like a typical politician, Callaghan agreed wholeheartedly with us and promised to change things. As he left the security gates, he turned and waved to us promising, 'I won't forget you, lads.' I was there for another two years. Nothing changed.

A more sympathetic visitor was Lord Hunt. He'd been made chairman of the parole board and was a well-respected public figure; he had even climbed Mount Everest. He visited me in my cell for a chat and discussed a book I was reading called *The Anatomy of Britain*. He mentioned that it had been written by a friend of his. I felt he was very dissatisfied with his job because he was powerless to implement his ideas. I asked him, if he went on future expeditions, could he find room for me? We had a chuckle over this remark and before leaving he shook my hand and wished me luck in the future. Lord Longford was a regular visitor, and one Christmas we even had a visit from a bishop in full regalia with crook and robes. He said prayers and blessed us all. He was a nice old boy and his compassion was appreciated.

One of the problems with prisons is the constant change of staff and governors. A new governor would change everything the previous governor had done and you had to start all over again. You would be given new routines and different rules and they twisted things round to suit themselves. In Leicester, we went on a hunger strike for 12 days over Cat A visits. We were joined by special-wing prisoners in Durham, Parkhurst and Chelmsford. I lost a stone in weight and it was the first time I'd been able to see my ribs since I was 16. The governor would get screws to fry up onions in the wing in an attempt to seduce your tastebuds. But we held out and stood firm.

The authorities had decided that visitors would have to be photographed and checked out by local police station officers. During visits, we were also required to wear sterile clothes, which would be left in reception, and then submit ourselves to a strip search. During the visit, there was to be no physical contact with wives or friends; your children would not be allowed to sit on your lap. The whole thing was so stressful and upsetting, you dreaded the entire procedure. We won our hunger strike but the victory was short-lived, because years later they got all their own way again and reverted to the same old rules.

After more than four years segregated with eight people, I was moved to Wormwood Scrubs in west London. John McVicar, the so-called 'No. 1 public enemy', took my place in Leicester. The change to the Scrubs was dramatic. It was like being dropped in the middle of Waterloo Station in the rush hour. All of a sudden, even though I was still a Cat A prisoner, I was in D wing surrounded by 300 men.

The hierarchy in this prison centred around Table 4 and I was able to exert quite a lot of influence here. So much so that at one point, Table 4 was mentioned in a governors' report, publicising the fact that they were giving some prisoners more leeway because they were a steadying influence on the rest of the prisoners. But in spite of us being a calming influence in the wing, we were not immune from being sent down the block if we misbehaved.

The diners at Table 4 included Buster Edwards, Jimmy Hussey, Gordon Goody, Roy Hilder, Frank O'Connell and Alan Gold. We selected who we had on our table. Dining took place in the centre of the landing at the bottom of the staircases in D Wing, home to the long-term prisoners. There were television sets on opposite walls at each end of the wing but little else. All you had were a few shops to work in, an engineer's, laundry and the gardens. A concrete exercise yard with goalposts lay between the wing and laundry building. On the other side of this was a patch of grass that we laughingly described as the 'bowling green' and a tiny aviary, and you never ventured far from there.

Although it was a Victorian prison, it had not been built on the star system, as most of the prisons were. That set-up allowed for the governor's office to be in the centre, from which the governor could survey every wing. For some reason, the Scrubs was built on a different system, comprising four separate blocks and no connecting corridors. Each block had its own exercise yard. The kitchens were in another block and when food arrived it was freezing cold and to be put back on hot plates and re-heated. It was really bad anyway, though, and you got cold meals all the time. Prisoners seemed to be permanently hungry. The meat was so thin it looked as though it had been cut with a razor blade. The prison authorities were again courting disaster. A hungry man is an angry man.

We were always sorting out problems at our table. At one time we had a row with all the black guys because they were getting out of their pram. Other problems would arise over currency or snout, as well as incidents of bullying and intimidation. The victims would air their anxieties at Table 4 and you would see other prisoners watching us, looking for telltale signs. Usually prisoners were seeking a bit of protection. Somebody was taking liberties or wanting to beat them up and they looked to us to resolve their problems. You could hear young prisoners on remand hollering and screaming in other wings.

By exercising a controlling influence, we were helping the prison authorities, so we also had to show them our authority could work both ways and that we could create problems as easily as we could solve them. That was the only power we had and we needed to exercise it, as I had to during a repeat of a Muhammad Ali vs. Joe Fraser fight on television. We were all mad-keen boxing fans in our wing and were watching the fight, which was scheduled to finish at 8.30pm. Bang-up time was half an hour earlier, although on special occasions they would give prisoners the extra time. It meant the screws would be late going home, though. On this occasion, the screws wanted to go home and banged us up early, though with several hundred men intent on watching the fight, a little diplomacy to keep them happy would not have been a bad thing.

One insensitive screw came over from another wing and turned off the set just before 8pm. I got up and turned it back on. The screws walked away growling and standing around ready for another showdown. Then another hard-case turned off the telly again. I turned it on again and nobody would budge. It caused a right scene at the gate, because there was a change of shift due and all the screws would have to stay behind. In the end, they backed down but were raving mad at me. They didn't want a full-scale situation on their hands, but the next morning I was called down by the governor and read the riot act. It was all right when I kept things peaceful, but they weren't so forthcoming in return. I was threatened with a 'sojourn' to Parkhurst or Durham.

Soon after I had arrived, I was sent down the block for three months for attacking John Barry, who had grassed on us in the McVitie trial. It was just before Christmas 1973. Barry was on remand for robbery and I saw him in the yard. Frank O'Connell (he was doing 15 for armed robbery), two other prisoners – one a lifer – and myself were being escorted across the yard to the bookbinder's. I spotted Barry playing football; he was still in remand gear and hadn't been weighed off. I got the ball and dribbled it for a little, then kicked it towards Barry and chased after it. I covered the yard in no time and he knew I was coming for him. The screws told me to come back, but I ignored them. As soon as I got near, I jumped him. The screws came running over and we all wound up in a big pile in the yard with Barry underneath. Frank pulled a screw off me and despite people holding me, I was still trying to batter him. I managed to sink a couple into him and ripped off his shirt and jumper in the melee. He was shouting at the top of his voice, 'I knew it was you, Foreman!' Typical of his kind, he was still grassing me up. He still couldn't keep his mouth shut.

I was dragged away and thrown down the block; nothing happened to Barry. Wheeler, the prisoner governor, was livid. He had virtually guaranteed Barry's safety when he was sent there from Wandsworth. Other friends of the Twins had threatened him there and that's why he finished up in the Scrubs.

Three of us – me, Frank and the lifer – were sent to the block and were brought in front of the governor every week so he could determine how long we'd stay there. I argued with him, asking why he had flaunted Barry in front of me when he knew he was a prosecution witness. I stayed down the block all over Christmas and the New Year. You only got number-one diet down there and my old mate from Leicester, Micky Kehoe, ran the gauntlet down the back of the punishment block to climb up to my cell window and pass food in to me.

Back at Table 4 after the punishment block, I continued helping young guys and protecting many a kid from being molested, often by just showing friendship to them. Roy Hilder, one of the chaps on Table 4, had been a customer in my pub and met Sue, his wife, there. They made a lovely couple. I used to keep my eye on him and at one point he had a confrontation with the biggest black man you'd ever seen. Roy had to stand two steps higher on the stairs so he could punch him in the head. I stood behind the black guy. When Roy saw me there, he chinned him, really knocking him out.

Another black guy who was formidable was called Daly and he had done a bit of fighting in his time. He ran around the exercise yard shadow-boxing with lead weights in his hands. Another inmate, a fellow called Proudfoot, had a confrontation with him while I stood by. Proudfoot was a Scouser, skinny and tall, with no muscles. Most of the time he just lay in his cell, smoking pot and listening to Eric Clapton. He was a throwback to the sixties, but like all Scousers he loved his football and was quite a good goalie. On this particular day, he went for a high ball just as Daly was shadow-boxing his way around the perimeter of the exercise yard. The two ran into each other and the ball went over the bar. Proudfoot had saved the goal. But by now Daly was growling and went for Proudfoot, who looked at me and the signal I read in his eyes was: Help! Help! He was a beanpole next to this gruesomely built ex-fighter, who was solid muscle from head to toe: 'I'm with you,' I told Proudfoot. In prison it's always a one-to-one. You never gang up unless you think a pal's going to get hurt. If it's a no-good bastard, you let him get battered. I encouraged Proudfoot to have a go: 'Go on,' I said, 'give him one.' As he shaped up to him, Proudfoot threw a right hander and poleaxed Daly spark out. Nobody could believe it. When he tried to get up, Daly's leg went into a spasm. I was laughing, 'See what you can do!' I told him.

Proudfoot's chest swelled as if to say, 'Don't mess with me.' I couldn't stop laughing. This pot-smoking, pallid and weak-looking beanpole, the type you kicked sand in the face of, knocked out Marvin Hagler with one punch!

Norman Parker had also wanted to do Daly. He came to me one day and told me, 'Fred, I have to have a row with Daly. I want to do him.' Now, Norman had already killed two people and was asking me to get Daly in the recess and knock him out. He knew what I was capable of and told me, 'If you can knock him over, I'll plunge him and finish him!' Was I hearing right? I asked him incredulously if he really wanted me to be an accessory to murder just before my release. Norman, being slightly paranoid, had not liked the way Daly looked at him but I told him not to wind himself up and defused the situation.

Table 4 resolved another potential disaster in the Scrubs in about 1974, when prisoners rioted over food and conditions. The food situation in the Scrubs was stupid. I picked up a bit of ham one day and it was as thin as tissue paper the way it was cut. Everyone was hungry and the food was atrocious. I threw the ham at a gold-braided prison chief and it stuck to his face like clingfilm. I told them they had to do something about the food. Not only were we getting cold food, but it was inedible too. If food is all right, the prison runs well. This followed riots in other prisons, including Parkhurst from which both Frankie Fraser and Martin Frape were afterwards dispersed. Frape joined us in D Wing in the Scrubs and now found himself in the middle of another riot. Prisoners at Parkhurst had tried to hang screws and cut their throats. About three hundred D Wing prisoners refused to go in their cells and all the other wings camped in the yard. Some prisoners had got on to the roof of our wing and we were feeding them for about three days. The whole prison was on red alert and surrounded by armed mufti wearing riot gear. Now the rioting prisoners began settling old scores and were fighting each other as well as trying to rip the prison apart. Me and the others on Table 4 were eventually able to talk some sense into everybody and resolve the situation.

One of the hardcases in the Scrubs was a flat-nosed geezer called Catino – we called him the 'Cat' for short. He was unpopular with other prisoners and had battered a few people with a can of beans in a sock – one of the weapons used in prisons. Cat claimed he was a post-office bandit, which gave him some standing. At the time, there was another prisoner there who'd been done for rape, although he protested his innocence. This fellow and his secretary used to pull girls in bars and clubs and take them home for little caning sessions, which he'd administer to their bare bottoms. He'd then take photographs revealing the marks and weals, but they were never brutally raped and were half-willing participants in his sex games. One girl screamed, though, and then another and that was how he came to trial. He was a businessman and felt really hard done by getting seven years.

While in prison he built up a scrapbook library on sex offenders so you could check out everyone's background. We never accepted him because of what he had done, but one morning he came to our table full of excitement to show us a picture of Cat in the *News of the World*. There was Cat posing for a boxing photograph wearing his shorts with the headline 'The Beast of Bedsitter Land'. Now we knew what he was really inside for. He was doing a 10 for attacking young students by knocking on their door and, as soon as it was opened, he'd chin them and rape them on the spot. On the following Saturday morning, we had our usual football match. He was on the opposition team and I was fullback. He came on with one of his hard tackles. As he raced for the 'dropped ball' his left foot came up between my legs and caught me on the inside of my knee. Instinctively I cracked him on the jaw with my right and gave him a left hook on his way down, catching him in the mouth and knocking out a couple of his teeth. The screws took him to hospital but nothing was said. He never grassed me up and the screws said nothing because they wanted him to get a seeing-to. I wound up with a couple of stitches in my knuckles.

At the time, my Danny and Jamie were attending the Italia Conti school, which was then in south London. Danny's classmates included present-day stars like Tracy Ullman, Sadie Frost, Lisa Maxwell, Patsy Kensit, Bonnie Langford, the late Lena Zavaroni and the Neves sisters, Vivien and Tracy. I used to bring the girls home when we lived in Dulwich and also went to all their concerts at Conti's. Now they were having trouble at North Lambeth underground near the school. Young yobbos were barracking the girls and putting hands up their dresses. It was all getting out of hand and the school wasn't able to control it. I was told of the problem and got Danny Oliffe to go there on my behalf and sort it out. He found out who the troublemakers were and went round to their fathers, one of whom was a local newsagent. He told the geezer, 'If you don't stop your kids molesting the girls, we'll come and batter the fuck out of you.'

The Shreward family, who owned the school, were very pleased that the problem had been resolved so quickly though they never knew how. In fairness, they were very good to us when Maureen had difficulty in paying school fees for both Danny and my Jamie and gave us a fair bit of leeway.

Shortly before I was moved from the Scrubs, I battered a certain screw. I attacked him because of the way he mistreated one of the Angry Brigade prisoners who were not dangerous people but misguided students rebelling like most other kids. This screw was notorious for his ill treatment of prisoners. He used to terrorise all the young prisoners and the borstal boys in the other wings, as well as other screws, and he was often drunk and causing trouble; he used to fling his hat to the floor and challenge people to a fight. On this particular night, one of the Angry Brigade, a nice lad who was very studious and intelligent (he got most of the answers right on Bamber Gascoigne's quiz shows) was off to education classes. He was running a bit late and came down the staircase with all his books, calling down to the main gate to let them know he was coming. But just as he got to the gate, the screw locked it and said he was too late, which meant he would miss his lessons for that week. The lad remonstrated with the screw, who was pissed again

I watched him as he grabbed the kid and his books and slammed him up against the gate. The books were sent flying and before I knew it I was tearing down the wing towards him. The other screws standing there warned me, 'No, no, don't do it, Foreman!' I took no notice, though, ran past them and leaped at him. He came down with my flying tackle and I knocked him halfway down the wing. I then got on top of him, wrestled him on to his back and sat on his chest. I was about 14 stone in weight back then. Pinning him down with my body I then started battering him until Frank O'Connell and Jim Hussey came up and pulled me off. The screws didn't interfere, but Jim and Frank stopped me from beating him up really badly. He had big claw-marks down his face and a black eye. There was no way he would have got up if I hadn't been pulled off him. They got him to his feet and, pointing his finger at me, he screamed, 'You're nicked!' The next morning, I was up in front of the governor.

A few months later I was shipped to Wandsworth – 'Wanno' – again. Some of the screws were sad to see me go, because I helped keep a happy equilibrium at the Scrubs. I was put into the mailbag shop for the last six months of my bird and then went straight back to Brixton on remand for the Marks murder trial. What with all the old faces there, going to Wandsworth was like returning home: Micky Kehoe, Tony Baldassari, Ronnie Stratton, Billy Murray and Charlie Dale were all waiting for me. Since I'd last seen Micky, he'd been out on licence and committed further armed robberies, so he finished up doing 18 years. Tony Baldassari was just starting a 10-year stretch. Ronnie Stratton was also beginning an 18, Billy Murray was on the tail-end of a life sentence for robbery. Tony Baldassari was a pal I'd known all my life and had once told me, when we were sitting together in prison sewing the mail bags, 'When this sentence is over, that's my lot. I couldn't face any more long sentences, Fred.' When he finished that sentence, he committed another armed robbery and was surrounded by armed police. Rather than face more time, he decided to burn the money and blow his brains out.

Ronnie Stratton was another armed robber and part of a very active firm. He came from a big family in north London and could sew a perfect mailbag. Then again, he'd spent many years practising! I refused to sew any mailbags and rather than see me on a charge, he'd sew some for me. He had been one of my customers at the Walk Inn and whenever he'd had a good touch would walk around with bottle of Scotch and gin, topping up people's glasses. Billy Murray was doing life for shooting a security guard, but that was accidental as they'd already got their loot and were driving away. Charlie Dale was another face and cut the cloth for the mailbags. I knew him and his brother Johnny Dale, who was a friend of mine for many years, got himself a bad name and was shot in the back. (Two Irishmen were charged with attempted murder but were acquitted.)

On his release from prison, Micky Kehoe got married and went into the printing business, although he kept certain other – more profitable, interests alive – he did very well but suffered a cruel death. He was out on his motorbike and was knocked over by an ambulance. Mickey had overtaken it to avoid a police escort for the Queen and while he lay on the ground, a police outrider accidentally ran over his head and killed him. The Queen stopped the cavalcade and asked after him but by then it was too late. It would have been the highest insult for Micky to be killed by a copper after all the years he suffered in prison – and tragic, just when he was enjoying his life again.

We were very sad when Ronnie Scrutton, who was well into his 18-year sentence, died of a heart attack while doing press-ups in his cell. He was a well-loved character and a terrific spender. Micky Kehoe and Ronnie Scrutton were of the old school. Armed robbery was their game and they were definitely two of the chaps.

CHAPTER 16
SNOOKERED

After I had served my 10 stretch for Jack 'The Hat' and been acquitted of Ginger Marks's murder, I tried to get my life and finances in order again. Most of my assets – the pub, betting shops, flats and houses – were sold while I was in prison. All that was now left was the 12-roomed house in Dulwich. It was a nice place with plenty of room for the family and the back garden looked out on to a wooded area, which made you feel you were in the heart of the country. It was lovely and Maureen had decorated it in style.

I had to get into something to earn a living, so my friends Micky Regan and Ronnie Knight put up £10,000 for me to invest in some pool tables, and together with my pal Ted (Ginger) Dennis, we started up a new business. At first it was hard work but it soon grew and we were able to repay the money and own the business ourselves. Things began to look good again.

All the people I had known in south London were under one wing when I came out. They were united and gave each other support. We were a formidable force of chaps. The Richardsons and the Krays were gone and it was just us and the Bermondsey firms and nobody was rowing, We had a virtual army. Three or four hundred people came to my homecoming party in the Angel pub, on the Lambeth Walk (which was right next door to my old club, the Walk Inn). Everybody was there. I had bought a complete set of new clothes for my big night – naturally, my wardrobe was all out of date. I spent all night saying 'Hello' and shaking hands with old friends, but I was really uncomfortable around the feet and I whispered to Maureen, 'I'll be well pleased to go home and get these bloody shoes off, they're killing me!' When finally I did get them off, I found I'd left the cardboard packing inside – silly bastard! Over the next three years we had a golden era, but then petty quarrels began to threaten our unity and civil war finally broke out. After a Customs officer was killed in a multi-million-pound drugs raid – of which more later – I fled Britain and went on my toes to America.

Ted Dennis and I had 60 pool sites taking in up to £3,000 a week. It was a good living and we got our sons to help us – Ted's Gary and my Gregory. Jamie would help occasionally when he was not busy in theatre or doing a TV series and my niece Barbie also did some part-time work for us. It was a good business and – best of all – a straight business. Then one day I received a phone call from one of our sites saying that a copper had called and taken our pool table away. This had also happened at several other pub sites. The bloody cossers were nicking all my pool tables with the cash inside and storing them at Camberwell nick!

And who should be in charge of the operation but Detective Sergeant Troon? Now there's a man with an axe to grind.

Ted and I went to see our solicitor, Tony Block. We met with police and asked the officer what he thought he was playing at. We showed him all the bills and receipts for the tables, cues, balls and chalk, and told him to get off his arse and 'put the fucking tables back' or he'd be the one to get nicked. This was costing us time and money when we were totally legitimate. Perhaps if we'd had the chance to buy some tables off the back of a lorry things might have been different, but we hadn't.

The police had to admit defeat and it was almost worth all the trouble to watch the fat cossers puffing and panting as they carried three hundredweight of slab-filled tables back to where they got them. Ted and I were used to handling them, but the police had no idea and made hard work of it.

While I was busy with the tables, Maureen went into the antiques business with Ronnie Oliffe's sister, Mary, who had a stall at Bermondsey market every Thursday. I put a bit of cash into the stock and they built up their little business, at the same time picking up bits and pieces for our home, which was looking better and better.

We progressed well from here. My Danielle and Jamie were at the Italia Conti theatre school and Gregory was in the music business, managing groups, as well as helping me with the pool tables. I went into partnership with my George in a bar of the Hotel Ellerslie in Crystal Palace. It was very successful and banged out every weekend. The owner was Billy Howard's ex-wife Jan and she was on her own now and needed to put the hotel on the map to boost the takings. There was a lot of building work to be done, so we pulled in Johnny McAvoy – a builder and brother of Michael, who was later convicted of the Brinks' Mat robbery – and Mick Regan to finance and enlarge the basement into club premises. We also sold a share to Brian 'Little Legs' Gifford, who was a bit of a mover and had other businesses, including a car showroom, warehouse and another club in Bloomsbury. Brian had wanted to get on the Firm with me for years and now that he had, he gave me a share of the car showroom and we were flying.

With all the money coming in, we bought Jan's share of the hotel when she wanted to sell out. I invited my old pal Micky Regan to invest and later we sold it on to Bill Best and his brother Dave so we all made a nice profit.

Once a month at the Ellerslie, we'd go on the piss with my Ozzie mates who formed the most successful shoplifting gang in Britain. Ronnie Oliffe introduced me to them when I wanted to buy some tom for Maureen. They were led by Ozzie Bruce and were all characters in their own right. Cadillac Jack, Billy Hill and the Bushranger were part of the team. They helped me out when I was inside doing my 10 by employing Jamie. Part of their operation was an illegal spieler in Earl's Court and Jamie was given the job of board boy, chalking up the winners and prices in the day's racing. They'd treat him generously with tips whenever they won a bet, knowing that Jamie was taking home the money to Maureen and helping with the expenses.

Another face who occasionally came into my club to drink was the actor John Bindon. John had a reputation for violence as well as being a ladies' man. He charmed society beauty Lady Vicky Hodge and had an affair with her that went on for more than 10 years. As an actor he'd won small parts with famous names like Michael Caine and Ryan O'Neal. He also appeared with Mick Jagger in *Performance* and in The Who's *Quadrophenia*. Home TV series like *The Sweeney* inevitably cast him in the role of a villain and he acquired instant fame after holidaying with Princess Margaret on the Caribbean island of Mustique as a guest of Sir Colin Tennant. The pair were said to get on famously. He poured her champagne and lit cigarettes for her, while she was spellbound by his cockney background and capacity for storytelling. But John Bindon was best known for hanging five half-pint beer mugs on his manhood. He was very fond of pulling his dick out and showing it off. It was like a baby's arm with an apple in its hand. Even Princess Margaret was not spared the sight of his manhood. While he was photographed naked on the beach, the princess strolled by, barely concealing a smile.

One Sunday in early November 1978, Ronnie Oliffe and myself were having a drink at the Ellerslie when there was a disturbance at the entrance hall. A chap called Johnny Darke had arrived and was drinking with his pals outside the main clubroom. He had a few words with Brian Clifford and chinned him. It's the old case of kick the dog and you kick the master, so Ron and I went out there to sort it out. A few punches were thrown and one of the offenders went over the stairs into my car park. It was not a major incident because it was a hands-up job and they didn't want any real trouble with me. The row was with Brian 'Little Legs'. But the golden rule is that you never make trouble in a man's place of business where he is trying to get a living. So after we got them out, I said to 'Little Legs', 'Come on, get some tools and we'll go and give it to them.'

He didn't want to know and told me, 'It's only a right-hander, Fred, forget it.'

Word travels fast and next weekend, who comes down the club but Johnny Bindon and a little firm from Fulham. Johnny said he had heard about the row and that he also had words with Darke but had done nothing about it because Darke had said he was a pal of mine, which was not true. I didn't have anything to do with him.

John said, 'I've got this for him,' and put his hand under his coat.

I thought, 'Oh no, he's going to pull out his dick again', but instead he pulled out a wicked-looking hunting-knife.

I told him, 'You do what you have to, John,' and sure enough, some weeks later they clashed at the Ranelagh Yacht Club and Darke was knifed to death.

When it came to trial, John told the court that he had been drinking with a mutual pal of ours, Roy Dennis on 20 November 1978, when Roy screamed out, 'I've been stuck.' Dennis was bleeding from a knife wound and was followed across the floor by Johnny Darke.

John Bindon told the court that Darke attacked him with a knife: 'I felt a sharp blow to my back near my kidneys. I looked down and could see the knife under my right arm. Darke sat astride me with the knife. He was quite calm. I was stabbed again. I felt weak and my head was spinning. Blood was pouring out of my chest and eye. Darke was standing a few feet away with the knife still in his hand. He was saying something like: "I'll cut your head off." Then he came towards me and swung his arm with the knife in it. I thought I was going to die. It was quite obvious he was coming for me again. I held my arm out with my knife in it. I was trying to keep him off me. But I can't remember feeling resistance to my knife when it entered Darke. But I was expecting to drop down any minute. The next thing that happened, people began separating us. Friends patched me up and put me in a car. They thought I'd better lay low so I flew to Dublin.' Some time later he gave himself up and faced trial for murder. It was proved self-defence. Much to his surprise, after a long trial, John was acquitted.

CHAPTER 17
OPERATION WRECKER

Back in the old days, long before the streets of London were awash with moody goods and foreign drugs, smuggling was an operation carried out in an altogether different manner to today. Ships carrying precious goods were lured on to the rocks at Cornwall by teams called wreckers, who would break open the vessels and nick anything of value to sell on the black market. These wreckers were ruthless, sometimes even murdering crew members as they robbed them blind – and it was after these gangs that Customs and Excise named their anti-smuggling operation that caught me out in 1978: Operation Wrecker.

Ironically, before that night a customs officer hadn't been shot for over 300 years, since the days of those wreckers. And the violent shoot-out in east London nearly ended in a murder charge against me. But let me take you back to the very beginning, to the Old Kent Road, where I had an interest with a close friend of mine and pal Ronnie Oliffe. It was an underground gambling club, situated over a second-hand furniture shop – the only one in its area. I know this to be a fact, because if there were any rivals we'd close them down. We found out there was a gambler frequenting this place, and dropping money like it was water.

Back in those days, south London used to be alive with gambling, dice, snooker crap and poker clubs – spielers. If you knew your cards, you could make a few quid, but soon word got around at our little spieler this punter was so terrible at cards that people were queuing up to play him. And he'd dropped enough cash over sixth months to buy the place twice over.

I soon found out the man was none other than Colin 'The Duke' Osbourne. While to many he was known as Duke, to our close family he was known as 'pasha'. This was mainly because his penthouse apartment in Sutton played host to harem-like gatherings where pipes were smoked and he'd hold court, telling stories about the Twins to a mixed audience. But in the East End, he was known simply as the man who looked after the Krays' arsenal. And The Duke was an old acquaintance of mine, going back to the 1950s, so when I heard it was Duke dropping the money I decided he and I had to have a long and serious talk. Duke decided to put me in on the deal, find a safe house for it and organise the wholesale of the goods.

Later, he had called me up at my brother George's minicab office in Peckham and told me he had a problem and he'd been let down over a safe pull-in for some cannabis: 'I need a flop to put it down,' he told me. 'It's here in a garage in the East End, hidden in a long-distance container yard in Aldgate.' Turns out he'd been getting a load of puff in from Afghanistan – old Afghanistani black – so I agreed to help him shift it. Cleverly, they tried to fool Customs by hiding the stuff in the floors and walls, so sitting in this big depot for long distance vehicles was this empty-looking 42-foot container, full of one-and-a-half tons of puff!

So on that day, Duke came to stay with me in Dulwich village, at my home. Just as dawn broke we left the house, and before the rush hour we arrived at one of my three lock-ups. There we put my car in and took out a crooked Ford Zephyr with all the cutting gear and scales (to cut all the gear out of the walls, and weigh it all).

Then we made our way to the lorry depot in Aldgate, to meet the driver, who I realised was Eddie Watkins, or 'Scatty Eddie'. The plan was for me to drive down in front for a few miles, then let them overtake to see if anyone was tailing, and I could see if there was any roadblocks up ahead. The roads were quiet, so I was behind it and in front of it so I was escorting it proper. There was just one fleeting second when I noticed one car parked in a lane off the motorway. It had an elderly man and woman in the sideline; they weren't talking, just looking. It bugged me.

Now, you've got to remember this was in more hippified days. Everyone was smoking pot, it was normal, and it certainly wasn't a serious offence. I mean, it's legal to smoke the stuff in Holland, ain't it?

So we arrived at our destination, with me still with this uneasy feeling. The guy that had the yard had a motorcycle, so I sent his son-in-law out to recon the lanes and the area for security, but he soon came racing back all excited just as we got to work with the cutting gear.

Just as we were about to get to work, we had driven the container into this yard where cars were piled up six high. So now was the time to cut the gear out. No one for miles around could see us in this narrow road flanked by vehicles. However, when the bike came back we had already arranged a plan B, which took us through a grazing field for sheep and back on to the motorway.

We left the chaps getting rid of the tyre marks in the yard by running up and down with a dumper truck, so there was no evidence of the lorry ever having been there.

'Get that lorry out of here quick! Meet you at the lorry stop at the coffee stall at Blackheath.' I said to Eddie, who drove straight there. But, when we arrived shortly afterwards, I said to Duke, 'You've bought me in for the funeral, not the wedding!'

I pulled the hood of my duffel coat over my head, sensing the police were taking long-lens photographs of me from afar. They were, but the cops had a feeling it was dangerous, and were waiting for the perfect time to swoop.

We had to get out of there, so we drove back down to Whitechapel, where our suspicions were realised. We got out at Blooms and Duke said, 'You can't help him Fred, he's nicked.' There the lorry stood in the road, lit up by the flashing blue lights of the cop cars surrounding it. 'He can't get away, it's over,' said Duke. So I reversed, to get the hell out of there before we were associated with the lorry and all the puff the cops were about to discover in its walls.

'They're on us everywhere!' moaned Duke, desperately, as we stood in the cold morning air.

I decided I wouldn't go straight home, so I got rid of the car, the scales and cutting gear and me and Duke went our own separate ways. I went to my old Nan's, and as usual the first words out of her mouth were, 'Fancy a bacon sandwich?' As I tucked into this delicious sandwich and a nice cup of tea – as only my Nan could make it – she switched on the news. What happened next made me nearly drop my cup and saucer and choke on the sarnie.

'Newsflash!' said the television. 'Customs officer shot dead!'

I couldn't believe what I was seeing. The weeds had well and truly blown into my garden. I never even knew he had a shooter – no wonder they called him Scatty Eddie. He'd shot a Customs officer dead, and for what? Cannabis. It was madness. You'd only get three to four years for that, even back then in the seventies!

As the long-distance driver, Eddie would have been looked on as a worker, and not a major player in the grand scheme of things. There was absolutely no reason to carry a shooter on this sort of work. He'd parked in a side street and jumped out of the lorry wearing an anorak in which he'd concealed a loaded Beretta pistol. He was spotted by Peter Bennett, an undercover Customs officer, and Detective John Harvey from Hampshire Drug Squad. They ran towards him and the Customs officer grabbed him by the arm, upon which Eddie shot him in his stomach, and fired through his own jacket so the officer didn't realise he was armed. The other copper chased Eddie as he tried to run away and brought him down with a rugby tackle. Eddie shot at him too, but only grazed his own stomach. A pensioner walking past then whacked him on the nut with a walking stick and Scatty Eddie was arrested.

I then realised that our conversation at the coffee shop would be our last. Now me and Duke certainly couldn't go home. I knew I could never return to my beautiful house in Dulwich, and the Duke had a lovely penthouse in Sutton he'd never see again.

It didn't take long before the police were smashing both of those places to pieces, looking for us. I'd had that house for 20 years and I lost it all – all furnished, the lot. But I knew I'd be involved in the inquiry if I stayed in England. As I suspected, it turned out they had photos of me on the Blackheath Green coffee stall. Operation Wrecker had been a success, but at what price?

Eventually, all the people closely involved with Duke and Eddie were arrested. Unfortunately, Scatty Eddie had been the architect of his own downfall. He'd come out of Maidstone Prison in 1976 with no money and built up the drug run with the Duke, making a lot of money in very little time. But he'd made the mistake of bragging about it to another prisoner, who'd grassed about their conversation. From that moment he became a marked man, and police and Customs set up Operation

Wrecker primarily to catch the Duke's gang. Before the swoop, they'd been watching these lorries make the run from Pakistan to England for 18 months, and learned that the gang had imported £10-million worth of cannabis in three years, which went some way to explaining Duke's high-rolling activities in spielers.

I had got involved in this event right on the tail end, and was angry at being associated with this major operation, and at having to go into hiding. Now, this little job was something I'd embarked on alone, without the rest of my firm. But of course the minute they found out about it, they were quick to help me out of this sticky situation. They all knew that I would cut the money up with the Firm, and they all would have played their part in dealing out the Pakistani black.

As it turned out, a good friend called John, whom I'd helped before (in fact, I saved his life once), got me a place over in Dalston. I had to get off the manor, you see, so that's where I went. This council flat belonged to a chap who'd gone over to Spain for a while. He'd said to my friend, 'Look after the place, and make sure you water my plants.' But I was amazed and amused to discover when I was taken there, that by 'his plants' he meant 24 giant cannabis plants! Here I am, on the run from a smuggling charge, and possibly an accessory to murder one too, and I'm holed up in a flat that looks like Epping Forest! Hitting the bloody ceiling they were!

So there I sat, in hiding, and the only contact with the outside world was phone calls from John. He'd ring up three times and on the third ring I'd pick up, to ensure I didn't answer to the owner in Spain, or any of his friends or family.

'They're spinning everywhere for you, Fred,' he told me, and I found out that in one place they'd even broken a man's nose by kicking his door down. He was a straight goer as well, with a medal from the Queen. But this was what they were doing, sending in dogs, and going in heavy handed – it was all in the papers.

After not being in contact with anyone and being stuck in this flat for days on end, I was so pleased when John, my pal, came over to visit. But I saw by the look on his face that it wasn't good news. Now I was already feeling very low. Just imagine – I'm wanted for a murder inquiry in the frame. They had photographs of me up on Blackheath, they were smudging me up good and proper, and from smuggling a bit of puff to a murder case, I was not having a great time.

Then John sat me down. 'Bad news,' he said softly. I took a deep breath. 'Your father's just died.'

I just sat there as tears filled my eyes and ran down my cheek. Life couldn't get any worse. 'But I've got your passport on the way,' said John, cheerily, 'So you can start a new life abroad.'

I knew that this little book would be my ticket to freedom. But it also meant that I'd have to travel alone, leave my home and family, my wife, and my sons Gregory and Jamie and daughter Danielle. It would be many years before I'd ever see them again. Also, I would not be able to attend my father's funeral or grieve with my mother and the rest of my family.

It was the only way out. If it was just the puff I'd have taken a four stretch and faced the music, but I knew I had to get away from this murder charge. I'd got Duke a passport too and I was cheered up when I saw his new passport photo. He'd changed his appearance so he wouldn't be recognised. Unlike me, who'd grown a beard since that fateful morning, Duke was a hippy-looking fella to start with, so he'd tidied himself right up and looked like a colonel in the army. I was pleased with it, and smiled, though I was still distraught at the loss of my father.

'At least the Duke'll be all right,' I said to myself, and wondered what I could do to cheer myself up. Later, I took the brave move of popping out to get some groceries. I fancied a real good chicken dinner – that would help. After all, I'd done a bit of weight, grown a beard and dressed up like an off-duty copper, with the blue shirt and tie, black boots and those waterproof three-quarter-length jackets the police used to wear. It was then that I got even more terrible news, as I opened the pages of the *Evening Standard*, and read that a man wanted in connection with the customs officer shooting had been found dead on Hackney Marshes.

It turned out that Duke had topped himself in the place he was holed up, on 1 December 1979. He'd already done 12 years jail in his life – plenty of bird – and couldn't face any more, so he OD'd. He liked a bit of drugs, Duke, and that was the way he went. I also read that the people who were looking after him dragged his body out on to the football pitch all suited and booted, looking all sharp.

I was devastated, as I thought he'd be good company over in America, and that perhaps we could go into business together. He left a suicide note with his solicitor, Tony Block, and in it he took the whole job on his shoulders, the puff and everything. He wrote that he financed it and did everything, but I knew that wouldn't help my case.

I tucked the paper under my arm and picked up a bottle of wine, a nice chicken, and some fresh vegetables, taking them to the counter – still in full disguise, as you'll remember. It was only when I came to pay that I recognised the mother and son behind the counter!

'Hello, Fred!' she said with a smile, as I pulled my cap over my face. 'Haven't seen you in ages!'

Of course, I got home pretty sharp! I put the chicken on the kitchen side, and went downstairs for a bit. When I returned to cook up my feast, I couldn't believe my eyes. The bird was completely red and pulsating. I focused my eyes and saw that it was being ravaged by red ants, they were bloody everywhere! I couldn't believe my string of luck. I carefully picked it up and sent it whizzing down the rubbish shoot to the communal bins at the bottom, and had just the bottle of wine for dinner. Could it get any worse for me?

It didn't take a genius to figure out that these fucking ants had come out of these cannabis plants and made tracks for my delicious chicken. So I got this spray, and did the entire flat in insect repellent, and resigned myself to more days of eating tinned food.

About a week later, I'm still waiting for my passport to come through and for all my money to be sorted out, because I wanted to go away with a nice bit of dough. Suddenly, there's a bang! bang! bang! on the door.

'I don't like the sound of that,' I thought. This flat was one of those council jobs with the entrance up the staircase, so you can see through the letterbox from the ground floor. And all I could see was people running up and down, and all these doors being slammed – bang! bang! bang! I could see boots and overalls, and people running around. 'That's it,' I thought. 'It's the heavy mob, the armed response unit.' You see, when there's a siege they move all the neighbours out because guns are gonna be used, and they don't want to cut any civilians down with stray bullets.

I remember thinking, 'Bollocks, if I'm going, I'll go out in a blaze of glory.' I reckoned I could take a couple of them with me. 'Come and get me you dirty copper!' Just like Jimmy Cagney! I'd been watching too many movies.

I stood at the stairs, listening as the banging and crashing got louder and louder, until I heard the mob at my front door. 'This is it,' I thought, clenching my teeth.

Next thing I know, the letterbox goes, and a card flutters innocently on to the mat. I picked it up with shaking hands… and couldn't control my laughter. I read it aloud. 'Environmental Health', it said. Environmental Health! 'Your flat needs fumigating,' it continued, and even suggested a date a week later.

Those fucking ants I'd chucked down the chute had infested the entire air conditioning of the flats and were bleeding everywhere! All over the shop! And I was thinking it was on me.

'I've had enough of this fucking flat,' I told John on the phone. 'They'll be in here within days, they've have to fumigate the whole block and they'll find these plants, and then they'll start asking questions.' But luckily, on that very day, my passport got sorted, and there was nothing holding me back. I opened the maroon leather cover and stared at the name inside. 'George Newbury', it read.

I couldn't believe it: they'd given me the identity of a known criminal. In fact, a man that had just shot Charlie Mitchell in Fulham. 'Bloody hell,' I said to myself, 'He's got more form than me!' But it was good enough for me, and I was soon set to leave London, and England – and life as I knew it.

CHAPTER 18
BREAKING AMERICA

My first mistake before leaving for the States was to buy a single, rather than a return ticket. Perhaps it reflected my inner feelings. I wanted to get away for good. But in practical terms, it meant that, when I arrived in New York, 'nerves a'jangling', I was stuck for several hours in the immigration department. They didn't like Brits coming over on one-way tickets. That might not have been such a problem if I hadn't been using the name of George Newbury. Apart from the seven stretch for shooting at Charlie Mitchell, he'd got a string of other convictions from robbery to assault. Standing there with my beard and false papers, which were being scrutinised all the more carefully because of the ticket, made me just a little anxious. But I kept my nerve. Somehow they didn't pick up on the convictions and let me through.

I breathed a sigh of relief as an old Glaswegian pal, Joe McClean met me at the arrival lounge. Joe had moved to America 14 years earlier and had married an American girl, Joanne, who worked for the Bethlehem Steel Company in Allentown, which was to be my new home. Joe worked for Paula Arlen, a slot-machine and video-game concern run by Dave Rosen, a lovely man who was well connected with New York families and was known as Mr Philadelphia. He owned whole streets of houses and gave generously to charities and other good causes. Joe and his wife took really good care of me and made me feel one hundred per cent welcome.

Allentown was a great little place, surrounded by beautiful Pennsylvanian countryside, very similar to England. (Billy Joel wrote a song about it.) We were conveniently situated at the apex of a triangle close to New York, Philadelphia, and Atlantic City. I felt very much at home there.

For the first nine months, I helped Joe run his business, learning all there was to know about it. In many ways it was very similar to what I had been doing in London with the pool tables, and which my partner Teddy 'Ginger' Dennis was still running in my absence. A great and loyal man, is Teddy. He looked after Maureen and Danni until they could join me and continued giving me a cut in the takings. Here in Pennsylvania, Joe and I and Mr Rosen went all over the state finding sites for game rooms, and bars that wanted to take our machines.

Joe and his gofer, Herbie Catts, took me around the nightclubs and sights around Allentown. It was really impressive. They also found me a luxury apartment in the Olympic Gardens, a prestigious place with nice mod cons where you could rent all the furniture you needed. They smoothed everything for me. The garden was beginning to look lovely again.

Soon after I arrived, my Jamie came to join me. I felt really bad about that, because his career as an actor suffered as a result of him having to go on his toes. He'd been doing really well with TV, stage and commercial work and had just auditioned for a French-produced film, *Quest for Fire*, about a family of half-apes, half-humans in the Stone Age. It won awards for best film around 1979 in the Cannes Film Festival and they'd badly wanted him to play a starring role. He was rehearsing for the part shortly before the Customs drama, but obviously lost it when he had to join me.

On his arrival, Jamie went straight to the George Washington Motel, from where I was meant to pick him up the next day, but my people in London had not got in touch and the result was that Jamie spent nine days waiting for me. By the time somebody told me, he was down to his last dollar wondering what had gone wrong. He wouldn't have been able to pay the motel if I hadn't come when I did. The annoying thing is that I'd been driving past this motel for days wondering when my son would arrive and he'd been there all the time!

We almost cried with delight when we saw each other. We cuddled and kissed. I love my Jamie to bits and never feel embarrassed at my show of affection for him. Now that one of the family was with me, things were a lot more settled.

Before you could open a bank account, you needed a social security number and for some reason I was given one straight away. I then opened an account with the First National Bank where the manageress was Nancy Beck, a tall, blonde, lovely English girl who missed the company of a well-mannered British gentleman and I made sure she knew nothing of my past. We built up a friendship that lasted throughout my stay. Jamie, in the meantime, had formed a relationship with a beautiful blonde girl called Betsy who worked for a large stockbroker firm. Jamie and I look back on the lovely Betsy with fond memories.

I began to invest money in video games and leased premises in Hamilton Street, Allentown. Dave Rosen helped me out there; he was so well connected and a brilliant businessman. He taught me a lot about running an enterprise. He would say to me, 'Always when you open a new business, just say to yourself, location, location, location. And never close a door on someone. Always leave it open just a bit to give them an out and they can also come back in.' This was good, sound advice from a man who knew everyone and had so much experience of life.

The apartment I rented was fine for Jamie and me but not big enough for the family and I wanted Maureen and Danni to join us once they'd sold everything off. Maureen had already emptied the bank accounts except for one in which there was a small amount of £75, which she had overlooked. (That money was to show up at a later date and be used against me to help secure a conviction when I stood trial for the Security Express robbery.)

For the moment, though, I was sitting pretty. I had nearly half a million dollars sitting in the bank and bought about 40 vending and video machines and rented a shop for a games room in Allentown's high street (Hamilton Street) as well as putting machines into several bars and clubs. I also bought a Chevrolet truck and Chrysler Cordoba car and still had enough left over to build a brand-new Georgian-style house with swimming pool and large grounds with cherry trees. It was all tastefully furnished, with lots of guestrooms. Jamie and I went out together working every day, finding new sites and meeting new people.

We made lots of friends and connections. Some Italians, who had nightclubs in the Balearic Islands off Spain and were connected to a New York family, gave me a lot of help so I did a few things for them in return. I met a lot of solid people from Philly (Philadelphia) and Atlantic City, which were only two hours' drive from Allentown. I would also drive up to the mountains and find sites in summer camps, bars, hotels and restaurants for my machines.

If a site was too large or I had too few video games or machines to fill the place, then Joe and his firm would fill half of it with his machines and I would get 50 per cent of their takings and do all the repair work and collections. In the meantime, Maureen and Danni arrived. Maureen was happy with the new home and Danni got a job with the Allentown theatre company, appearing in several Shakespearean productions. Gregory was still in London doing his own thing and coming to visit us every now and again with his new wife, Lisa. A number of our close friends would also come to rest up and take it easy for a month or two. The only drawback to our happiness in America was that, unknown to me, Maureen and Danni missed their friends and family in London. So much so that they would sometimes cry at night. I tried to make it more homely for them and even bought the girls a Maltese terrier, whom we called Pasha after the Duke. Otherwise, things couldn't have been better for us. Apart from all the capital and property we owned, we now had a tidy sum of cash in the bank.

I was getting reports from back home each week on how different businesses were going, from spielers to clubs and minicab firms and little drinkers like the 'shush' clubs. There was restlessness among the firms who had been strongly bonded while I'd been in London. It worried me and it was disappointing that I couldn't go back to help sort out their problems.

When I was there, all the south London firms would go to boxing shows, which were regarded as major events. The venues were held at good hotels like the Kensington Palace and we'd come fitted out in evening dress. While I was away, a lot of silly jealousies and squabbles resulting in tension between the different groups began to arise and came to a head one night at one such boxing event. Ronnie Oliffe, Paddy Onions and all the Bermondsey people who used to drink in my pub and had supported me, were at this show with Alfie, Jerry and Peter Hennessey. They were all good, solid chaps but sat at different tables, raising money for a charity. The boxing show was run by Beryl Gibbons, who was the licensee of the Thomas A'Becket, and the only woman boxing promoter in England. She took over from her husband Tommy, a boxer and promoter, who by now had died from cancer.

During the evening, an argument broke out between Peter Hennessey and Paddy Onions. Neither Micky Hennessey nor I was there, otherwise I'm sure it would not have happened. But all of a sudden the argument sparked off a fight, splitting the loyalties of the different factions right down the middle. Paddy had come out of the kitchen and grabbed Peter Hennessey round the back of the neck and stabbed him about a dozen times in the back. While he was on the floor, chairs and bottles were smashed over him. Peter was a good friend of mine and there is no way he should have been treated like that. If he'd been a wrong 'un he would have deserved it, but he was one of our own. Good company and a well-respected thief and one of the chaps. In addition, all his family were friends of mine. Paddy Onions's family were also friends of mine as were Ronnie Oliffe's. We were all connected in one way or another and such a split should never have occurred.

The result was that Peter Hennessey died and a couple of people, including Paddy, were arrested some time later by police. Another kid, Jimmy Colman was also arrested. Although hundreds of people were present at the venue, nobody saw anything and Paddy and Jimmy were acquitted for lack of evidence. Nobody, not even the waiters, would give evidence against anyone. They were good, solid south London people. But the damage had been done and the dangerman was now Mick Hennessey, Peter's brother. The others knew he wouldn't stand for what happened. No way. Now everyone was on tenterhooks wondering what was going to happen and where it was going to come from. When and where was the comeback?

The sensible thing for survival is to hit before you get hit. I'd helped Micky before, when he stabbed and killed Dicky Horne at a party. Horne had put a glass in the face of Bernie Hennessey, another of Micky's brothers. So there was little question that he was likely to carry out a revenge attack for Peter. Micky Hennessey was a man of few words. He'd come round to my house, read the paper, then suddenly get up and say he was popping out. In the two or three hours he'd been with me, he'd not said two words. People were a bit frightened of

Mick, and Paddy Onions's mob were not at all happy. Mick was driving down Bermondsey with a pal when they struck. Two men on a motorbike drove up beside him as he stopped at traffic lights and blasted him with a shotgun. The assault nearly took Mick's head off. The motorcycle roared off. Mick's pal took him to hospital and police came to see him. He was lying there with this big hole in his neck and they were round his bedside telling him he was dying and to tell them who was responsible. He told them to fuck off and mind their own business. It was touch and go, but he survived.

I felt frustrated over in America when I heard the news. But there was nothing I could do from there. My mate Micky Regan then asked if Micky Hennessey could come over to visit me. This further divided south London and put Mick Regan in the middle, too, because he had been friendly with both sides. We had all been unified and ours was still the main firm, so over he came, though he needed a lot of convalescing to rebuild his strength. He stayed with me for a month or two.

Although Jamie was still with me, things had got a lot better for him in London and he was able to slip back without being arrested. By now they realised he had only been driving me about because I'd lost my licence and they had nothing on him.

Mick Hennessey had been thinking deeply about what to do. He enjoyed the States and came out working with me. But now he'd made a decision. He said, 'I can't let it go, Freddie.'

I responded, 'You've got to do what you have to do. I wouldn't insult you by asking otherwise. Your brother has been killed and I can't ask you to stop. But do me one favour. Leave my little mate out. Ronnie Oliffe had no part in it. I blame Paddy for this. He kicked it off and done the villainy. What you do about that is up to you. No one could have asked me in George's situation to leave it out.'

A while later, Paddy was shot through the window of his house. A bullet lodged in his jaw. A guy called Davie Barry, from up north, was suspected of being the gunman. Some time after that, Paddy was shot and killed outside his wine bar; he died on the pavement. People hoped that with his death, the whole situation was resolved and the thing could now be laid to rest, but it wasn't. Dave Barry was taken into police custody and while he was there he was suffocated, supposedly while resisting arrest. People in south London were still tooled up and now a situation had developed where everyone was trying to wipe each other out.

There was also unrest between the Philadelphian and New York families, who were engaging in deadly internal warfare at the time. They were all trying to get a bigger cut of Atlantic City's casinos and the media used to publish a score card: how many bodies were found in car-boots or wearing concrete overcoats. The families even took over local TV stations and named intended victims over the air waves. I'm afraid the Philadelphia side who helped me when I arrived were on the losing end and suffering badly.

The Balliteri family in Allentown became good friends of mine. I used to frequent their nightclub and we did some business between London and the States on precious metals and other ventures. There's nothing like sharing a bit of money to bond friendships. They also owned car sites, and I bought several motors off them.

When I emptied cash from the machines, I had to be careful of the hold-up firms, usually Puerto Ricans or blacks, and that got a bit scary, so I asked for some help. They supplied me with a .38 revolver for back-up.

Jamie and I had our little rows with gangs of blacks and Puerto Ricans. We punched a few of them out and stuck our guns up noses when necessary. Jamie became very adept at taking care of himself. I once had to bar a couple of guys who were battering the side of one of my machines saying, 'It ate my quarter, man.' That sort of treatment wrecks the mechanism and these were expensive machines. The two guys I had barred came back a few days later with some friends and I thought we were going to have some trouble.

They came up to me and the best approach was to confront them head on. I told them, 'I don't want you in here any more. Now fuck off!'

To my surprise they said, 'OK, Mr Fred, no problem.'

That was easy, I thought. As I turned to walk away I realised why they'd backed down. For standing behind me were three massive Hell's Angels, all dressed in black leather, standing with feet apart, defiantly chalking their snooker cues. They were praying for the opportunity of a good row. I'd never seen anybody tooled up so openly. They carried huge hunting knives in their belts and down their boots, but although they looked threatening with their leather hats, studded belts, tattooed and muscular arms, they were good as gold. They never gave me any trouble and I welcomed them on my premises. They loved Jamie and his English accent. We taught them cockney rhyming slang and phrases like: 'Leave me out', 'count me out', 'drop me out', which they loved mimicking.

The police never gave you any hassle, but when they'd come into the games area looking for someone, we'd watch a line of cops march in single file, never guessing who they would arrest. They'd march past a group of Puerto Ricans and blacks and suddenly turn around and pounce on one of them, cuff him up and drag him off to the nick.

I was probably the only white guy in Allentown able to drink at an otherwise all-black bar around the corner from my shop. I'd put some machines into their premises and the guy who owned it let me set up a little card spieler, which I bankrolled. There was quite a lot of poverty around and I'd occasionally give some of the younger boys $5 notes. You could see they'd not eaten for days; typically, they would make straight for Wendy's or McDonald's. All the black and Puerto Rican girls called me 'Poppa Fred'. I was like a father figure to them.

In the summer, the city fathers would arrange concerts at which big bands like Count Basie's and Woody Herman and his Herd played in Allentown Square. The black community would arrive and set up chairs hours earlier to get a good pitch. When I came on the scene, they'd wave: 'Down here, Poppa Fred', and give me a front-row seat.

We were always being asked to barbecues and parties by neighbours and friends and I reciprocated their generous hospitality. It was now 1981, and everything was going smoothly. But in spite of all the comforts, Maureen and Danni were still missing England. When I said we could go back for a short holiday, which would also give me the chance to sort out some business, they were over the moon. I asked Joe to take care of the games rooms while I was away. Pals had told me that it would be a lot safer to come back now as the heat was off. My George Newbury passport presented no problems at Heathrow and I spent about two weeks seeing friends and family and being very discreet about my arrival.

After seeing all the opportunities in America, and seizing them, it took a little while to acclimatise to Britain again. I'll never forget going to Miami, where two things struck me as summing up the American way of life, both of which were pertinent to my philosophy. One was the name of the hostelry overlooking the harbour: the Last Chance Bar and Restaurant. The second was the name of a luxurious yacht gliding up to the restaurant: it was called *One Hit*.

I'm not advocating that a young man should turn to crime, but let's face it, what chance have you got if you have no qualifications or education? So that must be the key: education and jobs to earn a living, which all governments should provide. In all the years spent in prison I never once met a prisoner who had been educated at Eton, Oxford or Cambridge – funny, that…

Back in London, I had a meet with a few friends one Friday afternoon: Micky Regan, Teddy Dennis, Roy Hilder, Ronnie Knight, Bimbo, a well-known entrepreneur and many more. We were at the Martin Harris Club in Gerrard Street, Soho, where Ronnie Knight's Sue was working as a barmaid. A fellow called Franie Daniels was also there. Along with many other people, I respected him over the years for his involvement in a robbery at Heathrow airport in the fifties. All his conspirators were arrested at the time and got up to 15 years' imprisonment, but after a fight with police he is said to have escaped by hanging on to the underneath of a police van. Later, in 1974, he was arrested but acquitted of the murder of Scotch Jack Bugg, who was killed in a gaming club in Mount Street, Mayfair. His body, wrapped in a carpet, was found by two off-duty policemen fishing off Seaford, Sussex. What a coincidence.

They talk about a Freudian 'slip of the tongue', but Daniels made his slip when he put a hand on my shoulder, just like cossers do when they're arresting you. While I was drinking with the chaps, I felt his hand grasp my shoulder: 'Welcome back, Fred. Nice to see you again,' he said. At the time, his mode of greeting didn't reveal his treachery and it was only 13 years later that someone told me the truth. Afterwards, Daniels had gone upstairs and was overheard making a phone call outside the men's toilet during which he said, 'They're all in here and he's wearing a beard.' He was the grass.

I had not been in touch with Ronnie Knight since I'd left for the USA and he was very surprised at seeing me there. When he walked in he told me, 'Now I know why the whole of Gerrard Street is alive with coppers.' That was my cue to make a run for it. I went outside with Mick Regan, who offered to walk me down the road. As we got halfway down Gerrard Street, the Old Bill came running round the corner in line formation, just like a rugby team. I managed to side-step and dodge between them and ran up towards Shaftesbury Avenue, only to see more cossers looking down at me. By now, Mick was already under arrest, as he had no need to run or try to escape. Next, I ducked into an alley that ran behind some Chinese restaurants right into a van blocking my exit and, before I knew it, I was surrounded by police levelling guns at me. One of the coppers was so nervous his hands were shaking. He screamed at me to put my hands up. I was handcuffed and they started walking me back towards Shaftesbury Avenue.

Even though I was handcuffed to two coppers, one of the heavy mob kept poking his gun in my back. I refused to go any further, telling them, 'If that cunt trips over I'll be dead with a hole in my back.' They then took me into a doorway of a shop and called for a police van. As we were waiting to be collected, Teddy Dennis and Bimbo, whom we'd left drinking in Martin's Club, walked by. They were signalling an offer of help and also wanted to snatch back a telephone number Bimbo had slipped into my top jacket pocket, which could have been incriminating. With so many police around, rescue was impossible, so they pretended to attack me. Teddy went for me, crying out, 'That's him, the flash bastard!' The pair starting to fight with me, pulling at me and panicking the coppers attached to me.

Holding my handcuffed hands up, I said, 'Go on, fuck off the pair of you.' It was a nice try to get me away, but without bolt cutters it wouldn't have worked. They did manage to retrieve the phone number, however. What a lovely gesture from these solid old boys. They don't come any better than Ted, Mick and Bimbo.

Mick and I were taken to Holborn Police Station and kept overnight. The next morning, I was taken to Southampton Magistrates' Court and Tony Block, my solicitor, rode his motorbike down from London to see me.

The police charged me with importation of cannabis and I was remanded to Winchester as a Cat A prisoner. At my trial in Winchester Crown Court, my defence counsel, John Gray QC, told Mr Justice Bristow that I had very little to do with the Customs incident and pleaded mitigation on my behalf. The prosecution, however, brought up all my past involvement with the Twins and my record of 10 for Jack 'The Hat' and so on. An unrecognisable photograph of me talking to Duke Osbourne and Eddy Watkins on Blackheath Common was produced too. In spite of that, the judge, a very decent and fair person, said I had suffered enough already through losing my hotel, pool-table business and my home. In view of the fact that I had already spent six months in prison, he gave me a two-year suspended sentence, at which I was highly delighted. I had been treated fairly for a change and I thank the judge for his consideration and leniency towards me and my family. Because Bristow had been so fair to me, I felt a bit sorry about letting him down during my two-year suspended. If you're still alive, Mr Bristow, I apologise if I let you down subsequently. It's not often you get treated with such civility.

While I had been in custody, Maureen and Danni had nowhere to live, so I found them a flat in Bermondsey Lower Road, on the Bonhomie Estate, kindly provided by a pal in the nick. It was a temporary measure, as our home was still in America. They were quite happy there and had their own street door. But police smashed it in one day and brought their dogs and a team of drugs squad officers. They searched the flat and all they could come up with was a joint the size of a thumbnail. They were charged with possession of cannabis and locked in cells overnight. The following day a kind-hearted copper at Tower Bridge told Maureen and my daughter Danni that I would be sent to prison for 18 years.

On my release from Winchester, I went with Maureen and Danni to Tower Bridge Court. While all the other cases were fined £10 to £15, he fined Maureen £35 for a dog-end. Later, I would often chip her about being a junkie whenever she started on about my life of crime.

I was given permission to return to America to sort out my financial affairs and then came back and got on with the pool-table business. I also began making trips to Spain in preparation for moving there permanently. I'd had enough of England. With money from America, I was able to purchase a few properties in a Spanish development called the Alcazaba.

For the first time in my life, I had to report to a probation officer. She was a nice young lady with an office above Camberwell Magistrates' Court and I got on very well with her. We even invited her to a benefit party for King's College Hospital in aid of the glaucoma department, where my George had been treated for years. It was held at the Frog and Nightgown pub in the Old Kent Road and we raised £2,000 for the doctors and nurses.

Some years later, George was standing in the far corner of the bar getting a drink for friends when he heard what he thought was the sound of a few lights blowing, making a popping sound. The barmaid had ducked down out of sight under the counter as George held out his hand for the change. By now all the other customers and band were flat on the floor and George was the only one standing. Several men had come to the pub doorway and began letting go with handguns at people behind George including, among others, Tony and Patrick Brindle. Fortunately, they missed their targets and no one was hurt. The would-be hit men legged it back down the Old Kent Road, while the firm standing behind George ran out after them, dropping to one knee, Hollywood style, and letting go with their own shooters. Afterwards they returned to finish their drinks saying to George, 'You didn't lie down, did you George?'

As he can't see very well and didn't associate the pops with bullets, he replied, 'I don't get down on my knees for no one.'

A few minutes later, the governor of the pub came out of the back storeroom with a decorator's ladder, climbed up the steps with a plaster board and trowel, saying wearily, 'I've got to get out of this fucking pub,' as he spread Polyfilla over the bullet holes in the walls. South London's a funny old place. But it was good to be back.

CHAPTER 19

SECURITY EXPRESS

Immediately after racing out of the Security Express building, the Firm that had just pulled off what the newspapers were already calling 'the robbery of the century' drove directly to a dimly lit farmer's barn near Waltham Abbey. If you've ever wondered why they call that safe place where robbers flee with their swag a 'flophouse', you've never committed an armed robbery. The sheer levels of excitement, adrenaline, and pure 'fight or flight' emotions coursing through your veins means that for the duration of the work, you've got the strength of 10 men. But it's like a drug: what goes up, must come down, and the after-effects of any robbery is sheer physical exhaustion. The minute you're safe, you literally 'flop' against the wall or on to the floor.

Inside the barn, the Firm took to the green sacks of cash using gardening shears that were hung to the walls. It was only then that they saw the true glory of their takings: over £7 million in cash. Piled on the sawdust, several feet high, were towers of used banknotes, columns of £50, £10 and £5 notes almost filling the small room. Some of the Firm had to stand back and simply admire it, to breathe in that unique smell of used currency.

The money was divided into different parcels for different parts of the Firm. What you've got to remember with bank jobs is that you can't keep notes when they've got scribble on them from tellers. You put one of them into your account and you're done for – one silly note can get you fucking nicked or bring it on you – so they had to get rid of them. And it was quite upsetting, I can tell you, burning thousands of used banknotes!

I wasn't sure what the others did with their lot, but I did hear that when the police found a load of the notes they said they smelt damp. Some people think it was looked after in The Fox pub, which makes sense, as it had a very damp basement. But that's nothing to do to me. I had my special place for my money, and a couple of other people's whack too – and I was very professional and methodical about divvying it up. I kept it in a vault, and I could go there any time or night and get it out and count it with all a counting machine. It was such a good hiding place that if I hadn't have taken the money out, they wouldn't have found it, even today. Once inside, I'd throw all the wrappers away and clean the money right up. The trick was to put it all in two-and-a-half grand parcels, otherwise they got too bulky – and anyway, it's easier to count: '£2,500, £5,000, £7,500...'

The whole country was on red alert, as the newspapers had warned the nation to be on the lookout for anything suspicious, like anyone shifting large sacks or boxes full of what could be money. But I can tell you this: I know that a large amount of that money was carried through one of London's busiest train stations in suitcases, straight past the newspaper stalls selling the very papers appealing for people to be on the lookout!

And as is always in the case, known villains were immediately checked in case they had any part in the robbery. Frank Cater, who had worked with Nipper Read and was now a commander of the robbery squad, worked on the case with about 60 police officers. Initially, 120 officers were assigned to the case and half a million pounds in reward money was offered. Unlike the Great Train Robbery, there had been no gossip about this job and no evidence left at the scene. The job had been carried out with textbook professionalism.

Unfortunately, there is one thing that villains can never guard against, and that is the possibility of someone grassing, or a gang member boasting about his role and throwing money around in such a way as to attract attention to himself, thereby endangering his colleagues. None of the chaps would ever grass or be silly. However, a man I did not know – and whose background should have been researched thoroughly to see if he could be trusted – blew the whistle some time later, which resulted in the arrest of John Horsley, Terence Perkins and William Hickson, and two of the Knight brothers: John and Jimmy.

The grass, Alan Opiola, was recruited by John Knight to help count and launder some of the money. Opiola was not one of the chaps, but a motor trader who was friendly with Knight. He rented a van to transport some of the money, which was traced back to him. He should never have been recruited, because he turned Queen's Evidence and served three years in protective custody for his treachery. John Knight and Terry Perkins were each sentenced to 22 years.

It had been all too much for Opiola. He told police how he stared in disbelief when he saw the rows of banknotes, four feet high and five feet wide stretching across a bedroom floor of his Southgate house. Before he turned into a Judas, he was paid £25,000 for his help. Another part of the haul was counted at Horsley's home in Waltham Abbey, and he hid nearly half a million behind a panel in the wall of his father's room. Horsley also offered to grass, but was not given the opportunity.

The police had put a surveillance team on Horsley, Billy Hickson and Terry Perkins. Questioned about the other two, Horsley implicated Hickson immediately. Horsley got eight years, Jimmy Knight eight too and Hickson got six for handling £30,000 of the money.

Detective Superintendent Peter Wilton was in charge of enquiries and I feared once the Knights were implicated they would start watching me. But while all this was going on, the key was to not change my lifestyle. That would give the game away. I continued to make the rounds, doing the pool tables with my partner Ted, despite having all this cash around me. I never bought a different car, or anything flash, as I was so careful not to draw attention to myself.

I waited for it all to quiet down and took a trip out to Spain. But I had to go to America first to sell my interests, my house and my gaming machines; the latter ended up in a hotel in Atlantic City.

I always intended to go to Spain after I got back from America. It had taken just one trip for me to fall in love with the climate, and it was just two hours from London. Johnny Knight had been arrested for the robbery nine months after it had taken place, and I wasn't going to take any chances. Innocent or guilty, the police would have kept you locked up for months before a trial and I'd made arrangements and property purchases in Spain well before the robbery. Johnny never thought he'd be nicked and had even volunteered to delay going on holiday to Portugal, so the Yard could interview him, but I wasn't going to make that mistake. Micky Kehoe drove me to the airport and I was to fly away to a life of glorious freedom – but not before a chance encounter.

After checking in, I found the gate and was patiently waiting to board when who should I see standing there, but Sue – Ronnie Knight's girlfriend. Barbara was still his wife, but Sue was his girlfriend and she was standing right in front of me, clinging on to this bloody great holdall bag. 'Where's Ronnie?' I asked her.

'He's already gone, he's over in Spain, and he's told me to bring this out to him!'

But there was more to come: we couldn't fit it all in the overhead locker! It was far too fat with used banknotes, and even the stewardesses couldn't get it in there. 'You'll have to put it under your seat,' they said. And so I travelled at 30,000 feet with this holdall full of cash tucked under my legs, all the way to Spain!

It was a bit of a liberty I suppose, but I didn't mind doing it. At that time I wasn't associated at all, so we happily landed at Spain, and I handed back the cash. We went off in our separate ways – or that was the plan.

While I was looking at different places to buy a place, I knew the Knight brothers already had a home out there, and so I said to them, 'Let's not sit on each other's doorsteps, let's spread out along the coast so we're not associated with each other.'

Johnnie had a villa he shared with his brother, Ronnie and Barbara Windsor, for years before the robbery. They were up in Mijas, and the guy who was building the villas up there, an American fella, gave us the price list. They were very reasonable, but I refused to buy one.

Instead, I finished up in the Alcazaba. It was only half finished, and they hadn't even finished doing the garden. The apartments were nice and cheap, though, so I bought six of them including a beautiful penthouse. I really got along with the owners, even loaning them money when they were short of wages for gardeners, security men and other staff.

I started making regular trips backwards and forwards to London over the course of nine months, about half a dozen times in all, gradually moving and getting myself organised until I got settled.

All was lovely in the garden again, though it was only to last an idyllic seven years. The Eagles Country Club and properties kept me busy, but not to the extent that I couldn't party. Almost every day was party time in Spain. I'd go out of my house, meet a friend I knew and we'd be off to various bars drinking and enjoying ourselves. Sometimes you were out enjoying yourself so much that you didn't get back home until the next day. I felt safe in Marbella, because I had done nothing wrong in Spain and had entered the country legally. And there was no extradition treaty at that time which could be used against me.

It certainly was an amazing period. I even had doctors flying over to give my wife Maureen HRT, as she had just started her menopause. As I was paying for Maureen to have the full treatment, I thought I'd treat myself. I first met a Dr Studd, who was a pioneer of the HRT treatment at the time. He had a surgery at the Lister Hospital on Chelsea Bridge and also at the King's College Hospital on Denmark Hill. We later flew a young doctor over who would make a small cut in your groin, fire a pellet in you, and put a stitch on it. It then dissolves and it replaces all the hormones that the body doesn't produce after a certain age, such as testosterone, and oestrogen.

We were both like teenagers again! I had all these doctors, and often bankers coming over too, and I used to wine and dine them. One of the famous haunts was the Navy bar, where a good friend of mine named Mel Williams worked. Mel and his lovely wife Sally knew everyone who was worth knowing in Marbella and they're still good friends today. He was the top entertainer in Puerto Banus at that time, and later wrote a book on his life called *Almost Famous*.

Apart from my Eagles Country Club, I was also vice president of the Marbella Boxing Club, which was run by Ricardo Cruz. We had a licence to put on a boxing show, Spain vs England, and invited the Eltham, South London Boxing Club to take part. We put on the fights at the Marbella Football Stadium. It was a terrific night's entertainment, which ended as a draw for the two countries and everybody enjoyed themselves. Every fight had been a cracker.

The licence we held was for only two promotions a year, so we had one to go. I invited Frank Warren – his uncle Bob was a face from the old days – to come over with Ernie Fossey to promote a show at the

Puerto Banus bullring. When Frank came over, we dined at my expense with the Spanish Minister of Sport and also the Minister for Tourism at the Don Pepe hotel. We were joined by a few of my old pals – hotelier, boxing manager and promoter Jack Tricket, Vinny Scarfo, a reputable car dealer, and Nat Busso, an MC and referee, all from Manchester, and we laid plans for a future fight venue. I didn't hear from Frank for quite a while. Then, out of the blue, Micky Duff arrived in Marbella with his entourage and arranged a world title fight between Lloyd Honeyghan and Gene Hatcher with Frank Bruno and Gary Mason on the bill. Ricardo Cruz had to share the promotion with Duff, as part of the deal.

Apart from a few problems with police we had a lot of good times, with lovely people enjoying a drink with their ladies and everyone was very polite to each other. A lot of family and friends would visit from time to time and my Jamie also had a lot of showbusiness friends who came by, like Ray Winstone, Glenn Murphy, Robert Powell, Jess Conrad (who once played the part of Jesus Christ, in the musical *Godspell*) and Lionel Blair. Silks restaurant at the time was run by Eddie Avoth, the Commonwealth and Light Heavyweight Champion of Great Britain.

Recently, I read some malicious account that Freddie Starr was gay. Well, Freddie used to come to my home in the Alcazaba and to our parties and believe me, he was all man. No way was he a poof, although none of us have anything against homosexuals. I've employed lots of them over the years who are still my friends to date.

Ronnie Frazer, a famous actor of his time, stayed at one of my apartments once at the Alcazaba. His doctor told him that if he kept on drinking it would kill him, and even recommended that he try a bit of puff. Ronnie asked me if I could get hold of any. So I gave him a piece the size of a large bar of soap! Ronnie didn't remember much about his holiday, and over the years he used to repeat this story to people and the bar got bigger with ever retelling of the story. But I must admit, it was a bit of a lump.

The actress Diane Keane had a problem with a bully, while she was having a drink with her husband, a film producer, in Mel's club, while I was having my usual drink at the bar with Mel. Suddenly it kicked off. The bully threw punches at the husband and a drink over Diane. I said to Mel, 'Open the fire exit door!' I grabbed the guy and ran him through the club, and outside into an alley, and left him in a heap, out cold. It was a nice little combination I put together on him, and he didn't know what hit him! The very next day, the Guardia showed up at Eddie Avoth's villa and took him up to the Marbella nick. Of course, they had to let him go, as they'd got the wrong man – but we still laugh about it today over a couple of drinks.

One geezer who took a liberty and didn't know how close he came to getting a good hiding was Roger Cook, the investigative TV reporter. I nearly obliged his masochistic streak when he buzzed my flat with a helicopter, trying to take sneak photographs of me. I was listening to some music on my headphones one day, and from where I was I could see Maureen lying on the terrace, sunbathing. Suddenly, she was on her hands, crawling into the house and pointing up at the sky. I took my earphones off and saw this fucking great helicopter almost in my apartment. Cook later knocked on my door, demanding to see me, and I was on the point of going out there and clumping him, but was held back by Maureen. Taking her advice, I let the Alcazaba security chase him off the premises, which they did.

Spain holds many poignant memories for me, two of which involved close friends of mine. Ding Dong Dell was accidentally killed on the waterfront at Puerto Banus. He had been on a golfing holiday with three others in the late Seventies and after a good drink at Joy's Bar on the harbour, got into his car; when he switched on the ignition, however, the car lurched over the harbour wall straight into the marina. He must have left it in gear. The other golfers got out, but it was too late for Dell.

One of my saddest incidents – and this was beyond belief – involved Jimmy Allen, a friend of mine for over 40 years who was due to leave Britain and come over to be with our friends in Marbella. Before he was able to do so, he was murdered in a cowardly attack.

Jimmy was a millionaire who'd built up a very successful business in scrap-metal, cars, plant-hire and commercial vehicles. He loved engines and knew all about them. He was the sort of man everyone invited to their homes. He'd only been in Spain a few days and already he'd been a guest on an ocean-going yacht worth millions, talking to the owner about its engines. Whenever he came to Spain, we'd meet up with him and his wife at Tony Dalli's Italian restaurant in Marbella.

They were great times. At the restaurant, a piano accordionist would come to our table and play Jim's favourite tune, Neil Sedaka's 'Hungry Years', and we'd meet up with the chaps and talk about old times.

Before his death in 1986, Jimmy had sold one of his yards for more than £600,000 and had taken a cruise with his wife, leaving his son Billy in charge of the business. Billy had been the apple of his father's eye. He'd been at the scrap-metal yard since he was a small boy and his father spoke proudly of him at every opportunity. As far as his father was concerned, he couldn't put a foot wrong.

After their cruise, the Allens returned home to find some problems with their business. Not long after this, Mrs Allen died unexpectedly. One morning Jimmy made his wife a cup of tea, and on returning to her bedroom he discovered she'd passed away in the night. Grief-stricken, Jimmy came to Spain to convalesce.

We looked after him. Without his wife, he was a broken man. I would take him out and even spend the night at his flat talking him through his trauma. He couldn't sleep. We made the mistake of going to Dalli's and when they played 'Hungry Years', tears streamed down his face. Slowly, though, he began to return to his old self and wanted to buy a flat in the Alcazaba.

Jimmy needed to return to England. Unbeknown to him, however, his son Billy had sold the family house so he'd booked into a hotel. The day after his arrival, there was a knock at his hotel door. The man who stood in the doorway claimed he had had a slight prang with Jimmy's Mercedes, and could they settle the damage without going through the insurance company. Jimmy turned to the bedside table to write out his details when, without warning, he was pushed face-down on the bed and smothered with a pillow. He lost consciousness, only to be awoken by his son Billy. Billy then took his father to hospital, where he lied to the doctors about Jimmy's supposedly deluded state of mind.

Jimmy discharged himself a short time after and went to stay at a friend's bungalow in Essex. He was attacked again, though – this time fatally. His head was smashed by an iron bar while he was asleep. Again, his son Billy was first on the scene!

I discovered later that police had received information that I may have been involved in Jimmy's death over a 'drugs deal that went wrong'. Police came to interview me, and two Scotland Yard detectives flew to Spain. They told me, 'Fred, we know it's bollocks [about my involvement] but can you help us in any way?'

I told them that the bastard who did this deserved all he got and that Jimmy had been my pal for 40 years. I told them I'd like to know who killed him myself and if they found out, to drop me a line.

My son Jamie was also questioned by police, because it had been alleged that he was trying to sell Jimmy's gold Rolex watch – which was entirely untrue. Jamie couldn't believe it. In a later statement, he noted, 'Romford Murder Squad phoned and asked me to call by regarding the death of Jimmy Allen. They intimated I could make a few calls first, to my father for reassurance, so I spoke to several people in Spain, including my father.'

Jamie continued, 'They sat me down and asked me how long I'd known Jimmy and the family. They also asked me if I had ever met anyone outside the gates of Barking cemetery at 11pm on a certain night. I didn't even know where the cemetery was let alone meet anyone there. They also asked about the watch. I told them: "Not in a million years, I'm an actor, not a fence."

'Police told me there was some talk about exhuming Mrs Allen's body but I didn't know if she had been cremated or buried,' Jamie said.

'The police believed me. They knew our people *never* talk to police but on this occasion I'd been given the green light to talk as I had nothing to hide.'

Billy was sent for trial and accused of hiring a hitman to murder his father and also for defrauding £2 million from his father's company. Strangely, the jury was not told Jimmy had died, let alone murdered, only that a hitman (Anthony Smith) had been approached but did not take up the contract. The jury found Billy not guilty of hiring a hitman with intent, but guilty of fraud and sentenced to seven years. I still find it very difficult to accept poor Jimmy's fate and hope that one day his murderer will pay the price.

You'll remember I said how keen I was to remain separated from Ronnie Knight while I was out in Spain? Well, I soon heard that Ronnie and Sue had come a cropper in a car crash. It was nothing serious, but their motor hit a tree on the hill and they came right off the road. When they opened the door, their car was perched precariously on the tree. To get out there was nothing but 15 feet of fresh air below them and they both fell to the ground! Scrambling back on to the road, they realised it was only the tree that had saved them.

The road up to their villa was a gravely hill with little lighting, and a sheer drop to one side with no barriers at all. People used to drive sensibly up there unless they'd had a few drinks. And I can only figure out that this crash was behind Ronnie's decision to buy a one-bedroom flat in the same apartment block as me.

Now, we'd decided to keep our distance from each other, so I was surprised that he decided to buy an apartment there, where I was already well established. Instead of coming to me and saying he wanted to buy somewhere, he just bought a little place and started to use it whenever he got a bit drunk down at the port. I later read, in his book, that he reckoned he was there first – but I have to ask how much further I have to be established in an area than buying six fucking apartments in the same block!

So, from being 20-odd miles away, now he's right on my doorstep. The very thing we didn't want to do. That is how, all these months later when they were investigating Johnnie Knight, my name was first brought under the spotlight. The police were investigating Johnnie, and they interviewed the manager of the Alcazaba, a Chilean called Juan Carlos. I later found out exactly what happened by reading a book co-written by Detective Superintendent Peter Wilton, called *Gotcha!*:

'Do you know John Knight?' the cops asked him.

'No.'

'Has he bought anything here?'

'No, no. I don't know John Knight,' Carlos said, and the officers thought they had drawn a blank. They packed up their papers in a briefcase, and went to the office door when suddenly, Carlos said, 'But I do know *Ronnie*.'

The officers turned back to him and said, 'Who? Ronnie Knight?'

'Yes, and his big friend, Freddie.'

'Freddie who?'

'Freddie Foreman.'

'Oh, *that* Freddie,' the policeman chorused, and immediately sat back down again.

Suddenly, I was in the frame.

Another factor that occasionally gave me trouble was the fact that other villains had found the good life in southern Spain and were not prepared to keep their heads down and enjoy themselves without making their presence known. Whenever there was national publicity about anyone wanted by the British police, the spotlight would turn on one of the famous four. I've already explained how once the Spanish were told about me, they'd haul me in for questioning whenever there was a major incident in Andalusia.

The police started to sniff around my bank accounts too, but luckily the bank managers were on our side and were always letting me know when the police were making enquiries. They even used to empty out my safety deposit boxes before the cops arrived! And they were really digging deep. You see, the Spanish love anything with a stamp on it. Show them anything from a judge and they'll open the doors up and let the cops in for a nose about. It was making all of us out there very nervous.

Me and two of the chaps out there started to keep an eye on these three English policeman who were investigating us. They were everywhere, and wherever they went, they carried around this big canvas kitbag of evidence and papers. I had a meeting with my pals, and decided, 'We've got to get this bag off these coppers.' We knew it contained all of their evidence of the investigation, as even when they were eating at a restaurant or sunbathing they would tie the strap of the bag around the leg of their table or chairs.

So we started stalking them, and plotting up on them in hotels, shops and beaches. Unless they had copies of all that paperwork, it could have put the investigation back years. It was a funny old coup really, because if we were to succeed in our mission, we would have had to go in heavy handed, point shooters at them and put them on the ground and it might even have got ugly.

'We don't really want to shoot coppers, do we?' I said to the other chaps. It so happened that one day, I was in the foyer of their hotel when the lift door opened, and who should be in there but all three of the robbery squad! They were too busy talking among themselves to notice me, their chief suspect, standing right in front of them. I just turned my head and walked away. And it wasn't long after that, that all concerned had a sit-down and decided that by nicking the bag we were only prolonging the inevitable.

Then there were approaches for us to go back and put our hands up to a handling charge. For a hundred grand – which was the approach – I would have done it, to go back willingly and get a five stretch for handling. The only thing was, who was gonna go back first? Johnnie Knight and Terry Perkins had been sentenced to 22 years each! 'Who's the first volunteer,' I asked, 'don't put your hands up all at once!' Looking back, my only regret is that I didn't.

My bank managers assured me that the money in my bank was in an American address and the police were not entitled to get access to it because it was not a British bank account. I'd already built my Georgian-style house, complete with pillars and a swimming pool in the States, and had a well-established gaming business in Pennsylvania. I still had the house and businesses in America because I planned to divide my time between America and Spain, so I could easily explain my wealth. I thought it was watertight.

But somehow they bent the rules and were able to examine deposits in Spanish bank accounts and the purchase of property. Unfortunately in my case, with all the money I had coming over from America, it looked as though I had profited from the Security Express proceeds in the same way as police had suspected Ronnie Knight, who was still keeping a high profile on the Costa Del Sol, even writing articles for the British press (and that's not to mention his high-profile wedding to Sue). Shortly after the police enquiries, the Madrid-based news magazine *Tiempo* wrote a well-informed six-page cover story about our lifestyles and listed properties allegedly bought with the proceeds of the Security Express robbery.

Efforts to extradite all of us 'names' continued and, when things got too hot, I would make for the hills until things cooled down again. While I cannot plead total innocence, I feel very strongly about the way the authorities went about the case. If you go down that road, then you are on the way to a dictatorship and you expose the ordinary person in the street to the whims and prejudices of police and other authorities. There was little if any evidence against me, but the British police were out to get me and they eventually succeeded, through using the press and media and getting on side with police in Spain.

As mentioned in *Gotcha!*, there was a meeting in July 1988, held in Madrid, with the intention of improving relations between Britain's Flying Squad and the Spanish authorities. And when the conversation inevitably turned to the British suspects of the Security Express robbery living in Spain, a senior Spanish officer turned to Cliff Craig (the liaison officer for the Metropolitan Police) and asked, 'Out of all the British criminals on the Costa Del Sol, which one would you like back the most?'

And Cliff replied immediately, 'Freddie Foreman.'

Peter Wilton went on to say, 'Out of all the renegades on the Costa, Freddie Foreman was considered by British police to be the nastiest of the lot.'

The press in both Spain and England nicknamed us the 'Costa Crooks' and 'Famous Five'. Scotland Yard said they wanted to interview me, Ronnie Knight, Clifford Saxe, Ronald Everett and John Mason for the Security Express robbery and the £26 million Brink's Mat bullion robbery in November 1983. Again, there was no hard evidence, but it planted the idea of us as guilty men, and by repeating it often enough, which the press did, the general public could be excused for accepting it as a truth.

The Spanish authorities were also influenced by the Madrid magazine labelling us 'Robbers of the Century'. In short, I began to get very, very nervous about the whole situation. I knew they were coming for me. It was only a matter of time.

CHAPTER 20
KIDNAPPED

They came – mob-handed – for me on the morning of Friday, 28 July 1989. Black Friday, as I now call it. The Guardia Civil sprang me and swagged me off to Malaga nick, then banged me up in a Spanish cell with a load of smack-heads and low-lifes – about a dozen – all like animals in a cage.

As far as the authorities were concerned, I was responsible for what the Spanish press described as the robo del siglo – 'robbery of the century'. Five of us were named and secretly photographed in our luxury villas. The sneak pictures of the 'Famous Five' were published internationally.

The Spanish coppers couldn't get me legally, so the bastards kidnapped and drugged me. They did this by tossing the rule book out of the window. I can see the irony of it now. They reverted to my tactics: off with the gloves and anything goes. You don't expect that from law enforcement agencies. They should be setting examples. Ha ha!

Although I had not yet stood trial for Britain's biggest cash robbery – the £7 million hold-up at Security Express' headquarters in the City of London – the Spaniards expelled me on the basis of a whispering campaign. Spain has a long history of notorious inquisitions and abuse of human rights. Now the Guardia Civil were intent on expelling me to face the music in Britain. Even if that meant snatching me off the street, shoving me inside a cell, and slinging me on the next plane to London.

It was then my sixth beautiful year living the life of Riley in this warm Mediterranean climate, amid palm trees, beautiful beaches and lovely ladies. Sun, sex and sangria. It was all there for the taking and I made the most of it. Life was unreal. Since my arrival in Spain in 1983, the Costa del Sol had been round-the-clock pleasure. I had gone there to retire at the age of 51, although I still had unfinished business in America and some loose ends to tie up back in England. But that didn't present a problem, as I'd been back home several times without getting arrested.

The first sour notes of this scenario were played at 10 in the morning, as I walked to the car park of the El Alcazaba, my luxury development in Puerto Banus, Marbella. The pool at the Alcazaba sparkled in the morning sunshine. The palms and gardens, beautifully kept and rich with flowers, turned the development into a colourful oasis. Behind my big duplex facing the sea, were the rugged and beautiful Ronda mountains.

July and August are the hottest time in Andalusia and I had dressed comfortably in shorts, T-shirt and sandals and was set to visit my wife Maureen, who had medical problems and was in a private clinic near Marbella.

I didn't notice anything unusual as I walked to my car. Had I been more observant, I might have seen a number of unfamiliar faces lurking about. Policemen in all manner of disguises had descended on my paradise. They were everywhere. Hiding behind trees, pretending to sweep pavements, or just sitting in cars. As I opened the door of my British Rover Sterling, they pounced. Suddenly I was being arrested by a group of plain-clothes officers and whisked off to Malaga police station.

I didn't struggle or resist, because this had happened so many times before. I had not committed any offences in Spain and had nothing to fear. I had also employed several lawyers on whom I knew I could rely if the going got tough. Even so, every time a major incident happened, the Guardia would take me in for questioning – every time they fished anyone out of the sea or someone was washed ashore, usually minus their head and hands – it was always me they questioned.

Raymond Nash's daughter had been kidnapped in Spain and they had me in the nick over that. 'British criminals,' I bluntly told them, 'don't do this sort of thing. We don't kidnap little girls. That's not our style. Your people, or other Europeans may do that, but not us.'

They didn't like that remark. But I was proven right. Marbella was tipped upside down and they finished up arresting two Italians and two Spaniards.

On another occasion, a Canadian businessman renting Billy Smart's luxury villa, was murdered. He'd been shot through the head in his car, which had then been set alight. He was cooked like a bit of roast pork and police found his charred remains in the mountains behind us. I knew the guy with whom he shared the villa. I'd been there for a couple of parties and it was a beautiful place, done out like a circus tent with a large swimming pool in the garden. Anyway, the police came around on a Sunday, asking me what I knew about the incident as if I had something to do with it. With that, they pulled out a folder containing horrific photographs of this guy. 'Do you mind!' I rebuked them. 'I don't want to look at them. I'm going to have my Sunday dinner in a minute.' (Maureen had just cooked me a lovely roast leg of pork!)

With the constant questioning, I was beginning to feel persecuted (which was nothing unusual). At the same time, I had a number of legal actions against me by different provinces intent on expelling me from the country. Pressure to get rid of me was growing by the day but, as I had done nothing wrong here, the courts would not sanction my expulsion. Thank God!

Although the Spanish had been told I was a suspect in the Security Express raid, the British police had no evidence against me. Nevertheless, Scotland Yard clearly hoped that the Spanish could boot me out on the strength of the whispering campaign and that I would go on the run. Scotland Yard thought I had a dodgy passport because they'd found an application at Petty France (the passport office in London) in the name of Walters, a pseudonym I had used to apply for the passport. They figured if they could get me on the run I would be arrested for passport offences, giving grounds for extradition, even though I'd never even picked it up from the passport office. (That's one thing that *Gotcha!* got wrong: I hadn't entered the country on a false passport.) Nevertheless, from that moment on, Scotland Yard wouldn't give up trying to get me back.

So there I was, slung into the cells at Malaga with the low-lifes around me. I called for my lawyer, but the police ignored me until I became such a nuisance that they sent over an interpreter to quieten me down. I was urgently demanding that he call my lawyer, who was literally across the road from the police station. 'Yes, OK, OK, Mr Foreman,' he promised.

Some minutes later, several policemen came downstairs to take me away. I refused to leave and held on to the barred door preventing them from pulling it open, insisting once more that they call my lawyer. The other English and Spanish prisoners joined my stand and helped keep the police at bay.

The Guardia responded by summoning the interpreter again. This time he approached me, smiling: 'It's all right, Mr Foreman. You can come out now, your lawyer is waiting upstairs.' I didn't think he would tell me wrong, so when they opened the gate I walked out. But as I got to the stairs they jumped me, the bastards. They grabbed my arms and legs and hung on to my clothes. As I struggled, more of them joined in. In all there were about a dozen Guardia trying to get me to a car outside the station.

'You fucking liar!' I shouted at the interpreter. 'There's no lawyer!' With that I hooked on to the stair railings and clung on for dear life. 'I'm not going anywhere till my lawyer arrives.' I knew the bastards were as desperate to get me to the airport as I was to stay. They were frantic in their efforts to separate me from the banister, in fact the Guardia still joke that my teethmarks remain on the doorframe to this day. But with so many of them it was only a matter of time before they cuffed me up and got me in the car.

They shoved me into the rear seat, a guard on either side. Two more were in the front. But I wasn't going without a fight. Once we were underway I threw myself forward, trying to make them crash so I could make my escape. I was desperate. I knew that if they got me to the airport and on to a plane I'd be on my way back home to England facing a 22-year sentence. Can you imagine me and four Guardia squashed in a poxy Seat car – sweating, swearing and swerving at 100 mph along the Marbella–Malaga Carretara? They'd stop at nothing!

In the meantime, my son Jamie and my daughter Danielle had gone to the nick to find me. On learning what had happened they went straight to my lawyer, Juan Carlos Ramirez Balboteo, whose sister, a local judge, issued them with a habeas corpus writ and joined the chase to catch up with me at the airport. Served with the writ, the police would have been compelled to bring me to court again before throwing me out of the country.

The Guardia took no chances. They had me firmly pinned to the seat of the car and drove straight on to the tarmac to a waiting plane. But as they opened the car door to haul me up the passenger steps, I broke free and made a run for it and crashed past Customs and Immigration, straight into the terminal among all the passengers waiting to catch their flights. Everyone looked with open mouths, rooted to the ground. Some pointed and stared.

As the police grabbed hold of me again, I shouted, 'They're kidnapping me!' I was causing mayhem, creating as much commotion as possible while uniformed Guardia with guns and sticks surrounded me. If I'd had a free hand then I would have grabbed a pistol and held them until my lawyer arrived, but I couldn't shake the handcuffs. Again they hauled me to the steps of the plane and for a second time I broke away. This time, wet with sweat, they chased me around the wheels of the plane, cursing with frustration. It was like the Keystone Cops all over again.

Eventually they picked me up – it took about six of them – and they carried me up the aircraft steps. I waited till they got about halfway, then thrust my leg under a supporting rail and, with a tremendous heave, pushed backwards. We all toppled over, landing in a heap at the bottom. This time they got the right hump. Grabbing my arms and legs, one of them started laying into me. Another tried to strangle me. One little fat bastard, I'll never forget him, was letting rip with a torrent of Spanish abuse, while punching me in the bollocks.

I could see the pilot looking out of the window, stretching his head around, worried about the commotion. 'Right,' I thought, 'the more I perform the better the chance of him refusing to take me.' Two policemen were already down, taken to hospital with injuries, and the rest of them were red-faced and dripping sweat. Unfortunately, they got me inside the plane and threw me face down on the floor, collapsing on top of me. Like them, I was exhausted. I lay on the floor with my arms still behind my back and turned my head upwards to see a male steward and two stewardesses.

The male steward was attentive: 'Would you like a drink, Mr Foreman?'

I was parched and grateful for his kindness. He poured a drink into a plastic cup and held it for me.

'That's very kind of you,' I said, gratefully. Soothingly, he replied, 'Drink it all, drink it all,' tipping up the cup to ensure it all went down.

But the penny dropped. It was cold and refreshing – but with a bitter aftertaste...

I looked at him and said, 'You bastard, you fucking done me, you've doped me right up.'

Apparently, all planes have sedatives for people who run amok. The steward smiled and gave a little look that said, 'Yeah, I've done you good and proper, no more trouble from you.' He was right.

I could feel myself going right away. But I was still arguing. I called for the pilot and although I couldn't see who I was talking to I was saying, 'I'm not going to go. I'll fucking stop you. You won't fly this plane back to England.' A voice replied that we were going to Morocco. 'Bullshit,' I said. It was obvious we were going back to England, but I was trying to fanny them: 'You are taking me to London and what you are doing is totally illegal and you will all wind up in serious trouble!'

When that didn't work, I once more threatened to wreak havoc on the plane. But I could feel the drowsiness coming over me and knew I'd be going over any minute. Just then I got a massive panic attack. Paranoia set in. Why were there no other passengers on board? Were they going to fly off with just me and dump me somewhere in the Mediterranean?

I hovered between sleep and a drowsy consciousness. They had lifted me on to the seats and I could hear what sounded to me like the muffled rage of the jet engines flying me away from my paradise. I lay across three seats, my arms still pinned behind me and the plastic handcuffs working patterns in my back. My hands were numb through lack of circulation.

I tried to reassure myself: 'I'll wake up in a moment and everything will be all right. It's just a dream. People are trying to rouse me but that's all part of this nightmare. I'm slipping back into unconsciousness. It was that bloody steward. There's a bitter taste in my throat... how can this be happening to me?'

How could it? I had fought and won all my legal battles against expulsion in four different regions: Andalusia, Madrid, Seville and Barcelona.

What's going to happen to me now? I'm looking at a 22-year prison sentence. I'll be leaving jail in a wooden box or struggling out on a Zimmer frame. This is it. My life's finished! They were taking me away from my palm-tree paradise to the cold reality of Brixton Prison.

CHAPTER 21
TRIALS AND TRIBULATIONS

The aeroplane shuddered as it dropped altitude. People were shaking me, telling me to sit up. I was waking up again, my head was in a fog. There was a dull pain in my wrists from the handcuffs. All the passengers got off the plane, leaving me and the three Spanish coppers. Suddenly I was surrounded by four members of the robbery squad. 'Christ! We're back in London!' I thought.

Scotland Yard's heavy mob, the robbery squad, arrested me on the plane. A skinny, young uniformed copper was with them and they asked him if he wanted to be famous. He swelled to twice his normal size as they handcuffed me to him. I looked out the window at the welcoming party. The police had been working overtime in stage-managing my return. But try telling that to a jury. Press and TV were in a wide arc waiting for me to step off the plane.

After they were satisfied the press had got their photographs, and the uniformed cosser had got his moment of glory, I was bundled into a van and sat between two fucking huge robbery squad officers. They put the uniformed copper in another van and he was jumping in and out of it directing traffic. I was then taken to Leman Street police station near Shoreditch, where Henry Milner arrived out of the blue to handle my case. I awoke next morning staring at the cold, sterile, white-tiled walls. My back ached from the hard wooden bench, and in later years I have had to have surgery on my hands due to those handcuffs cutting off my circulation. The reality of my predicament set in. I appeared at Bow Street Magistrates' Court the next day, where I was remanded in custody and sent to Brixton Prison. My life of luxury, enjoying endless days of pleasure shaded from the sun by palm trees around a swimming pool, was now a distant fantasy.

I was sent reeling back in a time capsule when they took me to Brixton. I was put in the 'cottage', the small wing where I'd been with the Kray brothers in 1968. It had its own little exercise yard separate from the rest of the prison. Vicky Darke, a nice boy who'd represented England in karate, was there. He'd been nicked for armed robbery. Mark Rotherwell was another inmate with whom I was friendly. There was also a black guy called Ferdinand who claimed he was an ex-mercenary but was really just a sadistic killer. He had two fellows pleading for mercy on their knees in a nightclub but stabbed them both. One died, the other was saved only by the skill of a surgeon. There was a little Canadian guy we called The Bear because he was hairy all over like a teddy bear, two IRA guys, and Charlie McGhee who was in for shooting a copper and had got a recommended 25 years. Between us we had one bath – the same one, stains and all, which I had shared 20 years earlier with the Krays.

Charlie McGhee used the black guy's bath water out of turn but thought nothing of it. Later, while he was playing cards, Ferdinand borrowed a pair of scissors from the screw and stabbed Charlie five times in the back: 'That's for using my bath,' he said as Charlie lay bleeding on the ground. One of the chaps smashed Ferdinand over the head with a heavy wooden chair and laid him out. Ferdinand was a dangerous bastard and I later found out he used to terrorise a family I knew who owned the Red Pepper restaurant in Puerto Banus. It was owned by Chris, a good friend of mine. (I'd eat there regularly, as it was the best in the port.) Both Ferdinand and Charlie McGhee were eventually transferred to Albany Prison and, some time later, the black guy found himself surrounded by the chaps on the sports field, one of whom was Charlie. Ferdinand was jerked about a dozen times and his nose was also sliced off in the knife attack. Because he was 18 stone, his blubber saved his life. He got his just deserts for murdering innocent people.

At Brixton, both Mark Rotherwell and Vicky Darke were fitness fanatics, so I used to work out with them. We had a couple of chairs and a broom handle with buckets of water for weights at each end. But for some reason, the governor stopped us from doing this harmless workout. Mark and Vicky also used to wrap cloth bandages around their hands and spar with each other at karate. They were two great lads. I was sad when Vicky got 18 for the armed robbery and missed his company when he was transferred. We met up again in Full Sutton. Mark was convicted of being an accessory to murder. After his release, he got a job on the door at the Ministry of Sound nightclub, but the newspapers did a piece on him and he was sacked. They never let you forget your sins.

When I first arrived at the 'cottage' (the most secure wing in Brixton Prison), I stepped out into the small exercise cage and was walking around on my own, a solitary figure, when I heard voices calling my name from one of the cell windows overlooking the yard. You couldn't see faces inside the cells, just a wrist and hand sticking out through the bars waving at you. I looked up to the window and asked who it was. If it wasn't two of my old pals! Tommy Wisbey and Jimmy Hussey informed me they'd just been weighed-off for a ten and seven years. We had a laugh about our situation, gave our regards to each other's families. Both were being moved to Parkhurst that afternoon. I said I might see them later.

About a week later, I heard a commotion early in the morning, keys rattling, doors banging, and someone was put in the empty cell next to mine. I was opened up and taken out for exercise and on my return saw this prisoner who looked very familiar. We stared at each other for a second or two, and he said, 'Is it Fred?'

I pointed a finger at him: 'Gerry? Gerry Conlon!'

It had been 15 years since I had last said goodbye to him at this very same prison. He was only halfway through his sentence but had aged considerably with the amount of bird he had done. His father had died after he had served only five years of his 30-year sentence. We gave each other a big hug to celebrate our reunion. But I had still better news for him, which he wasn't aware of: 'Great news, Gerry,' I said, 'you're home on Thursday.' He couldn't believe me. I asked him who was here with him and he told me Paul Hill and Paddy Armstrong, who was in a cell down the end of our landing. I told him to get Paddy but we couldn't get Paul because he was up on the next landing. They came into my cell and sat on my bed while I made a cup of tea. He still couldn't quite believe it, but said, 'Now I know why the screws have been so bloody civil to me for a change.' I told him again that the radio had said he would get one court appearance and be released. When they heard the 4pm broadcast confirming what I'd said, Gerry and Paddy leaped up from the bed and jumped up and down in the air like a footballer who'd just scored a cup-final goal. Full of emotion, the pair held each other as tears streamed down their faces. The next day they were released, and rightly so.

While I was still there awaiting trial for the Security Express robbery, I received the news of Charlie Wilson's murder in Spain. Charlie, his wife Pat and their family had been old friends for many years and I was very upset to hear of his death. I'd known Charlie since his teens, but when he first arrived in Spain it was my Janice who found him the *casetas* (small house). He spent a fortune adding high walls, a tower and various security measures that made the place look like a miniature Parkhurst. In fact every week we drive by the walls had gone up even higher! But it was here that he was eventually killed.

The *Guardian*'s report of the incident, published on 26 March 1997, read as follows:

The man widely believed to have killed great train robber Charlie Wilson seven years ago has himself been shot dead... the Roff killing was the latest in a feud that began on 23 April, 1990 when a tall young man on a mountain bike arrived at Wilson's home near Marbella in Spain, shot him twice and fled, probably with the help of a getaway driver. Wilson's cousin, Norman Radford, said then: "Charlie's death has upset a lot of big names out here. They are not happy men." Roff, from a south London criminal family, escaped in May 1988 with two other prisoners described by Scotland Yard as "dangerous and potentially violent" after over-powering their guards on a prison coach in Essex en route from Albany Prison on the Isle of Wight to Blunderston in Suffolk. One of his co-escapers, William Edmonds, was also questioned about the Wilson killing.

I was even more upset when I read an article originating from Spain based on information from a well-known conman who goes under the name of Joe Flynn. The article alleged that I had arranged Charlie Wilson's murder from my cell in Brixton over a drug deal that had gone wrong. Of course, time has since proven that I had nothing to do with it. The man who put the contract on Charlie – Roy 'The Lump' Adkins – was shot dead in Holland. Adkins's close friend, Micky Blackmore, who went to Holland on his release from Maidstone to reclaim Adkins's money, was also shot dead.

In the meantime, I have not forgiven this mongrel dog Flynn for getting money by causing distress to Charlie's wife Pat and other members of her family as well as my own. Maureen and Pat had been very good friends as well and this cast a slur on all of us. Pat Wilson immediately issued a strong denial, saying the article was completely untrue, that I was a personal friend of Charlie and his family and that this was a malicious article written by someone unscrupulous enough to cash in on lies. In her words: 'Freddie was a friend of the family and a complete gentleman.'

I'll never forgive that bastard for causing so much upset to a grieving widow in an extremely turbulent and tragic time and I hope I run into him one day. In the meantime, if any of my friends would like to say a little word in his ear to explain to him where he went wrong, I would be eternally grateful.

In normal circumstances, the case against me for the Security Express robbery would never have come to court. The evidence was too flimsy. The prosecution case depended on the alleged confession to Spanish police, a defunct bank account holding £75, and deposits of money whose source they could not prove. When armed guards are put around prison vans bringing you to the Old Bailey, it can have highly damaging implications, though. What must a jury think when they see television and press photographs of police sharpshooters? A steady build-up of articles about my friendship with the Krays and my past convictions and even acquittals were other factors that must have influenced the jurors. Then, at the trial itself, police told the press that, 'A tight security net was thrown around the Old Bailey... and jurors will be guarded by police throughout the five-week trial.' One juror was taken off the case because of claims of 'nobbling'. We certainly didn't do any jury 'nobbling', but I did later hear exactly why this particular member of the jury was removed.

I remember him well, as I could tell even by looking at him that he was on my side, that he was likely to go with a 'not guilty' verdict. So I tried my best not to even look at him, for fear of doing anything that might change his mind. Regarding the other jury members however, such as the older ladies, I'd walk in and give them a polite nod. It was my way of counteracting the methods police had used to make me look like a monster.

Anyway, it looked to me that this one fella used to like his drink, and was forever looking at his watch to see when he could escape to the local boozer for a swift one. I was told that one afternoon, while standing at a urinal, he heard a voice from behind him say, 'On that Freddie Foreman trial, are you? Well you'd better find him not guilty or you'd better emigrate to Australia.'

Of course, this frightened the life out of him, and when he told the police minders who accompanied him everywhere, as they did the rest of the jury, it was brought up in court and he was told to step down. Now, I can tell you that was absolutely nothing to do with me or my associates, and I can also reveal that it is not uncommon for Old Bill to pull such tricks to damage someone's case if it isn't going their way. I mean, why would I have nobbled someone who already looked like he was on my side?

When I sat in the dock the next day, I could feel the hostility of the jury. There were no more nods or smiles. They'd turned against me and the robbery squad had done their business. From then on, I noticed a hostility in the jury towards me; I could see it in their eyes. I later heard that the prosecution were seen to be enjoying bottles of champagne that lunchtime, in celebration. The jury was told that the man had suffered a family bereavement, but they had already found out that he had been supposedly nobbled. I was given the opportunity to have a retrial, but that would mean a jury from a provincial town like Maidstone, and they were notorious for finding people guilty. I decided to stick with the London jury, a decision that in the end resulted in a not guilty verdict for the robbery.

My crime was more to do with upsetting the establishment, who are much more concerned about property than they are about human suffering. Laws were made to protect the wealth of the rich, to keep the world safe for millionaires. I was a professional, honest thief who represented a threat to them and that is why they've always tried to put me away and keep me inside for the whole term of my sentence.

I don't blame them, but I am fully aware of what the press can do. They all have their connections with police officers and get their stories from coppers who feed them little titbits of information. It's been that way ever since I can remember. I know that police computers would have been alerted each time the parole board sat to review my case and sure enough, as regular as clockwork, there would be a rehash of an old and damaging story about me in the newspapers and bang would go any chance of parole. So I never held my breath when it came around.

By comparison with other crimes, my nine-year sentence for handling money from the Security Express was harsh. No one was hurt or injured, no poor people suffered. Women and children were not molested or hurt. No old lady was robbed of her life savings by some unscrupulous solicitor or conman, yet I was made to serve nearly all my sentence. Why? Because I hurt the establishment, who have shares in companies like Security Express and in the insurance companies who had to pay out.

That's why I received nine years. Violent rapists and sex offenders have got much less. Other prisoners sentenced to 10 and 12 years were all out on parole while I was still serving my nine. With such inequality, I am surprised that the authorities can't comprehend the anger and bitterness of so many prisoners. One of the reasons I have written this book is to counteract the number of misleading stories about me in the past. I want to set the record straight.

My trial opened at the Old Bailey in March 1990. I was charged with robbing security guard James Allcock of £6 million, receiving stolen cash of £363,280 and using a false name to obtain a passport. One of the first prosecution witnesses was Captain Domingo de Guzman of the Guardia Civil, who had spoken to me in Marbella in November 1988 through an interpreter. My Spanish lawyer, Mrs Susana Fernandes, who was present at the meeting with Guzman, testified at my trial that I had *not* made a statement, as the Spanish police had alleged. Michael Worsley QC, the prosecutor, admitted to the court that my guilt hinged on the 'alleged confession' and the fact that I 'suddenly came into an enormous amount of money'. All

Scotland Yard's heavy mob knew me to be someone who does not talk to police or make statements. To do so in Spain would have been suicide, as I was fighting extradition proceedings at the time. The prosecution also knew that I was not skint because of the money I had from America, and although I deposited large sums in the Allied Irish Bank in London, the source of this money could never be proven.

While awaiting trial, my Jamie went on his toes to Spain because police wanted to arrest him simply because he'd deposited money into my account. Until that time, Jamie had been working regularly on TV and for commercials, so now it meant that while I was awaiting trial he couldn't get acting jobs in Britain. The day after Maureen's visit to me at Brixton prison, police burst into my son Gregory's home at 5 am, demanding to know where his mother was. Fortunately, he didn't know where she was as she'd booked into an hotel. But we had to get her out of the country because they wanted to arrest her, too, in connection with the robbery.

On 4 April 1990, exactly seven years to the day after the event, I was found not guilty of the Security Express robbery, but the jury did find me guilty of handling the cash and of the passport charge. The next day, Judge Stephen Mitchell QC passed sentence. He jailed me for nine years for handling, a further nine months' concurrent for the passport charge, and a concurrent year's prison for breaching my two-year suspended sentence at the Winchester trial. The judge told me, 'I disregard the fact that, due to your resourcefulness, you were able to escape justice for so long and were able to enjoy a life of relative ease and security in Spain.' As if that wasn't enough, police were reported in the press as saying that they had received a tip-off that I'd offered £1 million to the underworld to spring me!

At my appeal, which I had been led to believe we would win because of the weaknesses in the prosecution's case, I was handcuffed between two large officers and led into court in front of all the appeal court judges. My barrister, John Matthews QC, argued that I should not have been charged with both offences – robbery and receiving – and as I had been acquitted of robbery, it followed that I should also have been acquitted of the receiving charge. The court deferred judgement, sending me back to Full Sutton to await their verdict. It took them about a month to search the law books for a precedent, which they found in a remote case in Hong Kong. They rejected my appeal on 12 March 1991. The precedent was as follows:

> *Theft and handling – alternative counts*
> FOREMAN [1991] Crim.L.R. 702, C.A., No.90/ 2141/S
> The appellant was charged with robbery (the Crown's primary case) and, in the alternative, with handling (by receiving) proceeds of the robbery. The jury were directed to consider the robbery count first and to consider handling only if they reached a verdict of not guilty of robbery. They acquitted of robbery and convicted of handling. The conviction was upheld. The acquittal of robbery meant that the appellant was innocent of that charge, applying *Att.Gen. of Hong Kong v. Yip Kai-foon* [1988] A.C. 642. It mattered not that the jury may have reached their conclusion because they were sure that the appellant was not a robber, or were not sure that he was, or somewhere in between. Where there are alternative counts of theft and receiving the Crown do not have to make the jury sure that it was not a case of theft before there can be a conviction of receiving.
> *Archbold News*, 27 September 1991

They had to go all the way to Hong Kong and dig up some poor fucking Chinaman to blank my appeal!

In the first week of December 1991, the Tribunal Supremo (Supreme Court) in Malaga, Spain, confirmed the decision of the Sala de Lo Contencioso. The Administrativo of the Tribunal Superior de Justicia of Andalucia, overruled my deportation by the civil governor Francisco Rodriguez Caracuel. After everything that had happened, they now confirmed I was wrongly expelled from the country. The Spanish High Court stated that my extradition: 'Does not abide by the rules of the Judicial Order' and 'overrules the extradition of one accused in the "Robbery of the Century", ordered by the Governor'. My solicitor, J. Carlos Ramirez, accused the Spanish police and governor of 'kidnapping, torture, and illegal deportation', and instituted a lawsuit against them that is still going on.

Only recently, a judge in England threw out a case against somebody who was illegally brought back to London from Poland, to face serious charges. He said because that person was returned illegally, and against his will, it was not proper that he should face a trial. That set a precedent that should have been applied to my case.

I was sent to the familiar surroundings of Wandsworth Prison and met up with my old pals Tommy Wisbey, Patsy Sullivan and Dogan Arif. I used to have pool tables in the Arifs' clubs and drank at the Connoisseur, their place in the Old Kent Road. Dogan was doing a 10 for drugs. He'd been wrongly convicted of the charge, having been the victim of a mistaken identity, but stuck to our code by not revealing who the other person was. When we were together at Wandsworth, I questioned him one morning about a scratching noise during the night and asked him if he was trying to dig his way out. Perhaps it was the black guy between our cells trying to escape, he suggested. We couldn't question him outright, as it was none of our business, so I had another restless night listening to this scratching sound. This went on for about a week until I spotted the cause. A large sewer rat had managed to squeeze under the cell door and was gamely waiting only a few feet away ready, to snatch the leftovers from my food tray. We looked at each other and finally he panicked first, eventually finding a gap through which he could wiggle his fat little arse and escape. I then plugged the gap with my towel. He never visited me again. Later, I was moved from Wandsworth to Full Sutton, where I met Mehmet – another member of the Arif family – who was doing an 18-year sentence for armed robbery.

In April 1991, Maureen visited me there and wanted to stay at a local hotel for a week so she could make multiple visits. She was 60 by then, but in spite of that, she was arrested in connection with the Security Express robbery. The police took her to London and put her in the cells for the night. It was disgusting: they left her in limbo for over a year while they were deciding whether to charge her with handling the proceeds of Security Express. At the end of the day they never charged her. None of this helped our relationship in difficult times.

While in prison, and since, I have undergone terrible feelings of guilt and conflict over Maureen. Guilt, because after all these years of being with her, I left my wife, and this subconsciously affected me in my dealings with other people. I knew what the problem was. I felt that people would no longer respect me after walking out on her. It also affected my self-esteem and made it difficult to cope. I was looking to find reasons to punish innocent people to assuage my own guilt and to destroy any relationship and chance of happiness because I felt I had lost the one thing that I had strived for all my life – respect.

I hurt the one I loved in order to destroy what we had together because I stopped respecting myself. I was looking at ways of punishing myself by trying to end a relationship with a lovely person whom I love very much. At the same time, I tried my hardest to make Maureen and the family come to terms with what I had done and to reassure them that I still loved and cared for them. Inside, I was hurting as much as they were, but I had made my choice of whom I wanted to live with. If your heart is with someone else, you will drive those around you nuts and be a pain in the arse.

I can't live a lie. I have only a certain number of years left to live and I feel it's only the beginning of a new phase in my life. I'm still reasonably fit and well and not ready for the pipe and slippers. The grandfather bit is all right and I like to be Poppa Fred to my five grandsons and see them as much as possible. But it takes time to adjust. I was on my own a long time and Maureen and I spent many years apart. She was obviously looking forward to my return and starting life again, but I just couldn't face life as it was before I went in for my last stretch. I had to change direction and then fate stepped in at the right time when I was in Spain and met Janice. We had no control over the situation. She changed my life and I haven't regretted one single day of it because she has made me extremely happy in every way possible and has stayed loyal and solid by my side since we first met.

After two years of being a Double A Category prisoner I was decategorised to single Cat A after serving another two years at Full Sutton. After the riot, I was then taken off Cat A and sent to Maidstone Prison. This is where I first met Eric Flowers, who was doing a 10 stretch for importing a lorry load of puff. I hadn't seen him since the time I put him and Ronnie Biggs on a cargo boat to Antwerp in the 1960s, on their journey to get their plastic surgery in Germany to begin a new life in Australia.

Poor old Eric died tragically in an accident at his beautiful Spanish home. He'd climbed on to the roof to adjust his satellite television dish and slipped off. It was very sad as he was a solid, sound man, and sadly missed by all the chaps.

I had been in prison since August '89, my first parole was due around June '93 when, as I expected, something would happen to jeopardise it. Sure enough, an article appeared in the *Sun* newspaper stating that the murder squad were about to interview me in Maidstone Prison regarding the shooting of three men. A few days later, the police from Ruislip Murder Squad arrived. One of the coppers was named Dave Thomas. They were very polite and did their interview in a civilised manner, obviously knowing that these three shootings had fuck all to do with me. The first name they put to me was Roger (the growler) Wilson, Tommy Roche and a chap named Don Urquhart. It was said that he was a friend of mine and was seen frequently in my company. To be honest, he may have been in my company while having a drink at the Eagles Country Club with about 300 other people, but I had most definitely no business interests with either him or Tommy Roche. In my experience, I knew that time would tell and that these three murders would be totally unconnected.

Subsequently, I have been proved right. At the time, I took it in my stride – they were just going through the process of elimination – and with my reputation, my name was always going to be stuck up. So I never held my breath: as I had never been allowed early parole before, why should this time be any different?

Where I arrived at Maidstone, who was the first one there to greet me? Reggie Kray – with a handful of phone cards and a box of chocolates. We hadn't clapped eyes on each other since 1970, when we were together in Leicester special wing. We were both very excited at seeing each other after so many years. I thought when I looked at him of all the years that had past, all the experiences and adventures I had on the outside and all of those years Reggie had been locked away. It made me very sad. It was an emotional reunion. Later that same day, I met up with Terry Perkins, who'd been kicked out of Blantyre House Prison in Kent and moved back to Maidstone. Poor bastard, he'd been jailed for 22 years for the Security Express robbery, the very same robbery that I had been acquitted of. He was near to the end of his sentence and about to be moved to Latchmere House, which is supposed to be the flagship of the British penal system. Everyone wants to get there at the end of their bird.

Unlike some prisons. At Blantyre House Prison, for instance, prisoners were expected to engage in some very odd practices. The governor encouraged grown men to do the hokey cokey, while holding hands with screws. I mean to say! And if you weren't prepared to accept the 'Blantyre House Attitude', you were out on your ear to another prison. They would never accept me, thank God!

Latchmere House Prison did not impress me either. While I was there, they prevented me from attending the funeral of Buster Edwards, even though he was like family to me. Nevertheless, I was allowed out to work five-days-a-week, returning to the prison at night.

I already had guilt feelings, as no doubt most readers of this book will have had when someone who they hadn't visited as often as they should have dies. I drove by Waterloo Station when Buster was still alive without stopping to see him. It was always so difficult to park there. But why didn't I take the trouble to stop and speak to him for just a few minutes? Maybe I would have realised he had a problem and was depressed and managed to do something to prevent him from killing himself. Unfortunately, I was still at Latchmere and on my outside work duties. I had to return to prison each night so every minute of the day was accounted for. Yet, if only I had made that extra effort I wonder if he would still have been alive today. He was the godfather of my children and I was godfather to his children. Such are the guilt feelings we all have when someone is gone and it's too late to put right.

Governor O'Neill of Latchmere House got me to sign a letter saying I would not attend Buster's funeral while I was out on the work scheme. All my family were there and it was my Jamie who read the eulogy – not Roy James's son, as was reported. Everyone praised Jamie on his oration and for his tribute to our dear old friend Buster. Prison authorities must think we are made of stone. But we are all very ordinary humans with the same feelings as everybody else. In Maidstone Prison, as in many others, we raised money for charity. We helped a little girl called Chelsea get an operation on a hole in her heart, so none of us was without compassion. In all the prisoners raised about £700 from their meagre wages (£4 per week).

The excuse given by the authorities for refusing me permission to attend Buster's funeral was that they did not want to attract publicity. However, unknown to the authorities, I still went to the flower pitch and paid my respects. That was on the day of the funeral. I mingled with the crowds and waited for his procession to come through Waterloo. I watched my family drive by in the cortege and felt unbelievably sad that I couldn't be with them.

A little later, I was on the receiving end of a further injustice at Latchmere, one that made me very angry. In preparation for my release in May, I was still on outside work duties. These involved collecting money for a cash-and-carry firm called Bootleggers and delivering it to them the following day. One night, I came back to the cells with my collection, which amounted to nearly £400. There was a search of the cells and they slung me out for breeching the prison charter by having too much money – even though they had authorised my job!

With only five months left to serve, I was shipped out to Wayland in Norfolk, a big security prison, so now I was back to square one. Fortunately for me, a warder serving at Norfolk, PO Clitheroe, knew me from years before and kindly arranged for my transfer back down south. PO Gibson from Springhill, my old prison in Hertfordshire, offered to accept me from Wayland Prison, but the governor would not have me back. Was it because of my birthday party, where the boys presented me with a cake in the shape of a Security Express van?

Mr Clitheroe then phoned Janet Wallsgrove, assistant governor to Mr Jones at Maidstone, who readily accepted me. They are the most humanitarian governors I have met in the prison system. I should have got parole like everyone else, but didn't. It will take me a long time to forget the woman responsible for sending me to Wayland. She grounded me for two weeks as my punishment, which I accepted as a man. But at the end of the two weeks, she shipped me out in handcuffs to Wayland Prison in deepest Norfolk and informed the parole board of her actions. They later refused my parole.

On St Patrick's Day, 17 March 1995, I was standing outside my cell door in Maidstone Prison when I heard a con say that Ronnie Kray had died. It came as a shock to me, as I was only talking to Reggie the day before and Ronnie had sent his regards to Joe Martin and myself. Also, Reggie had phoned Ronnie every day and there was not the slightest hint of any danger. When Reggie had asked him about his condition, Ronnie said, 'Hang on a minute, I'll call the doctor.' Ronnie was more concerned about the £50 in stamps that he owed Reggie and said that he would send them on to him as soon as he could. No one suspected what was to happen.

I asked to be taken over to Reggie's wing and comfort him in his hour of need. It was an emotional time for Reggie, Joe and myself. As soon as Reggie saw me, he burst into tears and I hugged and comforted him as best I could. He asked me to be a pallbearer, which I said would be a privilege. We'd had a long friendship that stretched over more than 40 years. A lot of water had passed under the bridge since then.

A jug of green hooch appeared from nowhere (after all, it was St Patrick's Day). In sad situations like these, a drink helps a great deal. I said, 'Just think about it Reg. Ronnie knew on what day to go. All the chaps up and down the country will be in pubs and clubs saying, "Cheers Ron, you're at peace now. No more troubles or worries."' I told Reggie that he must be strong and survive and carry on with life and live for both of them because as long as he lives, they will not be forgotten.

I stayed with him all day. Governor Jones was coming over to see us after lunch, so Joe and I were able to stay with Reggie over the bang-up. The chaps kept us happy with more jugs of the green stuff – and believe me, it was needed. Reggie would show us a catalogue of some watches and point out one he had ordered for Ronnie. It was a very sad day. I shall never forget how every minute there was a gentle knock on the cell door and another con would come in and pay his respects and then leave us alone.

After lunch, we were not hungry, but sandwiches came by the plateful: tuna, ham and more green stuff. We three huddled together, talking about old times. How funny Ronnie could be without knowing it.

Governor Jones called us all down for a chat. He is a good man who was always helpful and understanding, He asked us how he could help. I was a little angry and told him, 'It's a bit late now, Governor. Reg needed help a few days ago when his brother was taken ill and he needed arrangements to visit Ron.' Reg was told that Ron had an ulcer and no one dies of an ulcer in this day and age. We can't accept the cause of death, nor the way Reg heard it – from another con who was listening to the radio. His brother Charlie saw it on TV. I said it was a common courtesy for families of hospital deaths or car accident victims to be informed first, but not the families of prisoners. I have seen dozens of prisoners get visits from the vicar or a governor to break bad news, but never such a disgraceful lack of sensitivity or compassion to a man who has lost his twin brother. When Reggie was allowed to visit Ron at Broadmoor, even after 27 years they were like Cat A visits. When Reggie visited Ron at Broadmoor, they still had two screws outside an open cell door, whereas all the sex offenders, rapists, child molesters and murderers had open-room visits. Because the visits were so bad, Reggie hadn't been down to see Ronnie for several months, so there was more guilt there. They had found the visits too upsetting for each of them, as Reg had received a three-year parole knockback.

I asked the governor if the truth could be told regarding the way Reggie and his family and friends found out that Ronnie had died, which he agreed to do. I saw his statement and we were all satisfied with his report. He also said he would try and organise for me and Joe to attend the funeral but would have to confirm this with the number one governor and get his agreement. I was later told that higher authorities had refused permission for me to attend the funeral, even though I had only two weeks left to serve of a nine-year sentence. They said it would attract adverse publicity. Reggie wanted me to be a pallbearer, but even then the authorities would only allow me to go in handcuffs, the same as Reggie: 'How the fuck am I able to carry a coffin while handcuffed to a screw?' I asked. I told Governor Jones they must be joking and that this was going to cause serious problems in the nick. Mr Jones contacted the parole board and talked them into the only sensible solution left: to give me two weeks' parole. Hardly a large concession.

Ronnie Kray's funeral was held at St Matthew's Church, St Matthew's Row – a few doors up from the Carpenter's Arms, the pub once owned by the Krays, and the corner of many memories.

When we buried Ron, we buried my past.

CHAPTER 22
FREDDIE TODAY

Since my release from Maidstone in March 1995, I have been kept very busy writing various books and embarking on many media projects, as well as meeting and talking with old friends, and slowly getting back into the London scene. Since the episode with Duke Osbourne and 'Scatty' Eddie Watkins in 1978, which preceded my three-year exodus to America, I had only spent one year in London. When I look back over the last 18 years, I realise now how little time I have actually spent on the city's streets. After getting the feel of moving around my home town again, my conclusions are that, although there is a lot of money being pumped into commercial business and different enterprises, the poor are still poor and the amount of homeless people on our streets is a disgrace. Even after all the hardships we suffered during and after the war years, I have never witnessed such poverty and desperation. People, especially the young, need a sense of achievement to give them a feeling of self-worth. I don't see that in the vacant eyes of these poor kids forced to sleep in shop doorways.

From the slow monotony of prison life, where you are conscious of every minute of time, once out in the free world all the clocks and events seem to increase at a rapid pace. The Grand National, Boat

Race, Cup Final, Christmas – where did the year go? Prison is like a time capsule; you come home and still think and live in the past. The pubs we used to go to have been pulled down – in fact, whole areas have been demolished and turned into supermarkets. A short-cut turns into a dead end and I'm constantly having to rely on the *A–Z* to get me out of trouble. You just don't know where the fuck you are.

The official line is that today I'm retired, but, in truth, the only time I'll ever really be retired is when my coffin rolls into the furnace. I've done my bird, and have been straight for a long time now, but trouble just doesn't seem to stay away from my front door for very long, even now that I'm in my mid-seventies.

There was a scandal in 2001, when a young girl from an advertising agency called M & C Saatchi persuaded me to appear in an advert, modelling Thomas Pink's posh shirts. I posed with Tony Lambrianou wearing their clobber, and the photographs appeared all over the place, which gave friends and family a real kick. Not everyone enjoyed them, however, and multiple complaints were made to the Advertising Standards mob. The Police Federation in particular were offended that two convicted criminals were given an 'undisclosed fee' for this bit of work.

Perhaps they'd prefer it if I chose to go back to armed robbery instead?

A lot has been made of my feud with Frankie Fraser, and one tabloid newspaper in particular delighted in reporting an altercation that happened near my home in north London:

'Despite a combined age of 145, they brawled at a cafe in an amazing 1960s-style gangland scrap,' said the *People*. 'Foreman, 69, laid in to his 76-year-old rival, flashing his fists faster than a pensioner's bus pass. He stunned customers by FLOORING Fraser with a right hook, then DRAGGING him along by his ANKLES.'

I refused to comment on this at the time, as I didn't want to justify that man with my time or words. Fraser wrote lies about me in his autobiography, unforgivable mistruths that sought to cast a shadow over my character. Regardless of my age, I have never stood for disrespect and I never will. I'll leave it at that.

One thing I do have a lot of time for is charity work, and it gives me a great amount of pleasure to be involved in fund-raising for causes such as the Make a Wish foundation, with Jimmy Quill, his wife Chris and family, and for Joey Pyle's charity, Zöe's Place Baby Hospice, which has been supported by a number of stars too numerous to mention and who would be embarrassed to be namechecked. It's with this charity work, and obviously through my Jamie's acting career, that I've found myself in the company of some fantastic stars and celebrities. When Jamie played Bill Sykes in the 2005 film *Oliver Twist*, I met the talented director Roman Polanski, and enjoyed a fantastic party with him in Prague. I also met Sir Ben Kingsley, who played Fagin, and, amusingly, I learned how his method acting dictated that even off-set he'd be hobbling around with Fagin's hunched back. When I saw him, I said, 'Oh, Ben! Are you all right?' and started rubbing his back for him! We still laugh about that now.

When I met Dale Winton at his book launch, he was very friendly too – and great company. He said to my Janice, 'I never know what to call Fred, should it be Freddie or Fred?' (I think he had a bit of a crush on me!), and Janice said, 'Call him what you like, just don't call him "Darling"!'

If you'd have told me back in the 1950s how things would be today, I would never have believed you. It's not through my own doing but, today, gangsters and respected criminals have become celebrities in their own right.

I spend alot of time in Spain, as the climate is not only good for the soul, it's good for the health. And, despite my treatment at the hands of the Guardia Civil, I still love the place, the people, and the weather. Just breathing in that sea air puts five years on your life, I can tell you. As I mentioned, though, trouble is only ever just around the corner, and life is not always just a whirlwind of celebrity parties and book launches. I was most upset when in 2005 I was arrested getting on to a plane back to Gatwick from Malaga Airport after a short holiday, and I was led away by two plainclothes police officers. I'd checked in, and was walking up the boarding ramp, these two coppers in sunglasses escorted me down into the bowels of the airport, where they've got holding cells. They looked like the Spanish Starsky and Hutch.

'You're coming with us, Señor Foreman,' they said.

'Where?' I asked.

'Back to Marbella,' they replied.

I couldn't understand what all this was about, but I'd been used to having every crime on the earth pinned on me for no reason before.

They were fingerprinting me and taking my photograph, and all the while I kept asking, 'Are you charging me for something or what?'

But I got no answers, and it was hours and hours before I could get through to Janice, who was in England, because I was so far underground my mobile had no signal. When eventually I did get through, I yelled down the phone, 'Get Porette! Get the lawyers down to Marbella nick!'

They drove me, handcuffed, back down to Marbella in a police car, and when I arrived at the Guardia Civil office it was like déjà vu, as all over the notice board was written 'Operation Foreman'! Can you believe that? Operation Foreman? The only operation I've been involved in was a triple heart bypass in the year 2000!

As it turned out, our family villa, which had been rented out for the summer, had been the focus of an investigation. There were all these bits of evidence labelled up from this beautiful little villa that sat up in the mountains and had tremendous views all across Marbella.

To my horror, the board was full of photographs of the computer and printer and various other equipment, as well a whole host of other stuff that obviously wasn't mine. Slowly, under questioning, I pieced together what had happened.

It turns out that agents had rented it out to these two Australians. Nice chaps, or so she thought. But, unlike me, they weren't there for the sunshine and the sangria. They were printing up moody credit cards on a grand old scale, plating up rental cars in the garages outside, and generally operating international crimes out of this address.

They were interesting characters, too, by the sounds of things. I later checked them out in an internet café, and when I typed their names into the computer, up came the headline: GANGLAND KILLINGS IN MELBOURNE AUSTRALIA! These fellas were involved in organised crime right up to their necks. Six people were shot out there in scenes that made that lovely bit of Oz look like 1960s London!

Turns out they had an amphetamine factory there and had got caught in the act, and once nicked one these Aussies said to the coppers, 'If you let me out, wire me up and I'll give you some bodies.' So they did and he shopped four major drug dealers, and six bent coppers. After doing this terrible villainy and getting bail, they went on their toes. They ended up legging it to Spain to hide out, and, while they were at it, pass the time by setting up a major credit-card-fraud operation – which was quite obviously absolutely nothing to do with me.

But the Spanish had pulled my file and they knew who I was, so I had to appear in court. And being a Friday night, I had to sit the weekend out in the cells – which, I can tell you, are no holiday home.

They put me in a cage with eight other blokes, all of different nationalities and in for various different things. You had to get your own mattress, carry it in to the cell and fling it on a lump of concrete to try and get some kip. It's an old family saying that I can sleep on a clothes line, but even that was hard because in this cage were Russians, Moroccans, a load of smack-heads, and they were pacing up and down, obviously more worried about their cases than I was about mine.

There were also several woman's cells down the corridor, and some of the prisoners in my cage had girlfriends in there, who were crying and sobbing all through the night. 'Sonja, Sonja!' one kept yelling down the corridor, 'Tell them this, and don't tell them that.' From what I'd gathered, they were all nicked for bringing over drugs from Morocco.

The toilet was a fucking hole in the ground, and you had to wait your turn to squat over it and try to hit the spot. The only water was from a dirty old dripping tap, and the food was paella they'd come round and throw at you. And this was not the treatment you'd expect at my time of life. I've got a bus pass, for fuck sake! I was later told you're not even meant to be in prison if you're over 72 years old in Spain.

Three nights I stayed in there. Three fucking nights. And, of course, when my brief, Carmen and the lawyers arrived, with a bottle of fresh water and all the skills to prove to these idiots that it was nothing to do with me, I went to court on Monday, was cross examined by the judge and released on bail. But the Australians were held for eight months in Alerin, the Spanish prison, until eventually the bail came down to 50 grand and as is normally the case, they paid it and fucked right off, to Thailand. But as Humphrey Bogart said in *Casablanca*, 'Of all the gin joints…'

In fact, I sometimes feel that my life is like a movie, what with all the strange episodes like this that have happened to me. It's been written that Bob Hoskins's character in *The Long Good Friday* was largely based on my life, and I can see the similarities in the script. It was a great film, and they're currently re-shooting an American version. It's much better than these modern gangster films. Most of them are unbelievable because of the ridiculous characters, though they can be enjoyable – in the way that a pantomime is enjoyable, I suppose. But they just don't relate, perhaps because I'm tarnished by a life spent in real crime,

That reminds me of the time Richard Jobson interviewed me on his television programme with the director and producer of *Gangster No.1*, which featured my son Jamie. There we talked about gangster films. They were discussing unnecessary violence on the silver screen, and showed that famous scene in *Casino* where the guy's head is put in a vice and squeezed by Joe Pesci's character.

'Was that unnecessary?' asked Derek Malcolm, the film critic for the *Evening Standard*, talking about the screen violence.

'Well,' I said without flinching, 'it all depends what the fella had done wrong!' And the whole studio fell about laughing!

We talked about a number of other 'gangster' films, and how close they are to reality, and the answer is: not many are very authentic. In *Get Carter*, Michael Caine did everything wrong. He was a grass! And he broke the criminal code by lollying them all right up – sending cops all the videotapes. But it remains a cult film.

Eagle-eyed readers might even have spotted me in Guy Ritchie's 2000 film *Snatch*. I've had a drink with Guy several times in my son's pub, the Punchbowl in Mayfair. Even Madonna's been in there, and they let her pull pints behind the bar! Whenever the Ritchies come in, I make sure there's no one hanging around, and organise a bit of security to keep the paparazzi away.

They had a birthday party in there once, like an Irish wake with song sheet and rebel songs. Guy and Madonna were in there, singing along! They later let her down into our pub cellar with her own movie camera, to take some film. My Gregory said, 'You know, through that wall is the vaults to the church where all the dead bodies are kept?' And Madonna freaked out because of all that kabbala stuff! She said 'Oh!' and was up the stairs like a shot!

Anyway, I thought I was turning up to the set of *Snatch* to just have a drink and be introduced to Brad Pitt, so I arrived at Caesar's Palace in Streatham, with Roy Shaw and Joe Pyle. They asked us to sit up in a box looking down to where they were filming the boxing match. But it turned out that rather than a meet and greet, they wanted us to appear in the film.

They sat us down overlooking the ring with some dolly birds and a few beers and suddenly the cameras started rolling, as Brad Pitt's gypsy character 'Mickey' refuses to take a dive and ruins a match-fixing ring.

I said to Roy Shaw next to me, 'We're being unpaid fucking extras, here!' The MC kept fluffing his lines and it was taking forever, so Roy leaned over the ropes and shouted, 'I'll fight the pair of you!', which relieved some tension. Of course, my friend Alan Ford was in *Snatch* also, so it was nice to appear in a film with him. Blink and you'll miss us! However, it wasn't the first time we've appeared together on celluloid, and this is a funny story I bet Alan is still dining out on...

My Janice was at night school studying Film and Media Studies, and for her course she wrote and directed a short film. I agreed to help, and my son Jamie appeared also, along with actors Alan Ford and Ronnie Fox. I'm sure Janice was the only one in her class whose film starred a real bank robber, and several famous actors!

We were sat in a vintage 1968 Mercedes car down by a Tower Hamlets council estate, and Alan and myself were wearing trilby hats and overcoats. The crew were all by the car, ready to film Ronnie and Jamie appearing from a tower block with a bag of tools, ready to screw a jeweller's. Me and Alan were tailing them, to iron one of them out.

But, just as we're about to shoot the scene, these two idiots in loud Hawaiian shirts came staggering round the corner. They were right trouble-makers, and real lumps too. And they saw us in our old car and the crew and came over, saying, 'Ooh, you're gangsters, are you, or are you actors?' Taking the piss, of course.

They'd just been thrown out of a pub, and were terrorising the estate, so I replied, 'Go on, fuck off, both of you.'

'What do you mean by fuck off?' they sneered. 'Nice fuck off or just fuck off?'

And with that I leaped for the door and went for one of them. But Janice and the assistant were holding the door shut and I couldn't get at them.

'Give me that fucking gun!' I yelled at Alan, who had a genuine pistol in a holster. We'd got it especially for the film, and, although it wasn't loaded, I wanted to pistol-whip these bastards. At that point, Jamie finally arrived on the scene with the bag of tools and all hell broke loose.

I managed to get out of the car and gave one of them a good right hook as Jamie chinned the other. I went right across the yard boxing him, banging him, and all the flats were alive with people coming out their houses to watch the filming.

Ronnie Fox hits one of them with the tool bag, and Jamie thumps him again, knocking him clean out. As peace was finally resumed, I said to Janice, 'I hope you kept rolling during all that action!'

On the floor these two geezers are lying spark out, so we piled into the two cars and screeched off to a second location to finish the film off. By the time we arrived, Alan was a bag of nerves, and kept saying, 'Fucking hell, I'm an actor not a gangster!' And he didn't get any better when Janice informed him that those blokes were in intensive care. There are probably a few people living on that estate who are wondering when that very realistic gangster film they saw in action will ever be released!

Although, if *Payback* – which is what it was that project was called – ever made it on to the silver screen, it wouldn't stir up as much trouble as Frank Simmond's documentary *12 Days of Freedom*. My admission in an earlier book, and on that television programme, that I disposed of Frank 'The Mad Axeman' Mitchell had the murder squad knocking on my door.

The Old Bill came round straight after the show, and took me down to Horseferry Road police station, near Victoria. They brought all these charges against me: preventing the coroner from doing his duty (by allegedly destroying the body), and perverting the course of justice (by allegedly tapping up witnesses in the Blind Beggar). I won't bore you with the technical details of the law and the subsequent changes they've made since I was acquitted of the crime, but I was placed on bail for a year.

Since then my name's been linked to a whole host of completely unrelated cases, even the disappearance of Lord Lucan! They famously found Lord Lucan's blood-stained car on 8 November 1974 – abandoned at the port of Newhaven on the Sussex coast. It is on the same coast where my 'little facility' is supposedly based, where they believed the bodies of Jack 'The Hat' and Mitchell may have been wrapped in chicken wire and weighted to sink to the ocean floor.

Of course, I don't know what happened to bloody Lord Lucan! But the theory that he killed himself after murdering his nanny is supported by the late casino owner John Aspinall. One of the last people to see Lucan before his disappearance, Aspinall said in 1994 that he believed Lucan's bones were 'lying 250 feet under the Channel'.

But it wasn't just Jack 'The Hat' the coppers wanted to know about. After questioning me, they casually asked about the Battle of Bow – and that was 40 years back. Of the member of our firm they shot in the head, they asked 'Did he survive?' It's no surprise they wanted to know the answers, because for people like the bank guard, Dighton – who shot the man in question in the back of the head – this would have been a weight he would have carried on his shoulders for 40 years.

I told them enough to finally answer their questions, and probably put a lot of people's minds at rest. I know how it feels: there's a lot of unanswered questions from my life. I don't want to hurt anyone, living or dead; important events will be taken to my grave.

We are all potential targets for false allegations and, in 2008, an inaccurate article about me appeared on the Internet. Whoever you are, there is always someone out there ready to knock you down. I can usually tell who is behind these kind of pieces from the style of their writing and the language they use. There's an old saying, 'a lie uncontradicted becomes an accepted truth', so I can't just let it go, can I? You would think that those who have broken the code that we live by would not want old wounds to be reopened and would think themselves lucky to be alive – but no. They can't seem to stand the thought that a man who has stood by all his friends, stayed strong in the face of adversity and done nothing but help people out of trouble never rolled over like all the other sewer rats that exist in the real criminal world.

You never forget a person who has given evidence against you or done you harm, no matter how many years go by. Some things still keep me awake and night and cause me to think very dark thoughts indeed.

CHAPTER 23
TIME TELLS ALL

It's true what they say: time tells all. And having outlived a good many of the chaps, I've had the fortune to be around to see what information the Home Office release to the public after the official 30-year time period. Because you never really know what is truth and what is fiction. When stories about past events are retold, they reveal how fact, rumours, half-truths and inaccurately remembered events become embroidered into legend with affectionate flair.

But, for me, the most shocking revelation came not from the government, but from two old pals who stopped by my Greg's pub one afternoon for a drink, in 2006. Bert and John used to work the doors at the Regency club, and popped in for a drink.

'I've got something to tell you about Jack "The Hat",' said Bert. I put down my drink carefully. Now they had my full attention. For the next half an hour, they took me back four decades and retold the entire story – which, I gradually came to understand, was something that had been weighing on their minds. 'The reason the Krays killed Jack "The Hat",' they said solemnly, 'was nothing to do with what happened in the 211 Club.'

Of course, I'd always believed that the reason the body was dumped on my doorstep was because the Krays had mullered Jack after his behaviour in my club, when he pulled a knife on the croupier in my casino with four of his mates. I'd heard the Krays had bollocked him after this ugly scene, and I'd always been led to believe that they straightened him out for me. Why else would I risk my liberty in disposing of the body?

I listened carefully as I learned the true story of Jack's final days. The week before the Krays mullered him, Jack 'The Hat' turned up at the door of the Regency, where Reggie Kray was rotten drunk in the upstairs bar. Jack attempted to gain entrance to the club, but was clearly drunk, and all fired up on 'phet (amphetamines). He had a shotgun and was yelling, 'I'm gonna shoot that cunt Reggie Kray!' Bert and John on the door were trying to talk him out of it, and there was a struggle, during which the gun went off. The guys did manage to prize the gun from his hands, but Jack escaped into the night.

Reggie came to the door, having heard gunfire, and asked, 'What's all the trouble?' but they didn't grass him up. They never mentioned to the Krays what happened, they went back to their drinking and the night finished.

Strangely enough, I still remember hearing a rumour at the time that Jack had let one go [fired a shot] at the Regency door, and I remember thinking, 'The Twins won't like that,' as they were being paid to look after the club.

Coincidentally, that same week, the Krays called on Jack 'The Hat', and asked him if he wanted to re-join the Firm. You see, he'd been paid handsomely to kill Lesley Paine and despite failing, he'd copped the money. That was the sort of fella he was. But when they approached him during a sit-down, he was pissed, and blurted out, 'Nah, you're only asking 'cos I came round the other night to shoot you!'

One Kray twin looked at the other, and in that moment Jack 'The Hat' had signed his own death warrant. They checked the story with John and Burt, who confirmed that is what had happened, and the next I saw of Jack he was rolled up, in a candlewick bedspread on the back seat of a battered-up old Ford Zephyr. Abandoned on my manor.

And these chaps are telling me all this 40 years later! I wouldn't have even got out of bed, let alone got rid of the body and copped 10 fucking years for it. That's the thing with the Krays, they never truly respected the risks people had to take in clearing up their mess, and it's only now both are passed away that I can tell this story, which reveals just how cheap the price of life was in those days.

Back in 1967, a car was sent over for me and the driver, Fat Wally Garlick, told me Ronnie wanted to see me urgently. When I arrived at the place, which was owned by Charlie Clark, who was an old cat burglar. There were other members of the firm there, all worried, and Charlie's wife was in the kitchen, nervously making sandwiches and cups of tea. It was a terrible atmosphere in that house, people looking at me with eyes full of terror. Ronnie was pacing up and down like a caged fucking lion, puffing aggressively on a cigarette, clearly in one of his psychotic murderous moods. I said, 'What's the matter, why have you got me here?'

Another of Ronnie's men replied, 'Ronnie's sent the boys out to get Billy G., to bring him back here so he can kill him.'

I said, 'Just like that? You're going to murder him... What's he done?' And I assumed that they wanted me to clear up the mess. Billy G. was a good man, a face whom I did bird with in Leicester – and Reggie was in there with him at one point. Billy was the unluckiest criminal I knew – in fact, I never saw the inside of a prison without seeing him in there. Somehow he'd upset Ronnie, who was right up for doing someone in. But this was never going to happen with me there. Billy is still alive today, and this will probably be a massive shock to him. If he does read this, I'd like to know what on earth he'd done wrong to be the subject of Ronnie's evil intent.

'It ain't as easy as that,' I protested, 'you can't walk away and leave them on the living-room floor for someone else to deal with.' There's a risk involved and Ronnie seemed happy to gamble with other people's liberties just because he wanted to muller someone. 'I'm not going to wait here for that, it's just not possible,' I said, 'there's no "facilities" to handle this situation.'

I'm explaining this to Ronnie and am about to leave when the doorbell rings and they have come back. There was a silence, with everyone looking at each other, waiting to see who would walk through the door. There was a big sigh of relief from Charlie Clark, as he would have to fork out for new carpets. One of the chaps winked at me, as he explained to a furious Ronnie that they couldn't find Billy anywhere. Of course, they were never going to find him, and in a way they saved his life. Whatever he'd said or done to Ronnie, he would have killed him for it – after all, Ronnie killed George Cornell for calling him a 'fat poof'.

Martin Fido's book *The Krays: Unfinished Business* dug out the evidence given by Chris Lambrianou, Tony Lambrianou, Ronald Bender and bystanders 'Trevor' and 'Terry' (whose surnames have never been made public), who were all witness to the killing. Trevor and Terry were croupiers from a local party and had been invited by the Krays to the party where they killed Jack 'The Hat'. Now, if this was premeditated murder, would they have invited every Tom Dick and Harry along to watch? Trevor and Terry's evidence was taken before the trial but never given to the defence and withheld by police. Why?

'Their statements are valuably free from police interjection,' says Fido. I believe these statements would have been priceless. It could have made a difference, as it would prove this could not have been a premeditated murder. Firstly it reveals that Ronnie and Jack 'The Hat' were arguing for a time, then Jack took his coat off and came back in wanting a fight. According to these statements, he was stabbed through his waistcoat, proving that he'd taken his jacket off for a fight. Trevor even admitted that Ronnie start the violence by glassing McVitie in the face, and telling him to 'fuck off'. This would have been the difference in court between a murder charge or a manslaughter charge, and certainly would have saved me a lot of bother in the courtroom.

Regardless of the charge, the price of life was cheap when the Twins were about. They would argue, scream and shout at each other like two jealous women, calling each other names, all through their lives. Yet there was a bond of loyalty between them. If anyone interfered in their arguments, they would both turn on that person and defend each other to the death. They were really one person split in two.

Charlie Kray was doing 12 years at the age of 72 while he was in Parkhurst, and became very ill. Charlie became not only an associate, but a close friend, and I went to see him about three days before he died. He said to me, 'I'm sorry for what the Twins put you through, they gave you a lot of grief.' That was an understatement. I told him, 'Charlie, you got it wrong, I did it all for you. You were my pal.' Wilf Pine was there by his wheelchair and overheard this conversation. He said to me, 'That gave him his respect back, Fred.' He was happy I'd said that to him. When our visit was coming to an end, the two screws nodded to me that it was time to go. They were OK guys, who even took the last photograph for us. After that, I left Charlie to talk to Di, his girlfriend. Despite a split, she was the one that still loved him at the end. Charlie said to me on the way out, 'Bring Jamie down, Fred.'

Charlie always liked my Jamie, and I replied, 'I'll come back next Wednesday, and bring him with me.' But as I stood at the door and looked back at him, time seemed to stand still as we held each other's gaze. We both knew really: he wouldn't be there on Wednesday. It was the last we saw of each other, that lingering moment in the doorway. It was a terribly sad moment.

Talking of the Krays, there are a few things I would like to have the opportunity to clear up, especially regarding their deaths. It's been suggested that I boycotted Reggie's funeral, but, although I wasn't in attendance, it was nothing as political as that. In fact, I had to get my lawyers involved to even have the right to go. On the day of the funeral, I was still on bail for that Granada TV programme business, and was due to appear at Horseferry Road police station that very day. My lawyer wrote to the police explaining the situation, and I got a very pleasing document back in return. Next to the section: 'No further action to be taken', there was a box with a tick in it, meaning they dropped it all and I was no longer on bail. I was relieved, but there were already tensions arising in the underworld about Reggie's funeral arrangements. They were being taken care of by Roberta Kray, his 'wife'.

When I say 'wife', Roberta was a freelance journalist taken inside the nick by a girl called Flanaghan, and a friend of the family. There she married Reggie to help him get parole. They much prefer a prisoner to go back to a home with a wife than just out on your own. And, after all, Ronnie had married when he was in Broadmoor, and, whatever Ronnie did, Reggie copied. Bearing in mind Reggie was a homosexual, the entire thing was a farce, and the fact that she announced she was 'madly in love' with Reg frankly made everyone laugh. How anyone could be in love with Reggie Kray? I don't know – you just couldn't get that close to him. Nobody could. Anyway, a lot of people had a grievance with Roberta organising the funeral.

You couldn't believe the people she invited. When you go to a funeral, the first 10 rows are close friends and family, and people you don't know so well are at the back and down the sides. Those are the fucking rules. But all Reggie's close friends were stood down the sides. The front rows were taken up by her friends, along with – you won't believe this – the pop band East 17 and other media types. It was all for publicity, you see. It was six-handed around the coffin and no one seemed to know who they were.

Paul Jonas, a local publican, laid out two grand for the wake at his pub, yet Roberta took all of her friends to a house in Kent, which caused offence. Jonas didn't fuck about when it came to food and his typically cockney spread – but it didn't get wasted, his pub was full to the brim with the Krays' real friends.

I had already experienced how Roberta worked when Reggie was on his deathbed. When I asked to go and see Reggie, with Wilf Pine, Joey Pyle, and Johnny Nash, Roberta kept putting us off. In the end, it looked like she'd never let us up there, so Wilf said to me, 'We'd better get down there, because it might be too late.' So we went up to Weyland, Norfolk, where Reggie was staying at a nice little place called the Town House.

That morning, we arrived as she was sitting on the bed, and she jumped up as if we'd gate-crashed the room. But Reggie perked right up when he saw us, and seemed to come to life again. He started to talk, for the first time in a while, and was asking us whether we had come by car or train. We had a lovely little conversation, regarding the time when he and Ronnie had purchased a country house with the help of Jeff Allen, just down the road from where we were.

As he was talking and chatting away, Johnny Nash noticed his mouth was dry, and he asked Roberta if she had a wet cloth to wet his lips. She barked back, 'I know what's best! I know how to look after him.' And had a right little tantrum.

When the doctor arrived, we left, but as I got up to leave the room, Reg said, 'You are coming back, aren't you?'

'We're going to the bar downstairs and we'll come back.' I told him. After the doctor had gone we returned upstairs, but Reggie looked like he was in a coma. He was completely gone, and didn't know what day of week it was. From chatting away and trying his best to put on a brave front, his condition had drastically changed. His eyes were now closed, his breathing was heavy and it was not a pretty sight.

Roberta moved away across the room, so I took her place on his bed and put my arm around Reg's shoulder. Fifty-odd years and a lot of water had gone under the bridge. There was a lot of baggage, but it was a very sad moment as I leaned over and said, 'Don't fight it Reg. Let go.' But it was obvious the doctor had given him the last injection. They keep giving you morphine near the end, until your heart can take it no longer, but you die without pain and in peace. 'I'll see you another time, another place,' I said, as he slowly drifted away.

I turned my head to speak to the chaps behind me. 'I think he's gone,' I said. Then, all of a sudden, he gasped! And it frightened the life out of us and we all jumped! But it was his last breath.

I was just glad that we had got to see him before he died. I went across to the bathroom for a moment to control my emotions. Wilf came and knocked on door, and asked, 'Are you all right, Fred?' I came out and the four of us went to the bar, and raised our glasses. 'To Reggie, the last of the Krays.'

I found it disgusting that Roberta Kray later wrote that we were unwanted as Reg lay dying. It was a disgrace what she wrote in her book. She even said that Reg didn't want us as pallbearers. He told me himself he did, just as I carried his brother's coffin. But the most amazing thing I read was her claims that she consummated the marriage when he came out of prison. He was dying and even with a hundred Viagras he wouldn't have managed to get it up!

Now, I don't want this chapter to be entirely about funerals, but I'd like the opportunity to say a few things about some of the chaps who've passed away, and how important they are to me.

As Shakespeare said, death is 'the undiscovered country, from whose bourn no traveller returns', and when you see someone close to death you can see it in their eyes. They wonder where they're going and hope that all their pals will be there to see them along the way. I recently saw the same look in Joe Pyle's eyes, another great friend who was there with me at Reggie's deathbed. Joey was one of the chaps I have lost in recent years, he died of motor neurone disease, a terrible muscle-wasting affliction for which there is no known cure. We had a benefit at the Caesar's Palace to raise money for him to have stem cell treatment in Ireland (we look after our own) but it didn't help. Perhaps one day they will find a cure.

I was so upset when Joe died, more upset than when Reggie went, because I've known Joe for over 40 years, and during the latter years of his life we became incredibly close. I have the utmost respect for Joey and the way he lived his life. I've never once heard of him refusing to do a favour or help out a friend in need.

Joe Pyle was a very humane person and comfortable to be around. He was warm natured and true to the chaps – that was the sort of person he was. I spent a lot of time with Joe towards the end, and even when he was dying we'd manage to do a bottle of Jameson's every time we met up. And while he had the oxygen tubes up his nose, he used to take them out sometimes and have a little sniff of the naughty stuff to perk his spirits up! He enjoyed life to the full, right until the very end. 'What the fuck,' he told me, 'I'm dying, I'm gonna have a good time!' And all the time he was making all the arrangements for his funeral and deciding what hymns he wants, he was laughing and we were celebrating. Celebrating the good times we shared and the life we had, rather than sitting there moping. I used to laugh as he couldn't make it all the way upstairs to go to the loo, so he'd go outside and water next door's hedge for them and then come back in!

On one occasion, I took him up to bed, when he needed help to get up the stairs, and put the oxygen mask on him and tucked him up! I bet you can't imagine that, of two old villains – I even gave him a kiss goodnight!

Towards the end, Joe gave me a tape of a song that was as important to me as it was hard to find in a record shop. It was called 'Sinner or Saint' by Sarah Vaughan, and it reminded me of a certain period in my life that meant a lot to me. 'I'll take you dear, any way you are, a sinner or saint,' she sang, 'Doesn't matter, what they say you are, I'll have no complaint.'

He also gave me two beautiful Hawaiian shirts and said, 'I won't be needing these.' Joey had taken his honeymoon in Honolulu, and now every time I open my wardrobe, I think of him.

Once again I was proud to carry my friend's coffin, with Roy Shaw, Ronnie Nash, Wilf Pine, Vickie Darke, and Ronnie Field; even my Jamie stepped in at one point. There must have been a thousand people there, and the police had to cordon off the whole area.

You never know what your destiny holds. When you get released from prison, you think all your troubles are over and the future looks great. This has been particularly brought home to me recently by the dramatic events that led to the death of four men I served time with. Prison has a way of bonding friendships when men and women are sharing hardship, pain and sorrow – it brings us all closer together. So when you hear of a tragedy involving one of your old friends, it hurts inside. One such event was the shooting of Lionel Jeffries.

Lionel was a very enterprising little fellow; we used to call him Hiram Holliday, as he looked like a Jewish bank clerk. In May 1987, Lionel, John Queen and Bobby Knapp hijacked a Post Office security van. Bobby Knapp is now currently serving life for killing a Pakistani tenant of the property magnate Van Hoogstraten. (Poor Bobby, he never intended to kill him, just to put the frighteners on, then a terrible struggle took place.) Anyway, they transferred 17 bags of money to their getaway car – they'd stolen £1,000,000. Unfortunately, some time later, all of them were arrested and sentenced to 14 years. But they did their bird like men – proper people; three of the chaps.

Lionel was already at Springhill with Micky Reilly and Pat O'Sullivan when they got the news on the prison grapevine that I was arriving on the Friday from Maidstone. So, being that they were already ensconced in the top huts, otherwise known as 'Park Lane' (two beds in a small room the size of a broom cupboard), they organised that for a 'nifty' (£50) to another prisoner – who was out within a few months – he would vacate his place; moving down the hill to 'The Bronx'. The Bronx was not exactly what you'd call a 'des res' – in fact, it was old 1942 air-force huts; 12 beds separated by a curtain with a small cupboard. Even though I'd still been pissing in a bucket at Maidstone, it was in my own cell and there's a lot to be said for one's own privacy. Unaware of the arrangements that Lionel, Mick and Pat had made for me, I was totally amazed at the reception I got. On my arrival, I was confronted with the governor, and chief prison officer threatening to put me on the first bus straight back to Maidstone for bribing and forcing a prisoner to vacate his hut! Obviously the guy had got a pull and spilled the beans, so to speak. So despite their efforts I still had to spend the next three months down in The Bronx until a place was found in Park Lane.

Anyway, we were all on the garden party. Lionel, Mick Reilly, Pat O'Sullivan, Dave Bullen and myself. After a back-aching week of hard but satisfying work, planting beds of daisies and pansies in front of the big house that was the main administration block of the prison, we all stood back to admire our work – the pansy beds looked really lovely. Then disaster struck. The next day, Lionel came rushing into the but frothing at the mouth, 'Someone's ripped up all our pansy beds!' This was now a case of life and death. Several accusations were thrown about, old arguments and enemies dissected. Who could, or would, do such a terrible thing – to us, of all people? Lionel finally came to the conclusion, 'It's a certain team down at The Bronx... Get the tools out!' (He could be a vicious little bastard when put out.) Then along came the garden screw, surveying the scene of devastation, noting our angry faces and clenched fists: 'Those fucking sheep have got through the fence again!' Not being country boys, we hadn't noticed the little round balls of black shit lying around the pansy beds for all to see. The evidence being obvious, the case was closed. So our next job was mending the fence at the bottom of the field. Meanwhile, Lionel threw stones at the sheep. It's amazing how every little incident in prison can be magnified out of all proportion.

Lionel Jeffries had always had a good name; he was a stand-up guy, and honourable where business was concerned. He was always a good money-getter and had plenty of bottle. Unfortunately, on his release he started to move around in dangerous circles. If he got in trouble with money, then I'm sure he would pay it back. But I'm afraid time ran out for Lionel. When he went on a meet to talk to those involved, he was blasted to death by two black guys on a motorcycle in Kensington High Street. Whatever the reasons are, or were, I think in his case the people overreacted. They could have given Lionel more time to settle his debt – he did his bird like a man and had never fucked anyone for money as far as I knew. A large number of chaps are not too happy about what happened to Lionel. It may sound strange to the average man in the street. But the chaps always gained respect, and took a certain amount of pride in putting their own liberty at risk when settling an old score.

Back at Springhill, Micky Reilly, who had been fitted up by drug officers to a 10-year sentence, fought his case for two years and eventually won it at the appeal court. Pat Sullivan got parole and Dave Bullen went to Latchmere. I followed Dave after a few months. But during my stay at Springhill there were a number of other prisoners due for release. One was a good friend of mine, Micky Williams, and I'll tell you more about him later.

Another was Lawrence Gibbons. I had known Lawrence for many years and did bird with him at Full Sutton and Maidstone. He got 10 years for a drugs offence. It took four years before his appeal and acquittal. So eventually, like Micky Reilly, he too walked out a free man. A car dealer by trade, on his release Lawrence left London to start a new car site in the coastal town of Margate. He had acquired a partner by the name of Richard Hilton, a face from that area. The car front was large, specialising in American motors and expensive models such as Rolls-Royces and Mercedes. They had even ventured into a gold and jewellery shop business together. Everything in Laurence's garden was rosy, until the time 'when that old wind blew in the seeds of weeds and all was ugliness', to quote an old Chinese proverb.

On the fatal night, Lawrence and Hilton had been drinking heavily and a silly row started. Lawrence challenged Hilton to a 'straightener' outside the house, where they had both been living with their families. Lawrence led the way, But Hilton didn't fancy his chances. So he took hold of a *Crocodile Dundee*-style knife from above the mantelpiece, I don't think he wanted to use it, but wanted to stop Lawrence from fighting with him. It all went horribly wrong, though. In the fight that followed, Hilton stabbed Lawrence, then, realising what he'd done, he helped Lawrence into his own Roller, drove to the nearest hospital, dumped him outside and did a runner. He hoped that a doctor could help save Lawrence's life – but it was too late.

Hilton later gave himself up to the local police and was eventually charged with manslaughter after two trials, the first being stopped when Hilton sacked his defence team and the judge awarded him a new trial. He got himself acquitted on a case of self-defence. So it was a very good result for Hilton.

Back to my old mate, Micky Williams. Micky had been thrown out of Springhill when I met up with him in Maidstone. He was a lovely man, kind and generous, big and strong (about 18 stone, 6 feet 2 inches), with a very happy disposition and an extremely infectious laugh. After his release, Mick made a bit of money and was doing OK. He had a nice flat just off Westbourne Grove, and also a penthouse apartment in Majorca, where he spent a few winter months of each year. All was fine and beautiful in his garden until, when getting out of his car one night, he was surrounded by three black muggers. They were after his Rolex watch. Two attacked him from the front but Mick put up a fight and was holding his own. Then a third mugger came in low from behind, grabbing both of Micky's legs in a bear hug. Mick was pitched off balance, and he went crashing face down, bouncing on the pavement. All three of his attackers then sat on his back, tearing the watch from his wrist, and ran off with Mick chasing after them. But Mick wasn't built for speed. Exhausted from the effort of fighting all three of them, Mick didn't know the damage that had been done to himself. Apparently, he had torn the main vein (aorta) to his heart, a result of the whiplash action of crashing face-down. He didn't know how serious this injury was, and thought it was just bruising. I went to see him, and we tried to find these muggers, but with no luck.

Mick decided to have a few weeks' holiday in his penthouse in Majorca. But after only a few days he had to return home. He was feeling really rough. Although he didn't know it at the time, his torn vein was leaking out blood internally. Back in London, he went straight to the Wellington Hospital in St John's Wood. After an examination, the doctors operated immediately, cutting him open from chest to abdomen, and leaving a scar similar to the zip on a tracksuit top.

My first visit to see Mick gave me a terrible shock. He had lost 4 stone and looked dreadful. I said, 'Just wait until you get well mate and we'll go and find those bastards who did this to you.' So Micky went back to Majorca to rebuild his strength. Then, out of the blue, I received a phone call, informing me that Micky had had a heart attack while he sat on his settee watching a video. He was dead – it was over very quick. I rang his old number to speak to his wife, but there was Micky's voice: 'Sorry we're not in but if you would like to leave your name and number we will get right back to you. Now would you get off the line there's a train coming, ha ha ha.' That oh-so-familiar laugh. It made my eyes fill and a lump come to my throat. I had got his answerphone. It almost brought me to tears, but instead my feelings turned to anger. Those three muggers had took a man's life away for a poxy watch. A good man who was worth more than those three put together.

Another such chap was Dave Ewing. He was a lot younger than myself, but we had met up over the years, never on the out, only in different prisons. Dave was a nice kid and I liked his politeness and respect. I would often loan him a score for petrol money, and he always paid me back – which was more than a lot of other guys did. Dave had suffered since he was a young man. They both got bird together, father and son, and big sentences too.

Another factor didn't help, and I know it affected him. Dave Sr had been in a pub and left on his own. On passing a housing estate he saw the fire brigade fighting a house fire and helping the family out to safety. Dave saw the mother of the family screaming that their little girls were still trapped inside, so against the advice of the firemen he ran inside to rescue the children, and carried the first of the two girls out to safety.

Then, he returned once more into the burning building to find the last girl, but this time he never came out. When the fire was extinguished and the smoke cleared, they found Dave's father at the top of the landing, still cradling the little girl in his arms. Both were dead. Although Dave's father had a criminal record and was looked on by society as a bad person, he was a man, and a brave man at that. He risked his own life to save two little girls and paid the price. But unfortunately that was not to be the end of the suffering for this poor family.

While in Latchmere, young Dave got a job as a motorbike courier. He was over the moon. He had all the leathers, and most importantly for him, something he'd never owned before: a driving licence! In fact, he was so proud of it he kept getting it out and showing it off to everyone. He saw this job as his last big chance to really make a go of things on his release. It was great to see him so happy and determined to turn his life around. So you can imagine the shock I got when I learned that for some unexplained reason his life was snuffed out as he left an off-licence after buying himself a six-pack. He had been shot in the chest by a police officer from an armed response unit. The officer responsible was charged with murder, and it is the first time such a charge has been bought against a policeman on duty. But later the case was dropped.

As well as telling all, time is also a great healer, and although the troubles and betrayals that accompany life in the criminal underworld are treated as life and death, life moves on. I even shook hands with Nipper Read! I went to Manchester to watch the Ben vs Eubank fight, and Read was on the boxing board of control. Jack Trickett from Manchester had given me ringside seats and I took Janice with me. When I arrived, I said hello to Barry Hearn, Nat Basso and Frank Warren, with whom I had discussed doing some promoting over in Spain, many years earlier.

'Nice to see you home, Fred,' he said, smiling.

I was shaking all these hands until suddenly I looked up, and who should have my hand, but Nipper fucking Read. I've shook his hand as he laughed away, and he said, 'No hard feelings, Fred.'

No hard feelings? He tried to life me off, and I later read in the book *Unfinished Business* what he thought of me at the time: 'Read once made an ungraded reponse on television, to the effect that he had been investigating about seven murders of which Freedie Foreman was suspected (this number probably includes several that were actually ascribed to the Krays at the time). Certainly Read made no bones about the fact that Foreman was the more dangerous criminal [than the Krays]. Read later said in a television programme that he cried tears of joy after getting seven people sent down. In total, 240 years were dished out. But I politely replied, 'No hard feelings, Nipper. You had a job to do.'

After I sat down, the chairman of the Boxing Board of Control turned to me, laughing, and said, 'I would have liked to have had a photo of that!'

EPILOGUE

Now that my career is over, I hope that I can relax and enjoy all the simple things in life that have been denied me over a number of years. In putting the record straight, so to speak, I take this opportunity to thank all our old customers and associates for their help and support over the years and to deny all those rumours, prevalent at the time, that we watered down the gin. Not true. The vodka, yes. And some of the staff were not completely honest when it came to handling money. Lots of them actually thought it was their own. Imagine! Some even got their money mixed up with mine. Never mind, as the song goes: 'You've got to give a little, take a little...'

Apart from my family, there are many other friends who have suffered and stood by me through all these turbulent years. I sincerely thank them. There are also many people from the legal profession, such as Peter Hughman, Tony Block and Henry Milner, who've worked hard for me. I would also thank the barristers and QCs, who include Tom Williams and Ivor Richard, my defence team in the Cornell, McVitie and Mitchell trials; William Denny, my QC in the Marks case; and John Matthews QC, who defended me in the Security Express robbery trial. Justice Bernie Caulfield also has my thanks and I won't forget how fairly treated I was by Judge Bristow at Winchester Crown Court.

When I wrote my book, *Respect*, in 1994, I predicted that computers would be the crime of the future, and I was right. Today it's all credit-card fraud and modern villains are earning millions without even getting off their sofas. Like the landscape, the London crime scene is constantly changing. The armed robber has been wiped out, and the 'jump-up' is a thing of the past, because everything seems to be online. You can't walk into an online bank with a shooter, can you?

Today no one even uses cash any more. Wherever you go in the world it's credit cards and chip and pin. If you visit a restaurant in Spain and try to pay with a 500-euro note, there'll be a steward's inquiry! They are affectionately known to the Spanish as 'Bin Ladens', because you hear about them but you hardly ever see one! Today, people only know how much they are spending when the bank statement arrives, when they get a right shock and have to sit down with a stiff drink.

It was enough to make me think about enrolling in computer classes at night school, but I fear it would have been too late for me. World War II started when I was eight years old. Over the next five years there were hardly any schools standing, let alone any prospect of a decent education.

Today's kids don't know how lucky they are. I was put out to hard work straight from school at the age of 14. A lot of children in this generation simply sit on the sofa all day and send text messages back and forth in a new abbreviated language (and often they're not paying for it either). That's why we have obese kids, because it's too much effort to get up and walk round to a friend's house when they can send an email instead. You can tell I'm up on my soapbox now. My Janice says to me, 'You should be on that TV programme,' and I'll say, 'And what programme is that, my sweetness, *Brain of Britain*, or *University Challenge*?' and she says, 'No,' with a smirk, '*Grumpy Old Men*!'

It's simply that I'm from another era, where criminals were gentleman, and I just can't understand today's youth. They'll rob old ladies and rape and kill for no reason. It's disgusting and I can't understand what the world is coming to. It's true, we are living in a very violent society. I blame the films and games kids watch – the violence is unreal. Yet the classics aren't much better. I'm a man who has read the entire works of Shakespeare while banged up in Leicester on a 10 stretch, and if you've ever read *Titus Andronicus* you'll know a thing or two about violence: the bloke's daughter gets raped by this other family, and then they go as far as digging her eyes out, so she can't see them again, cutting her tongue out, so she can't say what happened, and to top it all they cut her hands off so she can't even point the finger at anyone.

I mean to say, that's going a bit far even for a boy from south London!

In hindsight, I can see where my problems started, but in my youth there was no hope for young boys and girls with little if any education at all. Only very menial and physical jobs were available with no future prospects for a better life, especially if you had a young family. To improve your standard of living you had to take short-cuts while you had the drive and energy (with all that testosterone rushing around your body!).

It's human nature that there's a bit of larceny in everyone. In my experience that even includes MPs, the clergy, law enforcement – you name it! We all like something for nothing, as long as we don't get caught. We have to bridge the gap between the 'haves' and the 'have nots', and the fat cats must spread their wealth around in a way that will make poverty a byword.

We must tackle the problems of illegal immigration, especially those people who only work in the UK to send cash back to their motherland.

Many immigrants I speak to work so hard here, but they are saving to buy a house back at home, or to start a business elsewhere. This money doesn't go back into the community or the economy but to foreign lands.

What's more is the bloodshed that accompanies a multi-cultural community, and how some religions prevent integration. On meeting him at a partner's christmas party, John (Mad Dog) told me about his childhood growing up in Ireland, and how one side of his street was Catholic and the other Protestant, and it was as simple as that. It's the same in Iraq, with the Sunnahs and the Shiites, killing each other on a daily basis. Let's get out of their country, give them their own border and let them get on with it! Here I go on my soapbox again, so thanks for listening to my ramblings for a moment, but after 76 years travelling the world I might just have got one or two things right.

And, while I'm up on my soapbox, I have to say that the Home Office don't seem able to tell the difference between their arse and their elbow. So much for compassion, heart and soul – forget it. Ronnie Biggs gave himself up at the age of 71. After suffering three strokes, he could hardly speak or talk, and had to use a chalk and slate to communicate to his son Michael. What did they do? Put him in a prison hospital? No, they locked him up in Belmarsh top-security prison. It's bloody disgusting. People complain that the government are soft on crime but not when it comes to people like myself, or Charlie Kray, or Ronnie Biggs. They'll always find room for us old boys, while preachers of hate, sex offenders and drunk drivers get off with pathetic sentences.

In my life I've been sentenced to 23 years' imprisonment, 16 years of which I've spent inside 15 different nicks in the UK and abroad, with much of that time in remand for crimes that ended in acquittal.

Just imagine that, if you will. Those missed birthdays, weddings, funerals, your children growing up, relationships beginning and ending. A whole decade came and went, and when I think about what I missed during that time it saddens me.

Locked up in a cell every day of those many years, sharing a cell only with men could be hell. In most cases, out of the entire prison population, you would only associate with five to ten prisoners on a day-to-day basis. And anyway, even if you worked for say, Fords of Dagenham you'd only have a handful of close friends.

It's like that when you live in a criminal society – all of your close friends are in your 'trade'. In my case, many of my associates are all ex-criminals, who are retired and too old to participate in any criminal activity. And, anyway, when you're my age you find that you have no more time to give to the authorities. You can't afford to slip up any more because you've got few years left to give them.

Of course, I still have time to think about opportunities to make an easy pound note because I still have the fire and desire to feel the excitement and buzz of a big score, but nowadays I can't even run and catch a bus. I'll be sprinting down the street, and I'll say to myself, 'For fuck's sake, Fred, you're 76 years old, take your time. Another will be along in five minutes!'

It's just in my nature: I've never been able to wait for traffic lights, and I'll dash across the busiest roads, I still carry heavy bags of cement up three flights of stairs, and just recently I fell off a tall ladder and crashed straight through a solid glass coffee table. I was doing heavy manual work and a week later I was in surgery having a triple heart bypass! I just believe, when it's your time to go, that old reaper won't pass you by – but somehow I don't reckon he's ready for me yet.

Luckily, I've been able to enjoy my freedom in the twilight of my life. I still love socialising and meeting new people, and particularly going to parties where I'm usually the last to leave the bar! I still enjoy the company of older friends – although I'm sorry to say a few of them are sitting in God's waiting room. The funerals I've attended in the last year have outnumbered the weddings.

I have a hard job getting to all these functions, because it's not like the old days when everyone you knew lived in London. Today my friends are global. For instance, I have a large family in Australia resulting from my brother Herbie emigrating there back in the 1960s. There are children of my father's sister's in South Africa, and my daughter's partner's family are in Argentina. I've got old friends in Spain and France, while my mates Tricky – singer of Massive Attack and actor – and Jim Manos Jr – the Emmy-winning *Sopranos* writer – live in Los Angeles. I keep promising to visit, but it's hard enough getting up to see my friend Big Albert Chapman in Birmingham. I don't think my bus pass goes as far as America!

It's true, the world is a different place, but at heart the criminal world will always live on. As one old score is settled, new grievances arise. New people are arrested as old prisoners are released. It's a never-ending, vicious circle. I suppose you could say I'm of the 'old school'. However much of a cliché it may sound, I believe in 'honour among thieves'. Thankfully, there are still many young criminals around who think as I do.

However, I do still hear some young criminals talking about being sent down at the Number One Court like it's something to be proud of, like it's a similar achievement to an actor playing the Old Vic, or a singer playing the Palladium or Broadway. I have appeared to my sorrow at the Number One Court at the Central Criminal Court of the Old Bailey on six different occasions. For accessory to murder, to GBH, murder, and armed robbery – none of which I am proud of.

But I must admit that I was used by people. A lot of people in the criminal community had the attitude, 'If we've got a problem, Freddie Foreman will put it straight for us. He'll settle the score.' I've put my life on the line so many times, and all too often for other people's problems. But this had to stop, because it's never been appreciated in money or in kind. And, believe me, I'm owed a lot. It's just time for the younger men to take over. Anyway, after saying all that, I'm still the same person, just a little older. I have to go now and pick up the phone to get something sorted, so beware, you would-be liberty takers with evil intent, that old reaper might be knocking on your door sooner than you think!

Pulling strokes and playing dirty games only leads to guilty feelings and, in some cases, nightmares. So pick your company carefully. As the saying goes: 'If you sleep with dogs, you'll get fleas.' Remember that bad deeds have a funny way of catching up with you when you least expect it. They talk about the long arm of the law, but the old firms still have a long reach...

Now try to stay out of trouble, chaps. And don't do anything I wouldn't do.

God Bless.

Freddie.